THE GREAT WALL
AND THE EMPTY FORTRESS

THE
GREAT WALL
AND THE
EMPTY FORTRESS

CHINA'S SEARCH FOR SECURITY

by

ANDREW J. NATHAN

and

ROBERT S. ROSS

W · W · NORTON & COMPANY

New York   London

For information about permission to reproduce selections from this book,
write to Permissions, W. W. Norton & Company, Inc., 500 Fifth Avenue,
New York, NY 10110.

The text of this book is composed in Sabon
with the display set in Sabon
Composition and manufacturing by The Haddon Craftsmen, Inc.
Book design by Jacques Chazaud

Library of Congress Cataloging-in-Publication Data

Nathan, Andrew J. (Andrew James)
The great wall and the empty fortress : China's search for security / by
Andrew J. Nathan and Robert S. Ross
p.   cm.
Includes bibliographical references and index.
ISBN 0-393-04076-3
1. National security—China.   2. China—Foreign relations—1976–
3. Taiwan—Foreign relations—1945–   I. Ross, Robert S. 1954–   II. Title.
UA835.N38   1997
355'.033051—dc21   97-6385
CIP

W. W. Norton & Company, Inc., 500 Fifth Avenue, New York, N.Y. 10110
http://www.wwnorton.com

W. W. Norton & Company Ltd., 10 Coptic Street, London WC1A 1PU

1 2 3 4 5 6 7 8 9 0

For Alexa and Chloe,
and for Joanne

For Betsy and for Rebecca,
Alex, and Emily

CONTENTS

MAPS

"He saw clouds of dust rising into the sky. The Wei armies were nearing Hsi-ch'eng along two roads. Then he ordered all the banners to be removed and concealed, and said if any officer in command of soldiers in the city moved or made any noise he would be instantly put to death. Next he threw open all the gates and set a score of soldiers dressed as ordinary people cleaning the streets at each gate. When these preparations were complete, he donned the simple Taoist dress he affected on occasions and attended by a couple of lads, sat down on the wall by one of the towers with his lute before him and a stick of incense burning."

—*Romance of the Three Kingdoms*, chap. 95

"Make an outward display of confusion while actually being well ordered. Show an appearance of hunger while actually being well fed. Keep your sharp weapons within and show only dull and poor weapons outside. Have some troops come together, others split up; some assemble, others scatter. Make secret plans, keep your intentions secret. Raise the height of fortifications, and conceal your elite troops. If the officers are silent, not making any sounds, then the enemy will not know your preparations. Then if you want to take his western flank, attack the eastern one."

—*Tai Gong's Six Secret Teachings*

"Where the Ch'in built a wall to keep out the Tartars,
The Han still light a beacon fire.
Beacon fires are lit without cease,
And fighting goes on without end. . . .
How well we know the curse of war;
May the wise rulers follow it only as the last recourse!"

—Li Po, "They Fought South of the Walls"

"Therefore one who is good at being a warrior doesn't make a show of his might;
One who is good in battle doesn't get angry;
One who is good at defeating the enemy doesn't engage him."

—*Laozi*

"Weapons are an important factor in war, but not the decisive factor; it is people, not things, that are decisive. The contest of strength is not only a contest of military and economic power, but also a contest of human power and morale."

—Mao Zedong

"The United States cannot annihilate the Chinese nation with its small stack of atom bombs. Even if the U.S. atom bombs were so powerful that, when dropped on China, they would make a hole right through the earth, or even blow it up, that would hardly mean anything to the universe as a whole, though it might be a major event for the solar system."

—Mao Zedong

"Experience shows that even if the enemy were to come now, we would be able to fight him with our present weapons and eventually win the war, provided we persevered in the people's war. With such a huge population, once our people and our army unite as one, no enemy can destroy us."

—Deng Xiaoping

FOREWORD

CHINA IS THE largest and economically most dynamic newly emerging power in the history of the world. It intends to take its place in the next century as a great power. If the country maintains political stability and a high rate of economic growth, it will realize its ambition. How its foreign policy evolves will affect the balance of world power in ways that are as important to Americans as to Chinese. How China is integrated into the world will determine whether a successful post–Cold War order can be created.

Some of its neighbors view China as a threat. But its posture is defensive. Where Americans see a potentially beneficent new world order, China sees danger. While the United States is separated from Asia and Europe by oceans and shares borders with two much weaker countries, which are allies, China sits at the center of the Asian continent, crowded on all sides by powerful rivals and potential foes. While the United States has a technologically advanced industrial economy and a population dispersed across a fertile agricultural plain that produces more grain than its citizens can eat, most of China's much larger population is crowded into the 22 percent of its territory near the coastline. Population growth presses the limits of grain supply, and the bulk of the national territory consists of thinly populated mountains and deserts.

America's position makes it militarily almost invulnerable to invasion; China's situation has invited intrusions for millennia. American security problems are abroad; China's most pressing ones are at and within its borders. The American military patrols the world thousands of miles from home; the Chinese army worries about deterring attacks and suppressing internal disorder. Global developments of recent years—the end of the Cold War, the breakup of the Soviet Union, the rise of UN peacekeeping, the growing importance of cultural and economic power, the increasing integration of world markets, and the rise of several Asian powers and groupings—have enhanced America's ability to exert influence around the world. The same developments have opened gaps in the military, economic, and ideological Great Walls that protected Chinese security for the past five decades.

This does not mean that China is a power of diminishing importance, as some say it is, because of the end of the Cold War. It is true that the West no longer needs China to balance against the Soviet Union as it did in the era of the strategic triangle. But now it is growing stronger and it can either become part of a peaceful new world system or disrupt that system. It can do so through direct military action in the Taiwan Strait, South or East China Sea, Korea, Central Asia, or India; by undermining the emerging liberal world order centered on the UN and on international law; by supporting rogue regimes, selling arms, and opposing the world antiproliferation order; or by undermining the world's trading system and helping destroy its natural environment.

The history of rising powers is not encouraging for the peaceful accommodation of China in the world order. Violent conflict accompanied the rise of Athens and Rome in classical times, of the Habsburg empire and the Netherlands in the sixteenth century, France in the seventeenth century, England in the eighteenth century, Germany in the nineteenth and twentieth centuries, and Japan and Soviet Russia in the twentieth century. When rising powers join the world system, they want to remake rules that they did not shape and that they do not see as serving their interests. The established powers find it difficult to share leadership with them. The leaders of established and rising powers have often failed to see beyond conflicts of interest, which are real, to deeper common interests.

Yet not every rising power can become a hegemon. If China is a rising power with enormous assets, it is also a vulnerable power with little opportunity to be expansionist or aggressive if it wanted to be. Its situation forces it to be concerned with defending its territorial integrity against antagonists who are numerous, near, and strong. We can expect conflict over China's role, but not what international relations specialists call a "hegemonic war," in which China would bid for dominant world power.[1]

Until the end of the Cold War, Chinese foreign policy under communism went through three periods: alignment with the Soviet Union (1949–60); revolutionary self-reliance in confrontation with both superpowers (1961–72); and participation as the swing player in the strategic triangle (1972–89). Each period entailed risk, yet China came through them with its territory and independence intact, and made progress toward the recovery of lost territories. The three shifts in Chinese strategy disguised a basic continuity: Chinese leaders' attempts to assure their country's survival and to affirm its international prominence in what they perceived as a hostile environment.

In 1989 communism collapsed in Eastern Europe, followed quickly by the disintegration of the Soviet Union. Politicians fanned ethnic animosities in the ruins of the Soviet empire in Europe and Asia. These developments raised new threats to the legitimacy of communism in China and the stability of its Inner Asian borders. They also changed the shape of the international system. The collapse of the Soviet Union left the United States unchallenged as the dominant world power. American victory in the 1991 Persian Gulf War showcased American military technology that was twenty years ahead of its rivals'. The United States enjoyed preeminence among the major industrialized countries (known as the Group of Seven) and the permanent five members of the UN Security Council. Although China wielded a veto as a UN Security Council member, it had to acquiesce in the rise of an interventionist, American-dominated UN or else take the side of outlaw regimes. The American-led West promoted increasingly inclusive anti–arms proliferation and international human rights regimes. China made costly compromises to join a world trading order over which it did not have much influence.

In defining a place for itself in a changing world, China faces fundamental dilemmas. To exercise a major-power role, it needs to collaborate with UN-based peacekeeping mechanisms, world trading norms, international human rights activities, environmental pacts, and arms control regimes. But in doing so it ratifies U.S. dominance and compromises its own freedom of action. To avoid an arms race in Asia, China must encourage a continued American military presence in the region. Yet it considers the United States unreliable and potentially antagonistic. It must trade more actively to avoid being left behind as the world economy grows, but it fears exploitation in a system dominated by more-advanced economies. China wants to take advantage of a period of international stability to concentrate on economic development, but remains in a position of strategic vulnerability in which it must maintain the capability to defend itself in potential military confrontations with Japan, Russia, and other global and regional rivals, including the United States. Yet military self-strengthening risks alarming other countries and setting off a spiral of mistrust.

China is a big enough power that its choice is not merely between obeying the world's rules or flouting them. It may join the international regimes that govern trade, human rights, weapons proliferation, and other interactions as much in order to change them as to obey them. If the world order bears differently on Chinese interests than on ours, the more China joins the world, the more we may be forced to attend to its interests.

China's foreign policy dilemmas will shape and be shaped by its domestic political conflicts. In the early years of Communist Party rule in China, the international environment helped determine the leadership's choice of the Soviet model as the template of Chinese development. Internal politics conditioned China's responses to crises in relations with the United States and the Soviet Union, and the crises in turn affected political careers and economic and social policies at home. Under Deng the core issue of domestic politics was how the country could join the world economically without losing its independence politically.

But throughout the Communist period, a small group of leaders and diplomats made foreign policy without having to answer to lobbies, a legislature, the media, or public opinion. Unlike the United States, China did not have the kind of global reach that entangled it in a host of distant problems where it had to compromise general principles. The authoritarian regime was able to conduct a geopolitically strategic foreign policy that took account of the country's weaknesses as an agrarian continental power, and took advantage of its location at the periphery of the two superpower camps.

Scholars have interpreted international politics through several theoretical lenses: the theory of classical realism, which stresses the struggle

for power among states; neorealism, which emphasizes the search for security under conditions of anarchy; neoliberal institutionalism, which ex-
plores the evolution and influence of international cooperative regimes.
In explaining specific nations' foreign policy, some scholars stress states'
pursuit of national interest, others adopt "constructivist" theories, which
emphasize the role of culture, ideas, and identities in affecting foreign policies, still others emphasize the role of individual perceptions in decision
making, and some prefer theories that analyze how policy results from
bureaucratic and factional processes.[2]

We draw on all these approaches, but predominantly on a combination of neorealism and the national interest approach.[3] We understand
China's behavior as a search for security under what international relations theorists call "conditions of anarchy," with motives similar to those
of other states. Our analysis of Chinese foreign policy assumes that decision makers use reason, but not that the actor's reason is perfect. We
acknowledge that limited time, imperfect information, perceptual biases,
and faulty logic often create strategic missteps. This approach differs
from explanations in terms of culture, personality, tradition, or emotion
not in asserting that a country's foreign policy is always right but in looking for a decipherable means-end relationship in the choice of foreign policies.[4]

We do not overlook the tragic aspects of international relations. We
are aware of the "security dilemma," the paradox that each state's attempt
to improve its security is likely to reduce the security of the other side and
stimulate countermeasures that in turn reduce the security of the first
side.[5] National interest is defined within man-made boundaries among
communities under conditions of failed trust. Foreign policies are rational, when they are at all, in only a bounded sense.

No form of misunderstanding is more common in international affairs than the ascription of emotional or cultural irrationality to policies
that are grounded in strategic motives. Chinese behavior is especially often
misunderstood in this way, perhaps because China's strategic situation is
so different from that of the other major powers, and because the Chinese feel safer in hiding the logic of their actions than in explaining them.
Such misunderstanding can be dangerous for friends and even more so
for rivals.

Since we generally lack inside information on the Chinese policy-
making process, we usually reason from actions back to motives, also taking account of the public rationale for policy. Both the consistent themes

of Chinese policy and the major shifts and apparent anomalies turn out to be explainable by strategic calculations. That is, they make sense in terms of the country's security situation, needs, strengths, and weaknesses, even if some of the decisions turn out to have been ill advised. We apply the same form of analysis to the foreign policies of the countries China deals with. Every country faces security challenges. Every country is in some sense weak and vulnerable—some, like the United States, less so than others. Not every country's foreign policy is consistently strategic. But in the period and for the countries we look at, realism often works as an explanation for both China and its interlocutors.

Domestic politics is a helpful second line of analysis, in China and elsewhere. We frequently have in mind theories of linkage that suggest how foreign and domestic policies are intertwined.[6] Domestic considerations affect foreign policy in every country, at times more so in China than in some other nations, in ways we will describe. Most of China's policies abroad are incomprehensible without attention to their impact on interests at home.

Chapter 1 describes China's geostrategic situation. In Chapter 2, we explore the historical patterns of foreign relations that emerged from this geostrategic situation, patterns that affect policy today. Chapters 3 and 4 cover China's relations with the two powers that have been most important to its foreign policy, the Soviet Union and the United States. China's relations with other countries have revolved around its attempts to check and balance Soviet and American power on its periphery, so these chapters include some discussion of Chinese relations with Inner Asia, the Middle East, Africa, and Latin America. In Chapters 5 and 6 we give separate attention to China's relations with its chief regional partners in Northeast Asia and in South and Southeast Asia.

Chapters 7 through 10 turn from regional to analytical foci, taking up policy-making, defense, foreign economic policy, and human rights. Chapter 11 describes the international dimensions of Chinese policy toward its border regions and unrecovered territories, including Tibet, Hong Kong, and Taiwan. Chapter 12 analyzes the foreign policy of the Republic of China on Taiwan, which seeks to maintain control over its own foreign policy without openly challenging Beijing's claim that China must be unified. In the conclusion, we argue that the rise of China need not present a threat if it is properly managed, and offer our suggestions for shaping a constructive course in its relations with the rest of the world.

For comments and suggestions we wish to thank Joseph Bosco, Thomas J. Christensen, Karl W. Eikenberry, Harvey J. Feldman, Paul H.B. Godwin, Steven M. Goldstein, He Daming, Charles Hill, Eric Hyer, Merit Janow, Harlan Jencks, Mike Jendrzejczyk, Ellis Joffe, Alastair Iain Johnston, Nicholas R. Lardy, John T. Ma, Karen Miller, Brian Murray, Ni Shixiong, Carl Riskin, Lawrence C. Reardon, Morris Rossabi, Orville Schell, James D. Seymour, Jack Snyder, N. T. Wang, Elizabeth Wishnick, Jieh-min Wu, Xu Shiquan, and Geoffrey Ziebart. We give special thanks to Steven I. Levine, who contributed to Chapters 3, 4, and 6 and carefully reviewed the rest of the manuscript, offering numerous suggestions that we incorporated into the final draft. Research assistance was provided by Michael R. Chambers, Amei Zhang, and Xiao-yin Zhao. For editorial exertions beyond the call of duty we are grateful to Steven Forman and Otto Sonntag.

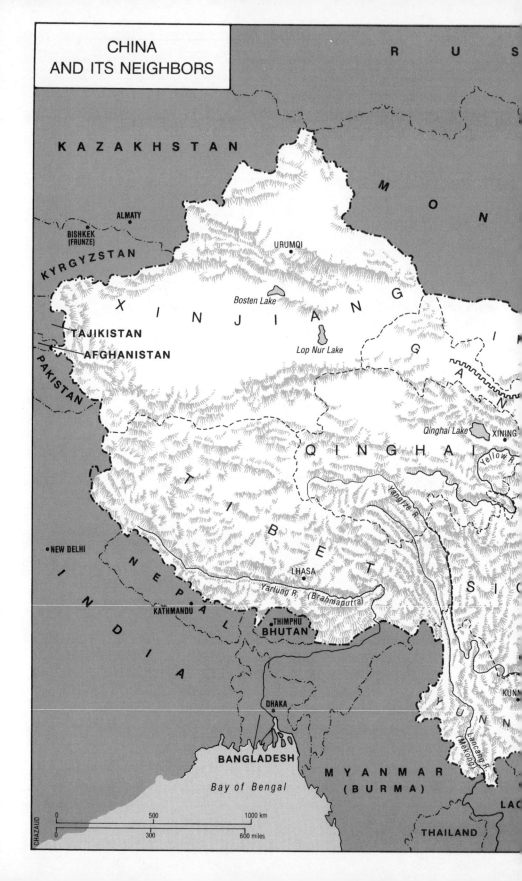

CHINA
AND ITS NEIGHBORS

R U S

KAZAKHSTAN

M O

N

ALMATY

BISHKEK
(FRUNZE)

URUMQI

KYRGYZSTAN

X   I   N   J   I   A   N   G   G

Bosten Lake

I

TAJIKISTAN

G

Lop Nur Lake

G

A

AFGHANISTAN

N

PAKISTAN

Qinghai Lake   XINING

Q   I   N   G   H   A   I   Yellow R.

Yangtze R.

T

NEW DELHI

N

I

I

B

E

LHASA

S I C

T

KATHMANDU

Yarlung R.   (Brahmaputra)

THIMPHU
BHUTAN

N

D

THIMPHU
BHUTAN

DHAKA

KUN

A

N

Lancang R.

BANGLADESH

Mekong R.

MYANMAR

Bay of Bengal

(BURMA)

LA

CHAZAUD

0   500   1000 km

0   300   600 miles

THAILAND

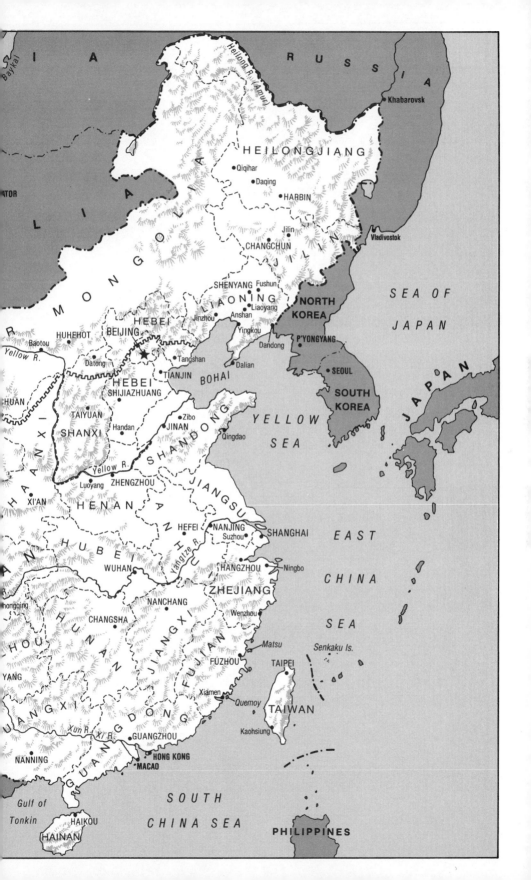

THE GREAT WALL
AND THE EMPTY FORTRESS

1

CHINA'S PLACE
IN THE WORLD

C HINA IS A vast country that some think will rival America as a superpower in the next century, yet it is militarily backward and ob-
sessed with preserving its territorial integrity. It is one of the United
Nations veto-holding "permanent five" and a member of the nuclear club,
yet it has no bloc of allies and claims to be an ordinary member of the
Third World. It is a critic of capitalism and at the same time one of the
top-ten trading nations in the world. Its vast rural interior nurtures an
inward-looking culture, while its long coastline is home to a cosmopolitan population larger than the combined population of all the East Asian
industrialized and newly industrialized countries.[1] It is a regional power
with global presence, from one vantage point standing at the periphery
of world affairs, from another at the center.

China's behavior often puzzles others. For centuries it placed itself
at the core of its own world order, oblivious to the power politics of Europe and the interstate law that it spawned. Today it defends a purist, originally European conception of national sovereignty. As a member of the
World War II antifascist alliance, Nationalist China gained a seat in the
UN Security Council. Under Communist rule soon after the war China

joined the Soviet bloc. It left the bloc to become a solitary state with only a handful of states friendly to it, in Asia and Eastern Europe. Then it entered into a quasi-alliance with the United States in the 1970s and 1980s.

China acts like a realist power on the world stage, yet insists its foreign policy is guided by principle. These principles were once expressed in Marxist terms; now Beijing says ideology should not count in international affairs. China has been portrayed as a dissatisfied power trying to upset the world order and as a status quo power favoring the international stability so necessary for economic development. It has been seen as inward oriented and as aggressive, as rationally calculating and as driven by cultural values and emotions. Its growing power has been seen as a force for stability in twenty-first-century Asia, and as a potential threat to world peace.

China's behavior begins to make sense if one looks at where it is located in the world, what assets and liabilities it brings to the defense of its own security, and how its leaders see their country's vulnerabilities. A good place to start is with what the Chinese government says officially about its foreign policy.

"AN INDEPENDENT FOREIGN POLICY OF PEACE"

China portrays itself as a Third World country that pursues "an independent foreign policy of peace." "Independence" means that China does not align itself with any other major power. Chinese spokesmen declare that their country seeks peace so that it can concentrate on development.

China says its decisions on foreign policy questions derive from the Five Principles of Peaceful Coexistence: mutual respect for sovereignty and territorial integrity, mutual nonaggression, noninterference in each other's internal affairs, equality and mutual benefit, and peaceful coexistence. The Chinese leadership originally enumerated these principles in 1954 when China was trying to reach out to the non-Communist countries of Asia. At the time the principles were intended to strengthen relations with neutralist countries like India and Burma, and to mollify Southeast Asian governments that were fighting Communist insurgencies and worried about the fifth-column potential of large Chinese minorities within their borders.

Today, with no change in wording, the Five Principles serve a new purpose. They offer an alternative to the American conception of a new kind of world order—one in which international regimes and institutions, often reflecting U.S. interests and values, limit the proliferation of certain conventional weapons and weapons of mass destruction, constrain mercantilist economic policies that interfere with free trade, and limit sovereignty by promoting universal norms of human rights. China's alternative design for the world stresses the equality of states in establishing international norms and the uninfringeable sovereignty of all states large and small, Western and non-Western, rich and poor, democratic and authoritarian, each to run its own system as it sees fit, whether its methods suit Western standards or not. The Five Principles explain why America should not be able to impose its values on weaker nations.

China says it "never seeks hegemony." In the 1960s "hegemony" was a code word for Soviet expansionism. In the late 1970s and the 1980s China extended the concept to Vietnam's domination of Cambodia and Laos. Today Chinese officials use the term to refer to a one-sided American effort to enforce its will on other countries in such matters as trade practices, weapons proliferation, and human rights. By saying it will not seek hegemony, China also tells its smaller neighbors that China's economic development and growing military might will not turn the country into a regional bully.

Chinese officials' position on most disputes around the world is that they should be solved by peaceful negotiations. This was their view on the war between Iran and Iraq, the struggle between Israel and the Arabs, and the conflicts in the former Yugoslavia. At the UN, China usually abstains or refrains from voting on resolutions that mandate sanctions or interventions to reverse invasions, end civil wars, or stop terrorism. Because China is a permanent Security Council member, its negative vote would constitute a veto, angering countries that favor intervention. By not voting or casting an abstention, it has allowed several interventions to go ahead without reversing its commitment to nonintervention.

Perhaps the most consistent element in Chinese diplomatic rhetoric is the idea that foreign policy should be based on moral principles. Moral judgments are almost impossible to avoid in the Chinese language. In the 1972 Shanghai communiqué, where America "acknowledged" the Chinese view that there is but one China and that Taiwan is a part of China, no translation into Chinese could convey the noncommittal flavor of the English term. The translation preferred by the Chinese and accepted by the Americans, *chengren,* implies recognition of a legitimate claim. Although realism is often a feature of Chinese policy and is valued as a political skill, no Chinese policy can be realistic that does not also include a moral rationale.

There are three other reasons why Chinese foreign policy rhetoric has been relatively consistent over time. First, in contrast to states with globe-spanning interests, China is still a regional power. Only in Asia does China face the sorts of dilemmas America faces everywhere: between conflicting long- and short-term interests, economic and political needs, the incompatible demands of friendly states, historical friendships and new alignments, or old principles and new realities. But in the Middle East, Africa, and Latin America, a few simple principles actually reflect Chinese interests most of the time. To oppose great-power intervention and defend sovereignty and equality among states is not only high-minded but represents China's national interest in regions where China cannot intervene itself. The farther one gets from China's borders, the easier it is for China to match rhetoric with interests.

Second, a weaker power strengthens its bargaining position when it insists on the inviolability of its principles. To the extent that Beijing can persuade other capitals that it never changes its mind, foreign diplomats shy away from raising issues Beijing has labeled closed. Even if concessions have to be made, the claim that they are not concessions preserves an appearance of power, which is itself an element of power.

Third, even when there are inconsistencies and trade-offs in Chinese policy, it is easy to hide them from view under the cloak of rhetoric because a handful of top leaders and a staff of professionals run Chinese diplomacy. The Cultural Revolution (1966–69) brought to the fore a group of leaders and diplomats who changed foreign policy rhetoric and practice, but only for a short time. Since then, even when domestic dissent appeared in the late 1970s and late 1980s, foreign policy has not been an important issue of debate. Dissident and off-the-record views differ from official ones chiefly in that they more openly acknowledge China's ambition to be a major power in the twenty-first century.

It would be wrong to call Chinese foreign policy transparent, if that means that policy derives directly from the principles the government supports. The declared principles draw their vitality and their meaning in specific circumstances from their service to national interests. They are open to interpretation as interests require, even to the point of disguising policy U-turns. Ultimately, rhetoric and strategy in Chinese foreign policy are as consistent as they are because they both respond to China's evolving geopolitical situation.

AN ASIAN COUNTRY

China's location in Asia dictates the priorities for its diplomacy. Japan and Korea, Vietnam and Cambodia, Tajikistan and Kazakstan are not distant but near. Refugees from Vietnam's economic troubles arrived in China not as boat people but by land. Foreign invasion of the small country of Cambodia was not a remote tragedy but a nearby threat. Clan wars in the new Central Asian republics involve kin of people living within China's borders. The prospect of war on the Korean peninsula looms larger in Chinese anxieties than actual wars in Central America, the Middle East, North Africa, and the former Yugoslavia. The leaders of Malaysia, Thailand, and Singapore are important figures for Chinese diplomacy. The Chinese pay close attention to the diplomatic potential of a regional economic grouping, APEC (Asia Pacific Economic Cooperation forum), which is on the periphery of American concerns. China sees the region we call the Middle East as "West Asia," part of an Islamic world that sweeps from Iraq and Iran through Central Asia into China's vast northwestern province of Xinjiang.

Distance matters less for a global power. Even though the United States is located in North America, it is also concerned with events in Asia, the Middle East, and Eastern Europe because it has investments, military bases, alliances, and raw materials suppliers almost everywhere. China lacks the worldwide interdependencies in economics and security that would cause it to be threatened by whatever happens anywhere. If China takes an interest in the Middle East and Eastern Europe, it is not because it relies on Middle Eastern oil (although it does buy some), or could be drawn into an Eastern European war, but because events in these areas affect it indirectly through states with which China has to deal in its own region, like the United States, Russia, and Japan. To the extent that China has interests outside of Asia, they are derivative rather than vital interests.

Although East Asia is distant from America and Europe, it is not a strategic backwater. During the Cold War it was the site of the Korean

War, two Taiwan Strait crises, the American policy of containment of China, a series of major wars in Indochina, and the Sino-Soviet border clashes. Cold War diplomacy was in some ways more complex in Asia than in Europe. In a region of great geographic expanse and ethnic, religious, and ideological diversity, Asian states were not all aligned along a single front by the equivalent of NATO and the Warsaw Pact. Instead, it was a zone of competition for the two superpowers. Eventually Asia settled into a strategic triangle involving China, the United States, and the Soviet Union. But China also conducted diplomacy within numerous smaller triangles: with the United States and Japan, the USSR and Japan, the USSR and Vietnam, Vietnam and Cambodia, South and North Korea, and India and Pakistan, among others. There were quadrangles, too—China with Vietnam, Cambodia, and Thailand; China with the USSR, Pakistan, and Afghanistan—and other, still more complicated patterns. Interstate relations in Asia were multilayered, more fluid than those in Europe.

The late Cold War was a time of relative peace in Asia, with the exception of Indochina. After the second Taiwan Strait crisis, in 1958, the risk of a Sino-American military clash receded. After the U.S. defeat in Vietnam in 1975, most of East Asia grew peaceful and stable. The ebb of revolutionary movements in Southeast Asia (many formerly Chinese supported) provided opportunities for economic growth that several countries were quick to seize. A spurt of development brought large parts of the region from the Third World into the developed world. East and Southeast Asia are now the source of a quarter of the world's GNP.[2] More than two decades of regional stability and growth have provided China with a sense of gradually diminishing threat and an opportunity to concentrate on economic development.

Located in the center of its region, China is a giant country surrounded by independent and assertive smaller countries, most of them different from it both ethnically and ideologically. Its regional relationships have been marked by mutual suspicion. China has historically exerted influence in many nearby countries, making them wary of its rising power today. Their suspicions are exacerbated by the presence, within their borders, of large communities of ethnic Chinese, whom they often regard as potential fifth columns.

A COUNTRY WITH MANY NEIGHBORS

China has more different political units as immediate neighbors than does any other country except Russia. On land, sweeping the map clockwise from the northeast, China shares borders with fourteen states: Russia, North Korea, Vietnam, Laos, Myanmar (Burma), India, Bhutan, Nepal, Pakistan, Afghanistan, Tajikistan, Kyrgyzstan, Kazakstan, and Mongolia. At sea Chinese claims abut or overlap with those of some of the same states plus six others: South Korea, Japan, the Philippines, Brunei, Malaysia, and Indonesia. In addition, China has boundaries with three entities that it claims but does not yet control: Taiwan, Hong Kong (until July 1, 1997), and Macao. And it faces a sphere-of-influence boundary across the Pacific with the United States. By this reckoning, China's immediate territorial interests overlap with those of twenty-four other governments.

China's land borders are the second longest in the world, after Russia's. The 4,000-mile border with the Soviet Union was for twenty-five years the longest unfriendly border in the world. At one point over one and a half million troops armed with nuclear weapons were ranged closely along the two sides of this line. The Soviet Union and China began to demilitarize the border and restore local cross-border trade in the late 1980s. But the breakup of the Soviet Union gave rise on China's borders to Russia and three Central Asian states, also setting Mongolia free from Russian domination. One regional actor was replaced by five. Each of the five has the potential to create tension with China over ethnic, trade, or security issues.

During the 1960s China concluded boundary treaties with Mongolia, Burma, Bhutan, Sikkim (now part of India), Nepal, Pakistan, and Afghanistan. In the 1990s it signed boundary treaties with Laos, Kazakstan, Tajikistan, Kyrgyzstan, and Russia. China still has unresolved boundary or territorial disputes with Russia, Tajikistan, North Korea, Vietnam, India, Japan, Malaysia, the Philippines, and Brunei.[3] Of all the neighboring countries, China has enjoyed alliances with only two, the Soviet Union and North Korea, as well as stable alignments with two others, Burma and Pakistan. Of these relationships the one with the Soviet Union turned to enmity, and now that China has established diplomatic relations with South Korea, the alliance with North Korea is fraught with tension.

In this century China has engaged in military conflicts with the United States, Russia, Japan, India, Vietnam, South Korea, and Taiwan. All remain potential military rivals. It is also conceivable that China might have to use arms against North Korea. The armies of the eight states just named all rank in the top twenty-five of world armies by size. While the United States enjoys a 6-to-1 advantage in troop strength over the combined armies of its immediate neighbors, Mexico and Canada, with whom military conflict is in any case unthinkable, China's army, even though the biggest in the world, suffers a net 2-to-1 disadvantage of troop strength compared with the aggregate militaries of its seven main regional neighbors, even leaving aside the more distant United States.

China's borders are easier to invade than to defend.[4] The long coastline is open to invasion from the sea. The inland borders are mostly mountainous and cold, difficult to garrison, and populated by minority peoples of doubtful loyalty to the central government. With the sometime exceptions of Vietnam and North Korea, China has had no buffer states on likely invasion routes between it and potential invaders. In contrast to those of the United States, China's most likely potential battlegrounds are internal rather than overseas.

For decades Beijing's planners left undeveloped the southern coastal provinces of Guangdong and Fujian, with their combined population of 96 million, in the expectation that the Chinese air force would have to bomb them in the event of a Nationalist or American invasion. Defense planners were prepared to bomb their own territory in order to deny invaders a beachhead. After the 1965 Tonkin Gulf incident increased tensions in Vietnam and as tensions with the Soviet Union increased, Mao decreed the removal of already developed industrial infrastructure from urban concentrations in the north and northeast to remote mountain valleys in the west and southwest. The transferred assets established an industrial "third front," dispersed and hidden to frustrate enemy attempts to destroy it from the air. For a time, two-thirds of all state industrial investment was spent in these remote locations. Productivity dropped and transport costs rose.[5]

War today looks unlikely, but defense planners cannot rule out the long-run possibility of war at almost any place along China's long continental and maritime borders. This strategic situation is just the opposite of that faced by American defense planners, whose home territory is so far from all conceivable enemies that invasion is not a serious concern in defense planning.

A CONTINENTAL COUNTRY WITH A HUGE, POOR,
AND ETHNICALLY DIVERSE POPULATION

China's territory is about the same size as that of the United States, but
at 1.2 billion its population is more than four times as big. Only 22 percent of China's territory is its demographic heartland, containing 66 percent of the population.[6] The heartland is roughly the size and shape of
the American Atlantic coast from Massachusetts to Florida, extending inland to include Pennsylvania, West Virginia, and Alabama, but it contains
five and a half times their population. Most of it consists of fertile, well-
watered agricultural plains and valleys that grow wheat and rice. This
densely populated area lies along the eastern side of the Chinese landmass,
at distances ranging from roughly 150 to 600 miles from the coast. Only
a small part of it is protected by coastal mountains against seaward attack. When Japan invaded in 1937–38, it occupied most of this area in
a year of fighting; in today's era of smart bombs, missiles, air troop transport, and nuclear weapons, the heartland is even more vulnerable to destruction.

Towering above and beyond the heartland is the other China, remote,
high, cold, and poor, stretching about 2,000 miles farther to the west. The
western thirteen of China's thirty provinces occupy 78 percent of China's
land surface, but contain only 34 percent of its population and produce
less than 22 percent of its GNP. They contain most of China's mineral resources as well as most of its ethnic-minority peoples (8 percent of the
total population). Except for the Yangtze River basin and the Chengdu
Plain, most of this area is mountainous and its people are poor.

Many of the minority peoples living in the west have doubtful loyalty to China, strained relations with the central government, and active
cross-border ties with related groups in neighboring countries. Nominally,
Beijing gives limited autonomy to 159 minority-occupied administrative
areas, ranging in size from province-sized regions to counties.[7] But most
of these districts are actually controlled by ethnically Chinese (Han) garrisons. They constitute the great rear area for the defense of coastal and
plains China, and its historical buffer from the political storms of Inner
Asia and beyond. The predominantly Han heartland has historically invested major resources to control this far-flung region, a subject we explore further in Chapters 2 and 11.

The Chinese population has grown rapidly in the last two centuries. In the mid-eighteenth century it was about 180 million.[8] The population increased despite wars and famines because the farmers found more and more intensive ways to cultivate the land. They went from one crop of rice per year to two where climate permitted, or from two crops to three. They started one crop's seedlings before the preceding crop had been harvested, then quickly plowed the newly harvested land and transplanted the seedlings from seedbed to field by hand. Elsewhere farmers fed silkworms by hand, picking and shredding mulberry leaves for many feedings per day. Short crops and tall crops, early crops and late crops were planted together in one field.

This economy and its technology did not support a projection of power beyond China's borders, nor did they require initiatives in inter-

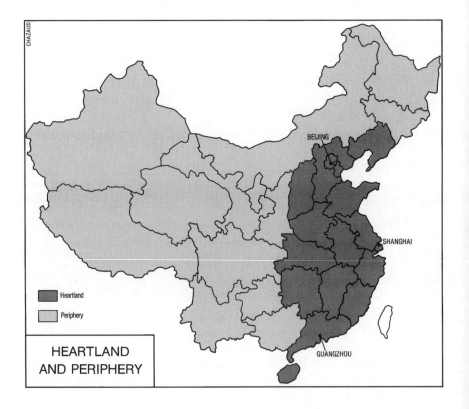

national trade or diplomacy. The economy produced little that could be sold abroad, needed little that was produced abroad, saved no money to be invested abroad, and offered no skills to attract investors from abroad. The economy was prosperous except during times of war and natural disaster, but so tightly balanced between population pressure and labor-intensive technology that no outside aid could have been bountiful enough to modernize it until it first released itself from its own economic stasis. The economy of the coastal region grew when the international economy was relatively open to Chinese exports, such as during the 1910s, but not fast enough to bring along the vast hinterland. For national takeoff, China had no alternative to self-reliant development. This meant squeezing the capital for industrial investment out of the small farmers. After 1949 China's Communist rulers turned inward to seek a bootstrap solution to the country's problems, aided only for the first decade by Soviet technology and loans. For two decades after its break with the Soviet Union, China was the only major country whose domestic economy was virtually unaffected by the international economic system.[9]

Only in the early 1970s, when industrial production amounted to nearly half of its GDP and foreign threats had diminished, did China begin to look to foreign trade and investment for part of the impetus to further development. Even today, when China is deeply involved in the international economy, its natural-resources base gives it the option of autarkic survival that is open to few other nations.

AT THE MEETING POINT OF WORLD CAMPS

During the Cold War, China was the only major country that stood at the intersection of the two superpower camps, a target of influence and enmity for both. In Europe the line dividing East from West was clearly demarcated and did not change for forty years. Except for a few small neutrals, every European country was on one side of this line or the other and was threatened by only one of the two superpowers. In Asia the demarcation line ran through the Sea of Japan between Russia and Japan, then cut across the Korean peninsula at the thirty-eighth parallel. But when it reached China, it became unclear. For a few years China stood on the Soviet side, but it soon broke away. Without formally joining the Western camp, it tilted to the West after 1971.

China was the largest and most powerful state not to stay in the camp of one of the two superpowers. It became what theorists call a "weak pole" in the international system, enabling North Vietnam and North Korea to use China to balance Soviet power, and for a time giving Cambodia and Burma an alternative to alignment with either superpower. But the rest of the smaller nations around China were aligned with one or the other superpower. Any expansion of its influence would bring it into conflict with the sphere of influence of either the Soviet Union or the United States.[10]

China found itself in the uniquely dangerous position of being alternately wooed and threatened by both superpowers. When China allied with the Soviet Union, the United States responded with a strategy of pressure designed to break the alliance. When China shifted out of the Soviet camp, the Soviets responded with similar pressures. Both superpowers at one time or another threatened China with nuclear attack. Only when the military confrontation between the Soviet Union and the United States eased could China also relax, taking advantage of the opportunities afforded by the end of the Cold War to deal on favorable terms with both former enemies at once.

The only development more dangerous to China than superpower rivalry would have been superpower collusion. That possibility took shape in the late 1950s with the Soviet push for "coexistence." The Soviet-American duopoly that Chinese diplomats feared never took full form. Had it done so, it would have exposed China to potential diktat in any area the superpowers wished. From about 1958 onward, Chinese diplomacy aimed at countering emergent U.S.-Soviet cooperation on arms control, European stability, and the Middle East.

FREE TO MANEUVER

Standing outside both superpower camps, lacking vital interests beyond Asia, uninvolved until recently in the world economy, and motivated more by the need to frustrate others' designs than by the desire to advance its own world vision, China surveyed the surrounding world with detachment and acted flexibly in pursuit of its central interest, to defend itself against the initiatives of others. Of all the large countries, China has had the greatest freedom to maneuver, act on grand strategy, shift alignments, and conduct a strategic foreign policy in the rational pursuit of national interest.

China is surrounded by smaller countries that are as anxious to maintain their independence of it as China has been to maintain its independence of the superpowers. Their fear of China's dominance and, for many years, its ideological hostility was not counterbalanced by the kinds of forces that sometimes draw nations together. China had neither the strategic power to coerce its neighbors to accommodate themselves to Chinese interests throughout the Cold War nor the dynamic economy to attract their long-term economic involvement. By confronting both superpowers, China put itself at odds with their clients. Among these clients, Thailand moved close to China only when it lacked strong support from the United States, and North Vietnam did so when it lacked strong support from the Soviet Union.

China sought to overcome its isolation by encouraging fluidity and multipolarity wherever it could. Because both dominant camps threatened its security and tried to restrict its freedom of maneuver, China's diplomacy in Southeast Asia, Africa, the Middle East, and Latin America aimed at breaking rather than at constructing alignments. Mao once said, "The world is in chaos; the situation is excellent." But the goal of China's multilateralist diplomacy was not to create a world of chaos, which might have threatened China in other ways, but to loosen the superpower vise that constricted its freedom of maneuver.

Its handful of national leaders were accountable to no special interests and bound by no public preferences. They were able to turn Russia from big brother to enemy, the United States from foe to friend, Japan from bogeyman to aid donor, South Korea from imperialist lackey to friendly neighbor. Leaders, diplomats, the controlled media, and the public sang the changing tune with one voice. China operated from a position of vulnerability and in a defensive mode, but its size and situation made it "a critical independent factor in the balance of world forces."[11] The authoritarian political system permitted the leaders to conduct the defensive, opportunistic foreign policy their international position required.

When the post-Mao leadership ended economic autarky and sought to join the community of nations, China's security improved but its independence of action declined. It entered the United Nations in 1971, encountered the rise of a worldwide human rights diplomacy in the 1980s, and experienced growing dependence on international markets in the 1980s and 1990s.

POWER AND WEAKNESS

History and geography set the agenda for Chinese foreign policy. Its first objective is to restore and maintain territorial integrity. PRC diplomacy seeks to reclaim the lost regions of Hong Kong, Macao, and Taiwan, to block outside support for separatist movements in Tibet, Xinjiang, and Inner Mongolia, and to deter invasion and military pressure on all fronts by building up the capacity for internal security and border defense.

A second goal is to prevent the domination of the Asian region by others while expanding cooperation with its neighbors. If China's location at the center of Asia surrounds it with potential enemies and involves it in complicated rivalries, it also gives it the potential to dominate the most dynamic region of the world. Should another nation dominate the region, it could turn its attention to dominating China. On the other hand, too strong a hand could make China's neighbors fear that China seeks to dominate Asia itself. A careful mix of military capability, economic power, and diplomatic involvement is needed to influence neighbors without pushing them into hostility.

Third, Chinese foreign policy seeks to create a favorable environment for economic growth. China favors stable world markets, opposes trading blocs, works for open access to developed-country markets, but bargains hard to delay the opening of its own markets. It seeks admission to the World Trade Organization with developing-country privileges that would permit it to increase exports to advanced countries while maintaining protection for its infant industries as long as possible.

China pursues its goals with a mixture of power and weakness. If size and extended borders render the country vulnerable, they also help it resist invasion. The vast hinterland provides room to fall back and "defend in depth." During the era of imperialism, China was not colonized. The foreign presence spread widely throughout the country, but except in certain coastal cities and foreign-concession areas it was too dispersed to become a dominating influence. The invading Japanese in the 1930s and 1940s were unable to secure rule over the whole country. Later neither the United States nor the Soviet Union wanted to get bogged down, as Japan had, in the vastness of China.

Population is at once a liability and an asset. Chinese military modernizers throughout the twentieth century faced great challenges in making modern soldiers out of the vast, mostly illiterate rural population, but that same population also makes China a potential military and demographic threat to its neighbors even without the most up-to-date technology. Merely by being so numerous, the Chinese affect the fates of the rest of the world whatever they do—when they emigrate, when they purchase grain on world markets, when they build roads and drive cars. They could strain world food resources by failing to feed themselves, or damage the global atmosphere by not reducing the rate at which they cook and heat their homes with charcoal briquettes. Because of its demographic size, no global problem can be solved without China.

Cheap labor is the basis of China's new export-led growth strategy. It has helped expand the Maoist industrial base into a major economy, which has been growing at a rate of over 10 percent per year since 1980, ranks ninth in the world, and is essentially self-sufficient in resources. By some estimates it could become the world's second-largest economy early in the next century, providing a strong basis for a sophisticated military machine. Chinese spokesmen are concerned that such estimates of national power based on economic size and growth encourage the rise of "China threat" theory. They insist that China is and will continue to be a poor, developing country that is in many respects technologically backward.

The fact is that China is in different senses both poor and rich. With a GNP per capita around U.S. $500, its per capita wealth ranks in the bottom tenth of all countries. Yet by quality-of-life measures, such as life expectancy and levels of education, China is stronger than this statistic suggests. The disparity is due partly to international exchange rates and to differential price structures: housing and medical care, for example, are cheaper in China than in the West. Finally, compared with some countries, China has invested more or more wisely in public health and education. Hence in "purchasing power parity" terms China's output per capita ranks near the middle.[12] The Chinese population is more educated, healthier, and better skilled than income figures suggest. In major cities many residents lead comfortable lives. Although housing is tight, consumer goods like television sets, radios, and bicycles are common. Food and clothing in most areas are plentiful.

China's location in the heart of Asia, the complexity of its regional environment, its abundance of difficult neighbors, its location between American and Russian spheres of influence—all the attributes that define China's difficult geopolitical position—also contribute to its strategic importance and its ability to achieve foreign policy goals. Despite its power liabilities, China has taken advantage of its situation to turn itself into one of the major world actors. China is in a diplomatic class different from that of other large developing countries like India, Brazil, or Indonesia.

A nation's influence consists not only of strategic and economic power but also of the "soft power" of values and ideas. China's opening to the world has reduced the mystique the Chinese "way of socialism" once enjoyed in the West. China has become vulnerable to international criticism over human rights, a subject we explore further in Chapter 10.

Population, territory, and location compose a kind of Great Wall that protects China from conquest. But like the Wall itself, they also point to the vulnerability of China's high civilization and rich agriculture to invasion. China has often been conquered—by the Mongols, by the Manchus, by Marxism, and in recent decades by modernization. But equally often the Chinese have enjoyed victory despite weakness by using superior strategy, a theme we explore in the next chapter.

2

LEGACIES

SINCE CHINA WAS drawn into the world of modern states 150 years ago, its foreign relations have reflected a number of persistent features. Among them are the notion of China as a central place with a self-sufficient civilization, a tendency to advise others to resolve disputes peacefully combined with frequent defensive uses of force on or near home ground, a moralist approach to international issues, skill at balance-of-power politics, and an obsession with the impact of foreign ties on the national culture and economy.

Yet history also means change. In one century China moved from empire to nation-state, became a republic and then the People's Republic, freed itself from semicolonialism to make itself diplomatically equal and economically self-sustaining, aligned with the Soviet Union, broke with it, and emerged as a major force on the world scene.

Continuity and change are not always easy to tell apart. Some continuities are perceived analogies between past and present, rather than the product of enduring influences from the past. Others are created from a malleable past to justify or disguise change. Or leaders may declare change in order to mask continuity. Even when continuity is real, it may not explain much. To say that things have always been done in a certain way explains neither why they were done that way before nor why they continue to be done that way now.

Of the five features of China's geopolitical situation described in the preceding chapter, only one can truly be called permanent—its location in Asia. Yet even the meaning of being in Asia is not fixed. Asia was once outside the European-based world system; in the nineteenth century it became part of it. The map of Asia evolved with the rise and decline of colonialism, the emergence and end of the Cold War, and the coalescence and splitting of nations. Five territories—Annam, Cochin China, Tonkin, Cambodia, and Laos—became French Indochina in the nineteenth century, then split into four states in the 1950s, and became three countries after the unification of Vietnam in 1975. After the Bolshevik revolution the loose Russian empire became a powerful Communist state, and in the 1990s the Asian part of the Soviet Union was replaced by Russia and five independent Central Asian states. As technology shrank the world in the twentieth century, America became part of geopolitical Asia.

China itself has had a shifting historical meaning. In ancient times the term Zhongguo meant "the states of the central plain," or was used to refer to various cities, states, and regions in what is now central China, and only later came to mean the Central State (Middle Kingdom), or China.[1] The first unified Chinese state, the Qin (221–206 B.C.), occupied a territory only about a quarter of the size of today's country. Over centuries members of the ethnic group who called themselves Han expanded from the central plain by conquest and migration to the south, west, northwest, and northeast, incorporating the territories of tribes living around them and assimilating many of the inhabitants. The Han territory in turn was conquered five times by Inner Asian nomads, who expanded China by becoming part of it. By the early nineteenth century, under the conquest dynasty of the Manchus (the Qing dynasty, 1644–1911), China was larger than ever before or since. But after another century's encounter with the West and Japan, by 1941 the area administered by the central government was about 60 percent of today's size, minus Tibet, Taiwan, the northeast (Manchuria), eastern Inner Mongolia, and a large chunk of the North China Plain. "China" is thus the ever-changing creation of population movements, warfare, and interstate relations.

HISTORY AND CULTURE

The mechanisms by which historical continuity operates are as elusive as those that drive change. One medium for both continuity and change is culture. Habits of action, attitudes and beliefs, and memories of how things used to be done affect present practices, but they do not do so irresistibly or in a predetermined way. Culture is a repertoire, neither dictating continuity nor preventing change. Like history, culture contains a host of possibilities, some more and some less relevant to a particular problem, providing in their aggregate a series of precedents for nearly any pattern of activity that social actors select.

For example, scholars have described Chinese culture as both peaceful and warlike. China was created by conquest, both when the Han invaded neighbors' territory and when Inner Asian neighbors took over the Han. China conquered, but was ultimately expelled from, Vietnam and Korea; its settlements but not its rule extended into what later became Russia and the Central Asian republics. China expanded when there was room to expand and population pressure on the land. It stopped when it ran out of room, met insurmountable geographic obstacles, or was turned back by other armed peoples. In this century Chinese troops fought mostly in civil wars or near the country's borders in wars that were primarily defensive. Internally, Chinese society has been violent when weak government, economic disorder, or social dislocation made violence attractive, peaceful when it was well governed and prosperous. Apparently, for Chinese as for Americans or others, violence is a matter not of culture but of need and opportunity. The Chinese are capable of peace as well as war, and cultural precedent does not tell us which they will prefer.

Similarly, Chinese culture contains elements of both moralism and realism. The historical epic *The Three Kingdoms* is in many ways a template for Chinese thinking about the role of human relations in international affairs. The legend tells of the struggles among three rulers who sought to reunify China in A.D. 168–265. Beloved by Chinese in all walks of life, the tales are told by village storytellers, enacted in operas and movies, and illustrated in almanacs, calendars, and pictures posted on doors. Some of the heroes have become gods worshiped in temples. Every literate Chinese has read the novelized version written by Luo Guanzhong in the late 1300s. Chinese diplomats and military officers often describe their maneuvers in terms of these stories. The very language is full of references to it.

The opening line of the book states the theme of balance-of-power realism: "Empires wax and wane; states cleave asunder and coalesce." In a world in which power is evanescent, the book glorifies the use of "stratagems" *(ji)*, deceptions designed to win battles against greater forces, if possible without using any of one's own forces. In the "borrowed arrows stratagem," the military adviser Zhuge Liang is ordered to prepare a hundred thousand arrows within three days for a coming military action, an apparently impossible mission. He does nothing until the evening of the third day, then sends twenty boats filled with straw across the river in a fog. The enemy camp shoots the straw full of arrows, which Zhuge brings back to his own camp. In the "defecting with a secret stratagem," also called the "personal injury stratagem," a loyal general accepts a cruel beating at the hands of his commander so that he can defect to the enemy's side to serve as a spy. The stories praise mirrors-within-mirrors deceit. People with steel nerves and quick wits disarm others' suspicions only to betray them. Leaders lose their power because they give trust. Intended treacheries are secretly perceived and turned against their perpetrators.

But cynicism is counterbalanced by a stress on loyalty and legitimacy. Perhaps the best-known scene is the "peach garden oath," where two of the main heroes pledge fealty to one of the contenders for power, Liu Bei. Nothing shakes their commitment through the rest of the book, and the novel is full of inspiring examples of self-sacrifice for the common mission. Liu Bei inspires devotion not because he is the most able general—that distinction belongs to the evil Cao Cao—but because he is the legitimate heir to the empire and therefore morally worthy (and a bit dull). That is why he can recruit an adviser like Zhuge Liang, who has a supernatural understanding of what the Chinese consider the decisive forces in war and politics: *shi, di,* and *shi* (time, place, and the correlation of forces). Yet neither Liu Bei nor Cao Cao manages to unify the empire. Stratagems win the battle but not the war. The Three Kingdoms myths provide repertoires of both loyalty and betrayal, effort and fatalism, idealism and cynicism.

Chinese diplomacy emphasizes the importance of giving and getting "face." Face has long been a central element affecting interpersonal relations in China. At the same time, the exchange of face can be a practical bargaining tool. The norm of face can warn other countries not to shame Chinese leaders by demanding humiliating compromises, lest tension escalate and cooperation become difficult. If China can convince its counterpart that its flexibility is constrained by concern for face, it can moderate its counterpart's demands. This strategy is particularly useful for the weaker party in negotiations, which China often is.

But China is not always equally sensitive to giving face to others. By citing the principle that "he who tied the knot should untie it," China can sometimes extract maximum concessions from a negotiating adversary. Face may then be given as a reward for diplomatic cooperation. Even then, the legendary diplomatic hospitality is manipulated for the domestic audience to demonstrate cultural superiority. When a foreign head of state visits China, Chinese television shows the visitor being graciously received by the Chinese leader, nodding appreciatively as the latter lectures him on the principles of international relations, and affirming China's importance before being shown to the door. If anything critical is said, the state-controlled Chinese media leave it to the other side to report it. Face is a traditional value that has been adapted usefully to modern diplomacy.

The problem of when and how cultural explanations apply also extends to the idea of China as the "Middle Kingdom." Imperial China regulated its relations with other states by a tribute system, under which foreign rulers were treated like vassals of the emperor. Historians have argued that this precedent affected Chinese ways of acting in the modern world of nation-states. Because traditional foreign policy was normative, Sinocentric, assimilative, hierarchical, ideological, and personalistic, nineteenth-century China had trouble adapting to the European-organized multistate system, which was egalitarian, nonideological, and contractual.[2]

Mao's worldview often seemed Sinocentric, as the leaders of pro-Mao Communist parties from around the world trooped to China to receive audiences and pay symbolic tribute. During the period of the strategic triangle, China allowed itself to be courted by the Americans as if it were an honorary third member of the superpower club. As the triangle faded in the 1980s, China continued to talk about its ties with other countries less in terms of practical cooperation than in terms of the partner's friendliness and acceptance of Chinese norms.

Yet the tribute system was only one form of traditional relations between the center and the periphery.[3] Even the heartland was ruled in a mixed manner, in the Qing dynasty by a foreign tribe, the Manchus, who superimposed themselves on the Chinese bureaucracy. Along the coast and in central China, government was bureaucratic. Toward and beyond the northern and western frontiers, one found a mix of military governors-general, Manchu Banner (tribal) garrisons, jasaks (hereditary princes), khans, hakim begs (governors), aksakals (representatives), tribute-paying theocratic and tribal rulers, and, even farther beyond, a few states that were linked to China as tributaries of Beijing's tributaries, as Sikkim and Ladakh were of the Dalai Lama. Relations with Inner Asia were often characterized by "pragmatism and diplomatic parity."[4] Dealings with maritime Asia involved what scholars have called a "maritime subculture" that was commercial, exploratory, and intellectually realistic. Chinese foreign policy can draw on precedents of pragmatic egalitarianism when it needs to.

The tribute system was a way of thinking about political relations that served Chinese ideological interests and those of some of its partners for a certain period of time. Like the Five Principles of Peaceful Coexistence, Sinocentrism was a concept sufficiently malleable that it could legitimate a range of diplomatic practices. We still need to analyze present realities to explain how and why Sinocentric elements have remained useful in Chinese diplomatic practice.

THE GREAT WALL AND THE EMPTY FORTRESS: CHINA'S STRATEGIC CULTURE

Two of the enduring symbols in Chinese strategic thought are the Great Wall and the Empty Fortress. The Great Wall was built over centuries as part of a military strategy to protect China from invasions by the Huns and other Inner Asian horse-riding armies.[5] The area within the Wall is cultivated, in the double sense of agriculture and civilization. It is rich, heavily populated, and attractive to invaders. The area outside the Wall is poor, uncivilized, violent, and threatening. The Great Wall is a symbol of weakness, because it signals susceptibility to invasion, and of strength, because it represents economic and cultural superiority and an ability to ward off invasion with feats of engineering and vigilance.

Militarily, the Great Wall belongs to a class of strategies of protracted defense. It builds on superiority of one kind to counter superiority of another. The opposition has mobility, concentrated force, and explosive violence. The defending side has the weaknesses of a fixed position and less ability to concentrate violence on a single battlefield. It tries to turn weakness to advantage by redefining the conflict as one of protracted defensive resistance. Drawing on the Chinese strategic board game of *weiqi* (Japanese "go"), the Great Wall strategy builds on the perception that one controls territory by surrounding it.

Marx observed that modernization "batters down all Chinese walls." The threat came from the sea in the mid-nineteenth century, in the forms both of trade and of modern military technology that could breach any wall. Chinese strategists still needed to protect a large, vulnerable territory but the aggressor was even more mobile and violent than before. Since 1949 China has erected new great walls of ideological discipline, economic self-reliance, and an army prepared for defense in depth. As we will argue in Chapters 8–10, Deng Xiaoping's reforms have partially dismantled some of these great walls while strengthening others.

The Empty Fortress is another symbol of mixed weakness and strength. In the story of the Three Kingdoms (see the epigraph on p. ix), when Zhuge Liang is outnumbered in the defense of a fortress-like walled city, he strikes all the military banners, orders his troops to hide, opens all the gates, and sunbathes on the ramparts in view of the enemy soldiers. They conclude that the city must be well defended and that Zhuge is trying to trick them, so they decamp without attacking. Zhuge's fortress is vulnerable, but he has troops on the way. He uses time, place, and correlation of forces to get through a tight spot on the way to a victory. The PRC has used deception in similar ways to magnify limited resources and deter enemies from military attack and ideological subversion (Chapters 8 and 10).

A popular saying has it that "of the thirty-six stratagems, running away is best." This is a witty summary of the thought of "China's Clausewitz," Sunzi, who says that it is best to win without fighting, and to fight once rather than twice. Sunzi advises the strategist to pick his time and place, strike when the situation is in his favor, and prevail quickly. "The important thing in a military operation," he says, "is victory, not persistence." Once victorious, the general should make friends of the enemy's troops and generals, lest he place too great a strain on his own people. "Those who use the military skillfully do not raise troops twice and do not provide food three times," Sunzi says. He adds, "If you are equal, fight; if you are fewer, keep away; if you are not as good, flee."[6]

Strategy consists in making the best use of one's strengths and the enemy's weaknesses. Thus Sunzi remarks, "Military formation is like water—the form of water is to avoid the high and go to the low, the form of a military force is to avoid the full and attack the empty; the flow of water is determined by the earth, the victory of a military force is determined by the opponent." The United States is a country that is industrialized and wealthy, is protected by oceans, and fights away from its own soil. It can pre-position more supplies of weapons and spare parts than it could conceivably need and use overwhelming technological force across a broad front to achieve rapid victory with minimal casualties. It might seem that for China the corresponding principle is the human wave and mutual attrition, but that strategy is second-best. Mao boasted about China's ability to sustain huge losses. But his purpose in doing so was to deter enemies. He actually viewed "protracted warfare" as a way to avoid losses by avoiding battles you cannot win and "fight[ing] no battle you are not sure of winning."[7]

As strategies, both the Great Wall and the Empty Fortress make sense for a heavily populated agrarian society, in which farmers are the main resource, serving at once as soldiers and as provisioners for the troops. From Mencius to Mao, Chinese leaders viewed the population as the chief productive and strategic asset—as did the military leaders of all states until the twentieth century. The kingdoms of ancient China could not wear each other down without destroying many of their own assets in the process, which is why Sunzi considered using force to be inferior to not using it. Only after Mao's death did the Chinese government begin to think that its population had become so large that it was a strategic deficiency.

PROBLEMS FROM THE PAST: BACKWARDNESS

If the meanings of China's cultural legacy are ambiguous, the past affects the present more starkly by the problems it bequeaths. China's encounter with the West left three problems that shape its international agenda today. The first is the consciousness of backwardness.

In the nineteenth century China found itself invaded and victimized, forced to grant extraterritorial privileges, sign "unequal treaties," pay reparations, and turn to the outside world for famine relief, development aid, weapons, and manufacturing skills. To gain its independence the country had to remake its technology, educational institutions, ideology, laws, and military and political systems on Western models. The imposition of colonialism on much of Africa and South Asia persuaded Chinese thinkers that nothing less than national survival was at stake in a Darwinian struggle among races. The Chinese became aware that their economic and technological systems were backward. This sense of vulnerability created the dominating issue of modern Chinese politics, the search for wealth and power. Left unsolved by previous governments, the problem remained to be addressed by the People's Republic when it came to power.

Like China, South Korea, Taiwan, and Hong Kong had low-wage economies, long commercial traditions, entrepreneurial talent, some manufacturing experience, and Confucian cultures. Over the first three postwar decades they registered growth rates of about 8 to 10 percent a year, in part by producing consumer goods for the West, and reached levels of GNP per capita that exceeded China's by five to seventeen times by the time Deng Xiaoping came to power in 1978.[8] But export-led development was not an option for China in the 1950s. Levels of global trade were smaller both in absolute terms and as a proportion of world GNP than they are today. Even had international markets looked more inviting, China could not have entered them. The West imposed a trade embargo at the start of the Korean War, which it later maintained as part of the effort to drive a wedge between China and the Soviet Union. China's Soviet ally was recovering from World War II and gearing up its own defense forces for the Cold War. It protected its domestic market for its own industries. It gave crucial but limited assistance, which came to an end with the Sino-Soviet split in 1960 (Chapter 3).

To develop self-reliantly, Mao and his colleagues devised a system modeled on Stalinism but with a number of unique features. They accelerated agricultural collectivization and created large communes with no private ownership of land, restricted the migration of rural residents to the cities, used ideological campaigns instead of material incentives to mobilize human energies, and applied political terror and indoctrination to make people accept low living standards. The population found itself organized into work units—communes, factories, offices, and schools—that controlled all aspects of daily life. The ruling party deterred opposition by mobilizing mass persecutions of designated "class enemies."

These measures enabled China to "rely on its own forces to revitalize itself" *(zili gengsheng)*. The party-state extracted capital from agriculture, used it to build state-owned industry, and returned the profits to more industrial investment. This led to rapid industrial growth in the 1950s, although growth slowed later under the impact of the Great Leap Forward and the Cultural Revolution. In three decades China made itself self-sufficient in nearly all resources and technologies, but it lagged twenty to thirty years behind world technical standards and remained hobbled by low levels of labor and capital productivity. Mao had improved public health and raised educational levels, but kept incomes stagnant. At the time of his death most Chinese lived in cramped quarters with poor food and clothing, few comforts, and no freedoms. Workers wasted time in the factories and fields, equipment rusted, electric power stuttered, and cargo piled up in the weather, waiting for space on trains. Much of Asia and the world had raced beyond China toward technical and social modernity.

When Mao Zedong died in 1976, the new leaders faced a crisis that was both economic and political. Chinese would not indefinitely tolerate frozen living standards in pursuit of a more and more grotesque vision of utopia. Because Mao had vetoed population planning, tens of millions of young people poured into the work force each year and had to be given not just jobs but productive work if living standards were not to continue to stagnate. The lumbering economic apparatus had to be redirected from extensive to intensive growth, from piling up capital assets to making existing assets more productive. Reform policymakers reckoned that the economy had to grow at a rate of 6 to 10 percent a year in real terms to put enough people to work and improve living standards enough to prevent an economic and social breakdown.[9] There was no way to do this without abandoning autarky.

Richard Nixon and Mao Zedong made themselves the unwitting godfathers of reform when they met in Beijing in 1972. By reopening contacts between China and the West, they supplied the strategic conditions that made reform possible. In 1978 Deng Xiaoping announced "reform and opening." Reform meant changes in the domestic economic and administrative systems; opening meant changes in economic relations with the rest of the world. Domestic and foreign policies were linked. Economic reform required less hostile political relations with the West, in order to relax ideology and justify combining socialist practices with market mechanisms. The opening to the West sped the transition from the inefficient Maoist mix of obsolescent Soviet-style heavy industry and mostly manual agriculture to a productive, rapidly expanding modern economy. Technological and managerial modernization required the import of advanced foreign technology through foreign investment and by sending students abroad. The decollectivization of agriculture released a flood of surplus workers; foreign markets supplemented the ability of Chinese consumers to buy the vast output of the exploding light-industrial labor force. The close links between economic relations abroad and society and politics at home made reform of foreign economic policy one of the most controversial elements of foreign policy under Deng (Chapter 9).

TERRITORIAL INTEGRITY

A second problem China inherited from the past is the issue of territorial integrity, which we examine in detail in Chapter 11. Traditional China saw itself not as a nation-state, or even as an empire with clearly identified subject peoples, but as the center of the only known civilization. In Chinese eyes, other kingdoms and tribes were more or less civilized, depending on how close they were to China culturally and politically. The Koreans and Vietnamese were the most cultured, partly because they used Chinese characters as their written languages. Others were less assimilated. China enforced clear borders with its neighbors,[10] but on both sides of the borders the Han heartland exerted a variable influence. China's cultural and political tradition stretched from the core provinces, through more remote southern and western provinces, to garrisons in territories dominated by non-Han peoples; to northern and northwestern border tribes and kingships extending as far as the edges of Tashkent and Samarkand in present-day Kazakstan; to a penumbra of other cultures that included those of Korea, Vietnam, Burma, and Nepal; and finally to barbarians so remote that some of them were mythological.

By the nineteenth century Chinese dominance in the border regions was increasingly insecure even in the Qing dynasty's Manchu homeland. Although the area was by then inhabited mostly by Han Chinese and had been incorporated into the bureaucratic empire as the three northeastern provinces (today called Heilongjiang, Jilin, and Liaoning), it was threatened by mounting Russian and Japanese pressure. In Xinjiang, Qing garrisons maintained a tenuous supremacy among a host of oasis states and nomadic tribes where Chinese settlers were recent arrivals. In this cosmopolitan region China was but one of many cultural influences, political forces, and trading partners, no more important than India, Persia, Central Asia, and Russia. Tibet, while formally still part of China, had coalesced into a loosely joined theocratic state as recently as the eighteenth century and maintained informal ties across the Himalayas to Nepal, Sikkim, and parts of India. A rising British India in the south and a rising Russia in the north ceaselessly promoted their influence at Chinese expense. Only in Inner Mongolia, where nomadic tribes were overwhelmed by Chinese settlers, was Qing control firm.

Toward all surrounding peoples the Qing practiced a policy of "impartial benevolence." In Qing eyes fights among barbarians of different degrees of closeness to China did not mean the transfer of territory from their empire to another, just adjustments of relations among their diverse cultural inferiors. So in the nineteenth century Beijing did not perceive a threat to its security in growing British influence in the tributary states of Nepal, Sikkim, and Tibet. The supremacy of Chinese moral and cultural influence seemed intact, and Britain was too small and far away to look like a rival. Beijing was also willing to grant special rights to non-Chinese authorities around the periphery to administer and tax trade and to discipline their own people living in Chinese territory, as in the Sino-Kokand accord of 1835. This type of arrangement provided the precedent for extraterritoriality in the Western-dominated treaty ports.[11]

When expanding Western powers reached the perimeter of the Chinese empire, they forced China to define its physical borders, starting with the Treaty of Nerchinsk in 1689. As China became a "semicolony" in the nineteenth century, it had to give up claims to varying degrees of paramountcy over Burma, Vietnam, Korea, the Ryukyu Islands, outer Mongolia, parts of Central Asia and Siberia—even in a sense over Russia and Britain, for the Chinese emperor unsuccessfully demanded that both countries' envoys kowtow to him as vassals. China reserved claims to substantial pieces of territory ceded to India, the Soviet Union, Vietnam, Burma, and other states. (The Republic of China [ROC] still does not recognize the independence of Mongolia, although the PRC does.) The process of border demarcation continues today.

The separations of Hong Kong and Macao also had their origins in the nineteenth century. The most difficult legacy of territorial consolidation was Taiwan. Taken as a colony by Japan in 1895, it was returned to Chinese control under the Nationalist regime in 1945. But after 1949 Nationalist-ruled Taiwan neither reunified with mainland China nor declared independence from it, posing one of the major continuing problems for PRC diplomacy (Chapter 11).

Besides defining its borders, China had to define the legal status of its citizens. In 1909 China adopted its first law of nationality, defining as Chinese the children of Chinese fathers anywhere in the world. This principle of jus sanguinis (legal status by bloodlines) was consistent with traditional thinking about the meaning of being Chinese. But it placed China at odds with most countries' view of citizenship as a juridical rather than an ethnic concept, and put China in the position of treating other countries' naturalized or even native-born ethnically Chinese citizens as Chinese subjects.

Yet China found itself unable to extend protection to its citizens abroad. Ethnic Chinese were victims of anti-Chinese riots and the Chinese Exclusion Acts in nineteenth-century America and of discrimination in Japan and Southeast Asia. Ultimately, claiming as citizens tens of millions of ethnic Chinese concentrated in Southeast Asia and scattered throughout the rest of the world was more a liability than an asset.[12] It was not until 1955 that the PRC began to extricate itself from this dilemma, when Premier Zhou Enlai announced at the Afro-Asian conference at Bandung, Indonesia, that overseas Chinese should voluntarily adopt the citizenship of their host country and give up Chinese citizenship. During the 1950s China reached agreements with North Vietnam and Indonesia that codified these principles and renounced the principle of dual nationality, and the same model was applied in the 1970s when China normalized relations with other countries in Southeast Asia.

Within China's borders as well, the comfortable ambiguity of tradition was replaced by problematic clarities. The emperor's subjects included people of many tribes, religions, ethnic and subethnic groups. Labels like Mongol, Tibetan, and Kirghiz covered people from scores of culturally distinct groups. The Han majority itself was a mix of people with a broad spectrum of physical characteristics, speaking eight major dialects and many minor dialects as different from one another as Italian and French, and treating one another with varying degrees of subethnic prejudice.[13] A clear sense of Han ethnicity was the creation of late-nineteenth-century nationalists intent on overthrowing the "alien" Manchu dynasty.

Modern social thought, influenced by Darwinism, required sharper definitions of identity. Reformers and revolutionaries in the late nineteenth century created a myth of Han homogeneity. The first flag of the new Chinese republic in 1912 consisted of five differently colored stripes symbolizing a unified state of five "races" (Han, Manchu, Mongol, Tibetan, and Muslim). In the 1950s the People's Republic started counting and classifying its people, eventually recognizing fifty-five official national minorities that are eligible for certain privileges. Many once extant groups had disappeared by this time; others were folded into the fifty-five accepted categories or classed as part of the majority Han. Some people who thought of themselves as Han were given government assistance to revive, or even create, minority-group languages and rituals.[14]

Several of the official national minorities are sizable groups with developed cultures, occupying strategically important territories and maintaining connections with non-Chinese populations across China's borders. These include the Tibetans; the Mongolians, who make up a significant part of the population of Inner Mongolia; and a group of related Muslim peoples, mostly Uighur, Kazak, and Kyrgyz, who live primarily in the northwestern province of Xinjiang. Only after 1949 did the central government have the ability to impose tight control over these regions, at the same time intensifying the Han influx that was overwhelming the original populations. Before and after 1949 local populations resisted Han rule in a variety of ways, violent and nonviolent. Their resistance threatened national security on strategic borders. It has also become an interstate issue because of the native populations' ethnic and political ties in Inner Asia, South Asia, and elsewhere in the world.

NATIONALISM

Problems of backwardness and territorial integrity engendered a third crisis, that of cultural identity. In a world of political and economic modernity, was China in any sense a great civilization? Was there something in its way of life worth saving, or was the search for wealth and power merely about protecting a piece of territory? Would the Chinese have to sacrifice everything that made them different in order to enter the path to development opened by the West? Such issues were reflected in the nineteenth-century debate over the limits of reform and in the intellectual revolution of the early twentieth century when contending groups of thinkers struggled over whether to save China through liberalism, fascism, or Marxism.

The Westernizing May Fourth movement of the early twentieth century was sparked by outrage at Western betrayal of China's interests at the Versailles peace negotiations, ending World War I. While European ideologies had their roots in European culture, China's ferment was reactive in motive as well as in content. Chinese used to think of outside cultures as pale versions of the central culture, whose power lay in its ability to civilize and transform others. Now the creative forces in Chinese culture got their power both from reacting to and from absorbing a more powerful outside culture. China's age of ideology thus differed from that of the West in that both the nation's problems and most of the possible solutions were perceived as coming from outside.

In 1949 Mao Zedong declared, "China has stood up." With his "Sinification of Marxism," Mao claimed to have combined a national identity with a cosmopolitan one, and to have forged a world-class model of thought and society that was distinctively Chinese. Whereas Hegel had declared China to lie outside of history, the center of world history had now moved to China. China was forging practices that would transform all humankind.

But Mao's death initiated a new period of debate over the cultural roots of his tyranny and the changes that would have to be made to put China back on the road to modernity. In 1988 an officially produced television documentary series, *Elegy for the Yellow River (Heshang)*, used language almost identical to that of late-nineteenth-century reformers to declare that China's inward-looking, land-bound civilization was moribund and that China would have to "join the blue sea" of Western culture in order to escape disintegration.[15] The authors of the elegy went into exile in the aftermath of the democracy demonstrations of spring 1989. The issue of cultural identity was taken over by conservative leaders who were concerned about cultural subversion by the West. Attacking "peaceful evolution" and "bourgeois liberalization," they tried to promote a nationalistic mix of Confucian and Sino-Marxist values.

As China joined the world decisively under Deng Xiaoping, the disagreement between those who favored and those who opposed Westernization (often referred to respectively as "liberals" and "conservatives") remained the fundamental cleavage of Chinese politics. The problem of cultural identity infuses every aspect of China's foreign relations, including policies toward security, foreign trade and investment, human rights, international academic collaboration, tourism, and the treatment of foreign news in the domestic press.

If a striving for national sovereignty is impelled by China's geopolitical situation as a weak country in the middle of a complicated Asia, it gains resonance from the experience of imperialism and the perceived tenuousness of China's territorial, cultural, and in some minds even racial survival. Schoolchildren learn about treaty ports and concessions (foreign-governed areas in Chinese cities), foreign leaseholds and spheres of interest, extraterritoriality (by which foreigners in China charged with crimes were judged under foreign laws by foreign judges), most-favored-nation (MFN) clauses that required China to extend low-tariff treatment to all its trading partners regardless of whether they did the same in return,[16] and foreign control over the Chinese customs, salt, and postal administrations. The memory of "national humiliation" is a strong element of Chinese rhetoric, but it is more than that. China's very vulnerability engenders an urge not merely to be secure but to take a turn at being a great power, capable of contending with any competitor throughout Asia.

Every nationalism is unique. In contrast to the self-confident American nationalism of manifest destiny, Chinese nationalism is powered by feelings of national humiliation and pride. In turn, it generates debates about why China is weak and how it can be strong, about lost territory, and about reclaiming a leading position in the world. Many Chinese see themselves as a nation beleaguered, unstable at home because insecure abroad, and vulnerable abroad because weak at home. To them it seems that China is always ready either to fly asunder or to be torn apart. With the fading of the Communist Party's utopian ideals, nationalism remains its most reliable claim to the people's loyalty. The only important value still shared by the regime and its critics, it unites Chinese of all walks of life, no matter how uninterested they are in other aspects of politics.

3

THE RISE AND DECLINE
OF THE RUSSIAN THREAT

T HE RELATIONSHIP WITH the Soviet Union was at the center of Chinese foreign policy for over four decades. From 1949 to 1960 the Soviet Union was China's closest ally. Then it became its main antagonist. In both phases PRC foreign policy in other parts of the world reflected the importance of relations with the Soviet Union. Only when the Soviet Union collapsed in 1991 did the relationship with Russia and the other successor states become one among many problems in Chinese foreign policy. In place of the Soviet challenge along a 4,000-mile border, China now faces a weaker Russia and three fledgling Central Asian states, Kazakstan, Kyrgyzstan, and Tajikistan.

The Soviet collapse has transformed China's strategic environment, as it has transformed that of the United States. But Chinese strategists prudently refuse to denigrate post-Soviet Russia. They know that the Kremlin still commands vast territories, enormous economic potential, daunting military capability, and advanced technology. And the Central Asian states, targets of great-power competition, politically unstable, and vulnerable to religious fundamentalism, occupy strategic locations in the Eurasian heartland and possess important resources, including oil.

LEANING TO ONE SIDE, 1949–1958

When the Chinese Communists took power on October 1, 1949, the concept of nonalignment was in its infancy, and neutrality was a luxury for small states on the geostrategic periphery. China's size and location made it the focus of superpower competition, while its need for economic reconstruction compelled it to seek foreign help. Mao Zedong announced in 1949 that China "must lean either to the side of imperialism or to the side of socialism. Sitting on the fence will not do, nor is there a third road."[1]

The need for security against the United States was the chief reason for the tilt. In a series of commentaries assailing the United States for supporting Chiang Kai-shek in the civil war, Mao warned Chinese intellectuals, most of them late converts to the revolution, that they must renounce pro-American sympathies. The United States would soon begin to construct a cordon sanitaire around China's periphery to contain the germs of revolution (Chapter 4).

The Soviets were permanent neighbors with a long history of involving themselves in Chinese affairs. Moscow had played a major role in the Nationalist revolution of the 1920s. In the late 1930s the USSR became Nationalist China's major foreign supporter in the Sino-Japanese War, sending weapons, military supplies, and "volunteer" pilots to China between 1937 and 1941. The Chinese Communist Party's relations with Stalin's government had never been close. Stalin supported Mao Zedong's rivals within the CCP until Mao became dominant, then maintained a liaison with an anti-Mao "Bolshevik faction." At the end of World War II, Stalin gave only intermittent help to the CCP in its struggle with the Kuomintang (KMT) to win the industrial base of the northeast, although that help was crucial in the party's effort to gain a foothold in the region.[2]

But as the CCP approached victory in the civil war, its liaison with Moscow intensified. Chinese began to participate more fully in the activities of the international Communist movement. Mao sought a meeting with Stalin in 1948, but the latter thought Mao should remain at his post during the crucial battles of the civil war. He dispatched his trusted emissary Anastas Mikoyan to confer with CCP leaders in China. In July 1949 Stalin welcomed Mao's first lieutenant Liu Shaoqi and other Chinese leaders to Moscow, where he apologized for having offered mistaken advice in the course of the Chinese revolution. Stalin aimed to cultivate a regime as pro-Soviet as possible and to preempt any Chinese tendency to act independently from the Soviet-led international Communist movement.

The partnership with the Soviet Union provided symbolic support in the international arena and showed the Chinese people that their new government had powerful foreign friends. The Soviets also helped resolve some of the domestic problems the regime faced in its early years. The CCP had won the civil war thanks as much to the crumbling of the KMT regime as to its own popularity. There was little public understanding of or commitment to the programs the Communists intended to introduce. Most intellectuals, business people, and landlords viewed the new regime with a combination of hope and suspicion. The new government faced insurgencies, bandit groups, and hostile militia all through the country. KMT forces remained active in the southwest and across the border in Burma. The Nationalist regime survived on Taiwan, and also controlled a number of offshore islands, from which it landed spies on the mainland and launched small attacks. Tibet was not yet in the hands of the People's Liberation Army (PLA). The CCP leaders waged a series of costly internal political campaigns to suppress opposition and establish security. Altogether, according to Mao, over a million "counterrevolutionaries" and "class enemies" were killed between 1950 and 1953.[3]

The new Chinese government felt it needed to achieve rapid economic development to build support at home and as a basis for military modernization. Given the scope of its economic problems and the wartime devastation of the Soviet economy, China clearly would have to rely mainly on itself to achieve its ambitious goal: self-sufficiency as a modern industrial-military power. The Chinese Communists were impressed with Stalin's record in building socialism in a generation and steering the Soviet Union to victory in World War II. By means of coercion and state planning, Stalin had squeezed capital out of a backward peasantry, mobilized a vast labor force, and rapidly built what appeared to be a world-class heavy-industrial sector that catapulted the Soviet Union to superpower status in thirty years. This experience seemed to prove that socialist planning was the royal road to growth in a backward country.

In China, as earlier in the Soviet Union, the countryside was the only possible source of the massive capital needed for rapid, self-reliant industrialization, since the industrial economy was rudimentary. On the basis of their analysis of rural class relations, the CCP leaders believed there was a large agricultural surplus that was being expropriated by the landlord class and used in extravagant living. They thought that after a period of economic recovery it could be tapped for capital through Soviet-style agricultural collectivization, and efficiently deployed for industrial development through Soviet-style central planning.

In December 1949, just two months after the proclamation of the PRC, Mao journeyed to Moscow, where battalions of international socialist dignitaries gathered to celebrate Stalin's seventieth birthday in proletarian-imperial style. Nonplussed by Mao's coyness in articulating the purpose of his visit, Stalin put the Chinese leader on hold for several weeks before the two finally got down to business, which was to negotiate a new Sino-Soviet treaty in place of the existing one signed by Chiang Kai-shek in 1945. Mao later complained that in Moscow, he "had only three tasks. . . . [T]he first was to eat, the second was to sleep, and the third was to shit."[4]

Negotiations lasted for several more weeks. On February 14, 1950, the two sides signed the thirty-year Treaty of Friendship, Alliance, and Mutual Assistance, which obligated the Soviet Union to provide "military and other assistance" to China should it be attacked by Japan "or any state allied with her." This was no small commitment. Stalin and Mao were convinced that as soon as Japan regained its strength, it would seek to reclaim the territories China and the Soviet Union had stripped from it at the end of World War II. Moreover, Japan was under American occupation, lacking foreign policy or defense autonomy, so there could be no mistaking that the United States was the ultimate target of the pledge.

China and the Soviet Union agreed on who was the common enemy, yet tough negotiations were required to resolve bilateral issues. Moscow wanted to retain its colonial-era controls over Chinese territory; Beijing tried to eliminate the vestiges of colonialism. Ultimately, the PRC had to swallow humiliating compromises. Stalin agreed to relinquish control over the Changchun railway and its base at Lushun by 1952. But he compelled China to pay for the Soviet shares in the railway and in other joint-stock companies and retained open-ended use of the port at Dalian. More important, secret protocols to the treaty granted Moscow the right, with no time limit, to transport troops over the railway and to import military equipment to Lushun without notifying Chinese leaders. They also prohibited China from allowing foreign business activity in Xinjiang and Manchuria, while Soviet officials in China charged with a crime would be tried not by Chinese courts but by Soviet officials in accordance with

Soviet laws. Moscow had compelled Beijing to allow the Soviet Union to retain extraterritorial privileges in its sphere of influence on Chinese territory. Mao was so humiliated that only a handful of Chinese leaders were told of the secret protocols, and he refused to vote in support of the treaty in the Politburo meeting that approved it.

Nevertheless, Mao did not come away from Moscow empty-handed. Stalin agreed to China's request for a five-year $300 million loan, and he agreed that China could use half of it to pay for Soviet equipment for the Chinese navy. The loan would also be instrumental in building fifty key industrial and infrastructural projects devoted to the recovery and modernization of Chinese heavy industry, defense industry, and energy production. Later agreements brought the total number of projects to 156 and the total value of Soviet loans to $430 million. The Soviets sent a large contingent of economic planners and technicians to help set up the Chinese economic bureaucracy and manage the projects. Although by today's standards the amount of the loans may appear ungenerous—and the Soviets did not supply any grants-in-aid—Mao was satisfied because he got what he had requested. Even at a time of great need, the Chinese leader was determined to avoid the burden of foreign debt that had left earlier Chinese governments vulnerable to foreign pressure. Soviet support has been characterized as the largest technology transfer in history. It was crucial to the success of China's First Five-Year Plan (1953–57), which laid the basis for the country's industrial economy.[5]

Most important, China was grateful for the Soviet security commitment. When war broke out in Korea, the Sino-Soviet treaty provided reassurance to Chinese leaders as they engaged the most powerful military in the world. Indeed, Chinese security concerns led Beijing to request that Moscow maintain its naval base at Lushun beyond 1952. Moscow transferred massive amounts of Soviet weapons and military equipment to Chinese forces in Korea, although China had to pay for nearly everything it received. The end of the Korean War ushered in a short period of optimism for PRC leaders. The industrial economy grew at an annual rate of 18 percent, and agriculture prospered. With its domestic enemies killed or cowed, the regime seemed politically secure.

Relations were not always smooth. China's economy suffered from the need to pay for Korean War equipment and supplies Beijing received from Moscow. The Chinese found many Soviet advisers condescending. Mao was exasperated by Khrushchev's failure to consult him before the Soviet general secretary attacked Stalin in a secret speech to the Twentieth Soviet Party Congress, in 1956. Beijing nonetheless supported Moscow's efforts to maintain discipline in the socialist camp, joining Moscow's criticism of Yugoslav revisionism and applauding Soviet suppression of the anticommunist revolution in Hungary.

In April 1956 Mao gave a speech titled "Ten Great Relationships," in which he foresaw at least a decade of peace, giving China an opportunity to divert resources from the military to promote light industry and agriculture, enjoy a modicum of political relaxation, and learn from the West whatever might be useful in science and management. In 1957, after the Soviets launched a space satellite ahead of the United States, Mao proclaimed that the "east wind prevails over the west wind," meaning that the communist bloc should now be able to roll back the global influence of the United States. The high point of Sino-Soviet cooperation came in 1957 when Moscow and Beijing signed the New Defense Technical Accord. The USSR promised to assist China in developing nuclear weaponry by providing Beijing a sample bomb and missiles as well as technical information.[6] Possession of nuclear weapons would enable China to resist American nuclear blackmail, reducing the need for direct Soviet involvement in any future Sino-American crises.

DIVERGING PRIORITIES, 1958–1960

So long as both sides adhered to a common strategy toward the United States, the foundation of the Sino-Soviet alliance remained secure. But near the end of the 1950s Soviet and Chinese priorities diverged. In mid-decade the new Soviet Communist Party secretary Nikita Khrushchev introduced the doctrine of peaceful coexistence between the socialist and capitalist worlds. By diminishing Cold War tensions in Europe, slowing the arms race, and stabilizing the division of Europe, Khrushchev hoped to buy time for the socialist camp to work out an internal modus vivendi in the post-Stalin era. This objective became even more urgent following the upheavals in Poland and Hungary in 1956. Khrushchev wagered his political future on the economic potential of socialism, promising his long-suffering people a better life.

China's willingness to go along depended on whether Soviet policy would help it achieve its own domestic and foreign policy objectives. The answer was no. The United States responded cautiously but positively to signs of Soviet flexibility in foreign affairs, but even after international pressure forced Washington's reluctant assent to talks with the PRC in 1955, President Eisenhower and Secretary of State John Foster Dulles were unwilling to enter into substantive dialogue with China. They remained committed to a so-called wedge strategy, designed to warm Soviet-American relations while keeping Sino-American relations in the freezer until cracks in the Sino-Soviet monolith deepened into fissures. And they were unwilling to antagonize right-wing Republican supporters of Chiang Kai-shek. They adhered to a policy of treating his government in Taipei as the legitimate government of China.

China's insistence on national autonomy also came into play. In April 1958 the Soviet Union proposed to build facilities in China to enable Moscow to communicate with its Pacific fleet. Shortly thereafter, responding to Chinese requests for assistance in building their navy, Moscow also proposed to establish a joint flotilla of nuclear-powered submarines based in China. Since China had no submarines, Moscow's offer could be seen only as a thinly disguised proposal for Soviet naval bases on Chinese territory. Meeting with the Soviet ambassador Pavel Yudin, Mao railed, "Yesterday you made me so enraged that I could not sleep at all last night." "You never trust the Chinese! You only trust the Russians!" he continued. "How would you explain to the rest of the world that you propose to build a naval 'cooperative.'? . . . If you insist on attaching political conditions [to our request], we will not satisfy you at all, not even give you a tiny [piece of our] finger."[7]

When Khrushchev visited Beijing the same year, Mao accused him of encroaching on Chinese sovereignty and seeking to "take away all our coastal areas." He warned the Soviet leader, "The British, Japanese, and other foreigners who stayed in our country for a long time have already been driven away by us, Comrade Khrushchev. I'll repeat it again. We do not want anyone to use our land to achieve their own purposes anymore."[8]

Changes in Soviet policy on nuclear cooperation further estranged the two capitals. Moscow worried that sharing nuclear technology with China would cripple its negotiations with the United States on a limited test-ban treaty. In early 1958 Moscow began to drag its heels on fulfilling its obligations under the 1957 nuclear-sharing agreement. In June 1959 it formally canceled the agreement, explaining to the Chinese that if the West found out about Soviet aid to the Chinese nuclear program,

Soviet efforts to relax relations with the West might be compromised. China later called this cancellation Khrushchev's "gift" to Eisenhower in advance of their forthcoming meeting at Camp David.[9]

Soviet policy on Taiwan also shifted. During their July 1958 meeting Mao failed to inform Khrushchev directly of his plans for imminent military action against the Nationalist-held offshore islands (Chapter 4). Still, Moscow was prepared to assist China in recovering Taiwan. But when China retreated from the brink, Moscow reevaluated its commitment. In October 1959, after meeting with Eisenhower at Camp David, Khrushchev again traveled to Beijing. There he not only reaffirmed his cancellation of the nuclear-sharing agreement but also warned Mao against testing the capitalist countries with force. He advised China to use "peaceful measures" to unify Taiwan and to "consider possibly granting temporary independence to Taiwan."[10] Moscow was apparently unwilling to sacrifice détente with the West on the altar of Sino-American confrontation. Juxtaposed with Moscow's refusal to side with Beijing in the escalating conflict along the disputed Sino-Indian Himalayan border (Chapter 6), the Soviet stance appeared to China to combine pusillanimity with treachery.

Relations with the Soviet Union disintegrated against the backdrop of China's Great Leap Forward. The Chinese had developed misgivings about the Soviet economic model. They expected faster growth and were disappointed at the inability of Soviet-type planning to resolve bottlenecks in transport, energy, and construction materials that emerged with rapid development. Despite agricultural collectivization, the proceeds from forced grain sales and the grain tax were disappointing. Mao experimented with a new set of more regimented rural collective institutions that he thought would spur production and improve the government's ability to control rural output. His experiments culminated in the Great Leap Forward and the institution of the communes.

The Soviet Union advised against the Great Leap, somewhat self-interestedly, since the communes made it look as if China was "entering communism" before its Soviet elder brother. As the Chinese Communists progressively abandoned the Soviet model, they also tried to fend off Soviet political influence by purging officials with ties to Moscow. Since Khrushchev had substituted his concepts of peaceful coexistence and peaceful transition for Lenin's classic theories on war and revolution, Mao posed as a defender of orthodox Marxism-Leninism against Soviet revisionism.

Dual Adversaries, 1960–1972

Still hoping to deflect the Soviets from their mistaken course, the Chinese initially expressed their disagreement indirectly. Even Mao's "east wind" remark contained a criticism, for it meant that the superior strength of the socialist camp obviated the need to placate the West. For years behind the scenes the Chinese fought for their ideological positions, but publicly they accepted compromise declarations that leaned toward Moscow's views.

In 1960 Beijing went public. From 1963 onwards Mao personally directed a series of polemics that excoriated Moscow's "revision" of Marxism-Leninism and its theory of the "peaceful transition to socialism," assailed the Soviet Union's credentials as the leader of the socialist bloc, and mocked Khrushchev's standing as a Marxist-Leninist. The Chinese later labeled the Soviet Union's attempt to dominate its alliance partners "hegemonism" and devised the insulting concept of "social imperialism" to describe Soviet efforts to gain influence in other countries.[11]

In retaliation, in 1960 Moscow terminated economic aid to China and abruptly withdrew its advisers. Two years later Moscow sided with India during the Sino-Indian War, the first instance of a communist state's breaking ranks with an ally in a war. When Khrushchev and President John F. Kennedy signed the limited nuclear test-ban treaty in 1963, China charged that the two superpowers were colluding to deny non-nuclear states the means to defend their national sovereignty. In October 1964, China's 1958 decision to continue its nuclear weapons program without Soviet support was vindicated by the successful test of a nuclear device (Chapter 8).

With China in the nuclear club, Leonid Brezhnev, the new Soviet leader, began to regard China as not just an irritant but a dangerous adversary. He doubled the number of forces in the Soviet Far East and Siberia, from about twelve divisions in 1961 to twenty-five by 1969. To deal with China, Soviet forces possessed several options. On the high end, they could launch a nuclear strike or a general ground invasion employing their vastly superior armored forces. More plausible scenarios were a limited nuclear strike on China's nuclear weapons program in Gansu and selected industrial sites, or a limited ground attack into industrial northeastern China, employing tactical nuclear weapons, which were favored in Soviet military doctrine at the time.

The Soviets did none of these things. But they encouraged ethnic unrest in Xinjiang, probing the possibility of carving a breakaway buffer state out of Chinese territory as they had attempted to do in the 1940s. There were frequent border incidents involving Soviet forces on the Chinese border. Chinese anxiety concerning the Soviet threat reached a new peak after Soviet-led Warsaw Pact armies invaded Czechoslovakia in August 1968 to terminate Prague's experiment with democratizing communism. Enunciating what came to be known as the Brezhnev Doctrine, the Soviet party secretary asserted Moscow's right to intervene in other socialist states by force of arms to defend socialism against counterrevolution.

China eventually balanced its Soviet estrangement with an opening to the United States. But throughout the 1960s the Americans were firm in the policies of containing China, recognizing the Republic of China as the government of China, and driving a wedge between China and Moscow. Unless the Americans made a reliable demarche to China and suggested flexibility on the Taiwan issue, the Chinese could not trust the possibility of relaxation and had to maintain their guard. The escalation of the American military presence in Indochina posed an additional obstacle to improved relations with Washington.

At odds with both superpowers, China mobilized for "people's war" against any invader (Chapter 8), deepening the sense of crisis generated by the Cultural Revolution (1966–69). Military clashes broke out along the eastern part of the Sino-Soviet border in March 1969. The most widely accepted explanation is that Beijing decided to occupy a Soviet-claimed island in the Ussuri River (named Damansky in Russian, Zhenbao in Chinese) to signal its resolve in the face of Soviet provocations.[12] Retaliating with massive force, Soviet troops ousted the Chinese, inflicting over a hundred casualties. Hostilities next broke out in August along the Xinjiang border. Moscow threatened nuclear attack, and the Chinese blinked by inviting the Soviet premier, Alexei Kosygin, to talks in Beijing to defuse the crisis.

But the militarization of the border continued at a steady pace. Soviet divisions were increased from twenty-five in 1969 to forty-five in 1973. Along the full length of the border, Moscow deployed its most advanced and lethal weaponry, by the 1980s including over 150 SS-20 intermediate-range ballistic missiles with nuclear warheads, the strategic Backfire bomber, and numerous tactical nuclear weapons. Soviet troops were supplied with advanced short-range missiles and sophisticated armor, including tanks and artillery.[13]

Soviet border deployments were complemented by other military and diplomatic efforts to "encircle China." The Soviets expanded their Pacific fleet, which included nuclear-powered submarines, two aircraft carriers, and numerous other surface combatants. Soviet warships roamed the Indian Ocean and established a strong presence in the Sea of Okhotsk, the Sea of Japan, the South China Sea, and the Strait of Malacca. To China's south, Moscow formed a close relationship with Vietnam, using economic and military aid to lure Hanoi to its side in the Sino-Soviet conflict. This strategy paid off not long after the unification of Vietnam when in 1978 Vietnam entered a formal alliance with the Soviet Union and then invaded Cambodia, extending Moscow's influence throughout Indochina. Soviet access to bases at Cam Ranh Bay and Danang enhanced Moscow's ability to project naval and air power into the Indian Ocean and the South China Sea. China mocked Hanoi's role as Moscow's junior partner, referring to Vietnam as a "regional hegemonist."

South Asia was another arena of rivalry. In 1971 Moscow signed a treaty of peace, friendship, and cooperation with India, which was still smarting from its defeat by China nine years earlier. Later that same year the Indian army assisted the breakaway rebellion of Pakistan's eastern provinces, which established the new nation of Bangladesh and weakened one of China's few allies and its lone foothold in South Asia. Moscow's open military pipeline to New Delhi fueled the modernization of the Indian armed forces, reducing China's advantage along the contested Sino-Indian border and sharpening Chinese anxieties about the security of Tibet, whose exiled ruler, the Dalai Lama, had taken refuge on Indian soil in 1959. Meanwhile, Indian public opinion inhibited even modest efforts to ameliorate Sino-Indian relations.

China's search for sympathizers took on an insurgent quality. Under the slogan "We have friends all over the world," China in the late 1960s and early 1970s engaged in a mixed bag of people-to-people diplomacy, state visits for leaders of international Maoist splinter groups, and relations with odd-lot Third World dictators. The Communist Party's International Liaison Department served as a second foreign ministry, managing relations with socialist countries and insurgent Communist parties in the Third World. Overall, China's foreign policy had an air of boastful self-confidence that others read as expansionist and aggressive, but which masked weakness and isolation.

THE STRATEGIC TRIANGLE, 1972–1990

In 1969 Mao ordered four retired marshals to analyze the changing global situation. Their report concluded that Moscow was bent on war with China and that the Soviet Union, not the United States, posed the greatest threat to Chinese security. Mao authorized contacts with the United States that led ultimately to Richard Nixon's historic visit to China in 1972 (see Chapter 4).[14]

China was driven out of its isolation by a combination of events: the 1968 Soviet invasion of Czechoslovakia, the 1969 Sino-Soviet border clashes, and the Indian victory in the 1971 Indo-Pakistani War. These made the dual-adversary policy too dangerous to sustain. At the same time, developments in the West had created an opportunity for rapprochement. The fires of anticommunism banked as the United States started to come to terms with its still unfolding defeat in Vietnam. Balance-of-power realism moved to center stage in the person of Richard M. Nixon. Recognizing the rising might of the USSR, Nixon brought the "wedge policy" of Truman, Kennan, and Dulles to its culmination. The United States reached out to draw China toward its side in the Cold War.

Global strategists labeled this the period of the "strategic triangle." It was remarkable that the third leg of the triangle was not a superpower like the other two legs, not a trading giant like Japan, or a prosperous and advanced region like Europe. Although backward and poor, China possessed the strategic location and diplomatic flexibility to challenge the security of either superpower. Aligned with the United States, China could help check Soviet power; aligned with Moscow, it could help expand Soviet power at America's expense.[15]

Participation in the balance of power helped Beijing deter Soviet attack in 1969–71, gain entry to the United Nations in 1971, assist the United States in extricating itself from Vietnam in 1975, and deter Soviet retaliation against China in 1979 when China invaded Vietnam. In a succession of U.S.-Chinese communiqués in the 1970s and 1980s, China was able to extract concessions from the United States in its policy toward

Taiwan. The opening to the West projected Chinese foreign policy into a period of global engagement. China moved into the mainstream of world affairs—establishing normal diplomatic relations with over a hundred countries, replacing Taiwan in the United Nations, and eventually participating in hundreds of international organizations, ranging from the Olympic movement to the Asian Development Bank.

China's search for multipolarity now proceeded within the international establishment rather than against it. To Moscow's encirclement of China, Mao counterposed a policy of counter-encirclement, seeking good relations with Soviet neighbors stretching from Japan through Pakistan, Afghanistan, and Iran, to Eastern and Western Europe. In 1972 Beijing normalized relations with Tokyo and six years later signed a peace treaty, formally ending World War II between the two countries. China tacitly backed the U.S.-Japanese security alliance while siding with Japan in its territorial dispute with Moscow over the Kurile Islands. After Vietnam invaded Cambodia in 1978, Beijing supported the ten-year Khmer Rouge resistance, heedless of the carnage Pol Pot had inflicted on his own people from 1975 to 1978.

China developed good relations with West European countries, chiefly through trade. It courted right-wing politicians like Germany's Franz Josef Strauss, who warned about the danger of Soviet expansionism, and found fault with East Germany, one of Moscow's staunchest allies. Beijing cheered efforts to strengthen NATO, viewing Europe's pacifist left as dupes influenced by the Kremlin's propaganda.

Among East European communist states, China's closest partner had long been anti-Soviet Albania, the weakest and most isolated country in the region. China had also developed cordial relations with Romania, whose leader, Nicolae Ceausescu, was trying to carve out a position of limited autonomy within the Warsaw Pact in the face of Soviet plans for bloc economic integration. Seeking to exploit dissatisfaction with Moscow after the invasion of Czechoslovakia, China mended relations with Yugoslavia, whose leader, Marshal Tito, it had earlier reviled in the crudest terms.

China feared that Soviet dominance in the Middle East would facilitate its victory over the West. Should Iran align with the USSR, it could provide the Soviet navy easy access to the Persian Gulf, jeopardizing the West's access to Middle East oil. China developed close relations with the shah of Iran. China was relieved when the Iranian revolution that overthrow the shah in 1979 turned out not to be pro-Soviet. During and after the Iran-Iraq war, China sold large quantities of arms to Iran, including short-range Silkworm missiles. China managed to improve relations at the same time with both Iraq and Kuwait. In the Arab-Israeli conflict, China offered consistent diplomatic support to the Palestine Liberation Organization (PLO) and lined up with most of the Third World in condemning Israel, even though Israel had been one of the first countries to offer the PRC diplomatic recognition in 1950. Only after the Soviet Union and major Arab governments began to reconcile themselves to Israel's existence did China ease its hostility. Trade and academic exchanges preceded Sino-Israeli diplomatic relations, which were established in 1992.

Chinese policy toward Africa and Latin America also followed the logic of its anti-Soviet posture. In South Africa the Chinese at first cold-shouldered the African National Congress, because of its close ties with Moscow, although later enlisting among its supporters. In the Angolan civil war Beijing provided military assistance to Jonas Savimbi's anti-Soviet/pro-U.S. National Union for the Total Independence of Angola, even though the Soviet-supported Popular Movement for the Liberation of Angola was the sole Marxist-Leninist faction there. In Rhodesia (Zimbabwe), China supported the Zimbabwe African National Union while the USSR supported the Zimbabwe African People's Union; in South-West Africa (Namibia), China supported the South-West African National Union while the USSR supported the South-West African People's Organization. The Chinese also devoted attention to Tanzania, Zambia, Zaire, Ethiopia, and Mozambique, where the Soviets were striving to establish their influence. In Latin America, Mao broke relations with socialist Cuba, a dependency of the USSR, competed with the USSR for influence among local communist parties, and sided with Latin American governments in diplomatic positions against both the Soviet Union and the United States.

FROM THREAT TO PARTNER

In May 1982, not long before he died, Leonid Brezhnev proclaimed Moscow's desire to improve relations with Beijing. He hoped to weaken China's link with the United States just as the Reagan administration increased its military pressure on the Soviet Union and challenged PRC interests in Taiwan (Chapter 4). China responded cautiously. Its leaders demanded that the Soviet Union overcome what they called "the three obstacles." The obstacles were the Soviet occupation of Afghanistan, Soviet troop deployments along the Sino-Soviet border and in Mongolia, and Soviet support for Vietnam's occupation of Cambodia. Each constituted a direct or indirect challenge to Chinese security.

Soviet troops had invaded Afghanistan in 1979 to prevent the collapse of Moscow's client regime there. Although Afghanistan's eastern extremity abuts China's Xinjiang province, Afghanistan's real strategic significance to China derived from its lengthy borders with Pakistan and Iran, two states China valued as bulwarks against Soviet expansion. China believed that Moscow's move into Afghanistan was part of the historical Russian push toward the south, foreshadowing increased pressure on Islamabad and Teheran to acquiesce in the expansion of Soviet influence. China also wanted to demonstrate its reliability as an ally to Pakistan and maintain solidarity with Washington at a time when the United States was pressing Moscow to withdraw SS-20 nuclear missiles from the border with China. Moscow started rectifying its Afghan misadventure in 1987 because of domestic and American pressure and military setbacks. By early 1989 the Afghanistan obstacle to Sino-Soviet normalization had been eliminated.

Soviet troop deployments along the Sino-Soviet border and in Mongolia embodied Moscow's direct threat to Chinese security. The new Soviet party general secretary, Mikhail Gorbachev, took the initiative to resolve this problem as part of the "new thinking" he introduced into Soviet foreign policy when he took power in 1985. In July 1986 he promised to reduce troop levels in Soviet Asia. The following year he withdrew a division of troops from Mongolia, and began to remove SS-20 and other intermediate-range missiles from the Sino-Soviet border in accordance with his treaty commitment to the United States on intermediate nuclear forces. In 1988, when Gorbachev further reduced the Soviet military presence along the border, Beijing reciprocated with troop reductions of its own. Meanwhile, progress was made in settling previously intractable border issues. By 1987 Moscow and Beijing had reached preliminary agreement on the eastern part of the border. The second obstacle was surmounted.

Soviet support for Vietnam's occupation of Cambodia was the most difficult of the three problems. Hanoi's easy victory in January 1979 over China's Cambodian client Pol Pot infuriated the Chinese. They were further humiliated a month later by the poor performance of their army in its limited incursion into northern Vietnam (Chapter 6). Moscow's economic lifeline and security guarantee enabled Vietnam to hang on in Cambodia over the next decade: hence China's insistence that Moscow squeeze the Vietnamese. Vietnam was a sinkhole for Soviet aid, and Gorbachev was trying to liquidate his predecessors' bad overseas investments. Moreover, the Soviets wanted to improve relations with China in order to reduce defense expenditures. The Soviets opened direct negotiations with China over the war in Cambodia, and leaned on Hanoi to withdraw. Hanoi was forced to comply. Chinese perseverance in combination with other circumstances had succeeded in removing the last obstacle to Sino-Soviet normalization.

Deng Xiaoping now agreed to a Sino-Soviet summit. In May 1989 Gorbachev flew to Beijing, where he was hailed as an apostle of change by students demonstrating in Tiananmen Square. But Gorbachev had come to honor Deng, not to bury him. His was the first visit by a Soviet leader to China in twenty years and the first by a Soviet Communist Party leader in thirty years. It formally ended the Sino-Soviet conflict, which had imposed such costly sacrifices on the people of both countries. Yet it was only the prologue to more dramatic changes. Two years later the Soviet Union collapsed, following a coup attempt by its old guard.

The shattering of the Soviet Union not only capped the dissolution of the strategic triangle but also marked the end of a Russian imperium that had prevailed along the Sino-Soviet border since the mid-nineteenth century. Chinese leaders faced a radically transformed political landscape across their Central Asian frontiers, in a region that had long been known as the "pivot of Asia," until its internal complexities had been covered over by the simplicities of the Cold War.[16] China had strong interests in Kazakstan, Tajikistan, and Kyrgyzstan, which border directly on China, and in Turkmenistan and Uzbekistan, which do not. All five republics remain economically dependent on Russia for energy resources and markets for traditional exports, but Chinese goods and merchants have made significant inroads. The Russian army maintains a strong presence in Inner Asia, where the position of millions of ethnic Russians, Soviet-era migrants for the most part, continues to erode in the face of nationalist efforts to create indigenous identities for the new states. Although the Soviet disintegration raised new challenges for China's own territorial integrity (Chapter 11), Beijing immediately extended full diplomatic recognition to the successor republics.

Beijing accorded high protocol to visiting Central Asian heads of state and heads of government, pursued negotiations over border issues left unsettled by the former Soviet Union, and promoted mutual disarmament along what were once highly militarized borders. China expanded road, rail, and air links with the region, eased visa requirements, and awarded customs reductions in order to encourage trade. China is near to replacing Russia as the main supplier of light-industrial products to the region. The potential for cooperation is especially great between Xinjiang and Kazakstan. China is Kazakstan's second-most important export market, with its chief purchases consisting of iron, steel, and metal products.

Kazakstan remains dependent on Russian oil, and Russia has been actively undermining Kazak efforts to develop and export its own petroleum resources. In 1995 joint exploratory work began on a pipeline running from Turkmenistan to the East China Sea through Uzbekistan and Kazakstan by a consortium of Japanese, American, and Chinese companies. This project is a component of Beijing's plans to develop a "new silk road" between China and Central Asia that would also include air, railway, and highway linkages. Given the good prospects for Sino-Kazak cooperation, China has not made a public issue of the fact that Kazakstan's Uighur population harbors a Xinjiang independence movement (Uighurs form the largest ethnic group in Xinjiang).[17]

Despite their natural rivalry in the region, China and Russia have a common interest in preventing the spread of Islamic fundamentalism. Muslim minorities inhabit provinces in both countries along their respective Central Asian borders. Secular leaders predominate, but should any of the Central Asian states come under the sway of fundamentalist leaders, they might promote secession movements in China or Russia and seek to incorporate these regions into their own countries. Moscow and Beijing are more likely to cooperate to contain fundamentalist influence than to try to manipulate fundamentalism to destabilize each other. This is another reason for both to seek influence in Iran and Turkey, nations that are competing to export their respective visions of pan-Islamicism and pan-Turkism to Central Asia.

COMMON GROUND, SHIFTING GROUND

In the new strategic situation, China needs to strengthen its relationship with Russia. As if to make up for the lost decades of hostility, the two sides now devote considerable effort to diplomatic and political links via summit meetings, exchanges of political delegations, and military exchanges. President Jiang Zemin and Premier Li Peng both received training in the Soviet Union in the 1950s. Even though the world they knew is gone, their trips to Russia must strike personal as well as political chords.

Chinese and Russian leaders engaged in an almost hyperactive summitry during the 1990s. Their outlooks converge on many international issues. Beijing is suspicious of U.S.-Japan cooperation, and Moscow opposes NATO expansion into Eastern Europe. Beijing and Moscow both complain that Washington applies the arms control guidelines of the Missile Technology Control Regime (MTCR) to them without seeking their formal participation in the regime or including them in the consultations among the formal signatories. The United States has opposed the transfer of nuclear energy technology to Iran by either China or Russia. Both resent U.S. criticism of their human rights practices—in Russia's case, in Chechnya. In a thinly veiled reference to U.S. foreign policy, Premier Li Peng told his Russian hosts during a June 1995 visit to Moscow that China and Russia "cannot let anyone teach us how to behave and how to live," a sentiment echoed by Premier Viktor Chernomyrdin of Russia.[18]

China and Russia also share parallel concerns regarding Japan. Both countries are suspicious of Japanese military and economic power in Northeast Asia. The refractory Russo-Japanese dispute over the southern Kurile Islands, which Japan calls the Northern Territories, inoculates China against fears of a Russian-Japanese condominium in Northeast Asia such as occurred between 1907 and 1917. Despite the allure of Russia's natural resources, the Japanese have been reluctant investors in the Russian economy and nickel-and-dime aid donors. In the Sino-Russian-Japanese triangle, China has better relations with each of the others than they have with each other.

With strategic animosity between the two countries at an end, border disputes appeared in their true light—as symptoms rather than as causes of conflict. An agreement on the eastern section of the border was signed in 1991, and one on the western section in 1994. The eastern sector agreement met opposition from local officials in the Russian Far East, who complained that Moscow had given away valuable lands to China. Nonetheless, both agreements passed the Russian Duma (parliament), and President Boris Yeltsin reaffirmed them during his visit to China in 1996. Although much work must still be done to demarcate the agreed-upon borders, the remaining issues are minor.

During the 1996 summit Yeltsin and Jiang Zemin joined the leaders of Kyrgyzstan, Tajikistan, and Kazakstan in Shanghai to sign a series of confidence-building agreements to reduce military friction at their respective borders. The five nations agreed to exchange information regarding troops and hardware deployments along the border, to limit large-scale exercises within 100 kilometers of the border to one per year, to give advance notice of these exercises, and to invite observers to witness them. These measures reinforced earlier agreements between Beijing and Moscow on military relaxation. The first, providing for troop reductions, no first use of nuclear weapons, and a wide range of cooperative exchanges, was concluded during Boris Yeltsin's 1992 visit to Beijing. In 1994 Moscow and Beijing agreed not to target nuclear missiles on each other, and to provide advance notification of troop movements and military exercises. The two countries conducted exchanges between defense ministers and service chiefs to discuss strategic issues. At the operational level, local border commanders inspected each other's positions to reduce the risk of accidental conflict.

Western sanctions imposed on military transfers to China after Tiananmen created an opportunity for Russia to become China's major supplier of advanced weaponry as well as of technology for upgrading China's defense industry. Since the collapse of the Soviet Union, Russia's military-industrial complex has fallen on hard times. The Kremlin can no longer afford to purchase many of the big-ticket items Russia's own defense industry produces. China's hard currency has become a vital source of income for Russia's ailing defense industries. China has purchased Russian-made jet fighters, high-altitude helicopters, submarines, and air-to-air and short-range surface-to-air missiles (Chapter 8). Ongoing discussions center on tanks, air-refueling technology, and advanced avionics.[19]

Russia still has the edge over China in certain branches of industry besides weapons. China has become Russia's main market for machine tools and other finished industrial goods. The Chinese have also managed to look past Chernobyl to recent advances in Russian nuclear energy technology. In July 1995 Moscow and Beijing signed a comprehensive technology transfer agreement that includes plans for Russia to construct a nuclear energy plant in Liaoning province, a center of China's heavy industry.

The positive outlook for economic ties between the two countries is encouraged by the complementarity of the Russian and Chinese economies in the border zone. The Russian Far East was devastated by Russia's industrial decline and lies well beyond the range of Moscow's limited capacity to provide substantial relief. Investment by Chinese entrepreneurs and cross-border trade have been instrumental in developing service industries in the area, contributing to the availability of consumer goods and local employment, and buttressing economic and social stability. China has promoted exports to Russia of grain, meat, tea, cigarettes, and other consumer goods, and in March 1991 provided a $730 million commodity loan to support such exports.

The growing two-way trade has not been without its problems. They include the transition from paying for goods by barter to paying for them with cash, Russian dissatisfaction with being the dumping ground for low-quality Chinese consumer goods, Russian protectionist measures, and Chinese inflation. Moscow is concerned about its inability to restrict the flow of Chinese traders, merchants, and farmers into the Russian Far East. The thought of uncontrolled Chinese migration into this thinly populated region is a nightmare for Russian leaders. Former Minister of Defense Pavel Grachev once charged that "Chinese citizens are peacefully conquering Russia's Far East," and the head of Russia's Federal Migration Service warned that "Chinese expansion must be stopped."[20] But the main targets of Russian economic nationalism are Europe and America, not China.

China and Russia announced "a strategic partnership" during President Yeltsin's 1996 state visit. But they are unlikely to revive their 1950s alliance. Despite tensions with Washington, neither can afford to antagonize the United States, nor does either face an imminent U.S. threat such as existed at the time the Sino-Soviet alliance was formed. Moreover, China cannot afford to disregard the possible long-term danger of a resurgent Russia. In a candid appraisal following the radical nationalist Vladimir Zhirinovsky's impressive showing in Russia's 1993 parliamentary election, one Chinese author remarked, "In view of the fact that Russia is still . . . the country with the largest territory, richest resources, and greatest number of nuclear weapons, its general mood of expansionism and national chauvinism mirrored in the current elections will naturally arouse the vigilance of various countries throughout the world."[21]

LIMITED PARTNERS

As the largest contiguous-to-China power, Russia must always be a prime concern for Chinese policymakers. Each of the two countries has reason to feel geostrategically insecure; each has the ability to threaten vital interests of the other. Their relations are affected now as in the past by ideology, culture, economics, and power balances involving third countries. Yet consistently the core of the Sino-Russian relationship has been each side's concern for security in the face of the other's might, and this remains the case today. At this fundamental level, each country's security is better served by the weakness of the other than by its strength.

Despite their vigilance for the long term, Chinese analysts believe that Russia today is in a decline that will be difficult to reverse. They consider it the least likely of China's neighbors to challenge Chinese security in the next decade. Although this estimate implies the possibility of better relations with Russia, such relations are not worth cultivating to the point that they threaten other important foreign policy objectives. Since Japan has been unable to resolve its border dispute with Russia and views the rise of Chinese power with concern, Tokyo could come to see cooperation between Moscow and Beijing as a threat to Japanese security. If Russian arms sales to China continue to increase, Washington, Tokyo, and China's Association of Southeast Asian Nations (ASEAN) neighbors might increase military preparedness against China. Rising Sino-Russian cooperation could provide ammunition to Americans who advocate the containment of China.

Thus, just as the Soviet Union was wary of developing excessively close security ties with China in the 1950s because of its desire for détente with the West, China may now have to resist Russian efforts to expand cooperation in order to avoid damaging its relations with other countries. But maintaining this balance is a relatively minor problem compared with managing the threat the Soviet Union posed during the days of the Sino-Soviet split.

4

THE AMERICAN PUZZLE

A MERICAN FOREIGN POLICY is as puzzling to Chinese as Chinese for-eign policy is to Americans. In the Chinese view, when the United States was a minor presence in Asia before World War II, it boasted of its missionary and educational good works while availing itself of the treaty privileges won by other imperialist powers.[1] When it became a global power after World War II, the United States sided with the PRC's rival regime on Taiwan, rearmed China's erstwhile enemy Japan, created military alliances to check China, and fought wars in Korea and Vietnam partly to contain Chinese influence.

China and the United States forged a partnership in the early 1970s, as Sino-Soviet hostilities escalated and the Vietnam War moved toward its bloody conclusion. Their anti-Soviet entente endured for nearly two decades. Formal diplomatic relations were established in 1979. Economic and cultural ties expanded, and Deng Xiaoping's reforms seemed to bring China toward convergence with American values. But the June 4, 1989, Beijing massacre of a thousand or more unarmed workers and students demonstrating for democracy crushed American optimism about China. When the U.S. government imposed sanctions, even Chinese who disapproved of their government's actions felt confirmed in their view of the United States as a temporary friend and permanent adversary.

Today the two countries cooperate quietly on many issues. But they are at odds over Taiwan, arms proliferation, trade, and human rights, among other issues. In the United States, China policy is a chronic political problem in a government divided both between president and Congress and along party lines, and Americans are debating over whether to "engage" or "contain" China. In Beijing standing up to the United States has become a fitness test for contenders in the post-Deng succession. A new Sino-American relationship must be built on the foundation that has already been laid, with its cornerstone of grievances from the past.

STRATEGIC ROOTS OF CONTAINMENT

Scholars have asked whether Chinese-American relations might have been put on a better footing when the PRC was established in 1949. According to the theory of the "lost chance in China," the Chinese Communist leaders in the 1940s were open to better relations with the United States, but doctrinaire anticommunism prevented American leaders from responding to CCP cues.[2] The result was over twenty years of containment from 1949 to 1972.

But U.S.-Chinese hostility during the Cold War was not a historical misstep that could have been avoided with defter diplomatic footwork. America's alignment in the Chinese civil war would have made it hard enough for two such different governments to work together. America supported the Communist Party's adversary, resisting the spread of communism in China and around the world. In addition, China's size and strategic location made its alignment a matter of intense concern to both sides in the emerging Cold War (Chapter 1). Had the PRC been tempted to remain neutral, it would have been subjected to intense pressure from both superpowers and would have been denied access to economic assistance from either side. However troubled the Sino-Soviet relationship, Chinese Communists had long been inspired by the Soviet vision of revolutionary development, and only the Soviet Union would provide economic and security assistance to the PRC. That the Chinese Communists would lean to the Soviet side was never in doubt.

It was inevitable as well that the Americans would view the Chinese tilt toward the USSR as a threat to their interests. American hostility toward China was partly ideological, to be sure, but it was rooted in the reality of competition for power between the two strongest countries to emerge from World War II. The addition of China to the Soviet bloc represented a major shift in the balance of power in Asia, a region of great significance to U.S. security. In the sense that containment grew from both the character and the circumstances of the protagonists, it was not a mistake but a tragedy.

It is true that Mao wooed the United States during and just after World War II. China had been fighting Japan for more than four years before the United States entered the war on December 8, 1941. The Nationalists and the Communists viewed the United States as a patron that could bestow great benefits, and they competed for its attention. Mao Zedong and Zhou Enlai persuaded some American diplomats, military officers, and reporters visiting their wartime headquarters at Yan'an that they were reformers whose rise to power would not harm American interests. But Washington preferred Chiang Kai-shek, firmly pro-American and apparently in a good position to keep power after the war. The United States denied the Communists the recognition and aid they sought. By the spring of 1945 the CCP had reverted to its long-standing public view of the United States as a bastion of capitalist reaction, and looked to Moscow for assistance as it prepared to resume the civil war following Japan's impending defeat.

In December 1945 President Truman, worried that the Soviet Union was gaining ground in China, dispatched General George C. Marshall to China to effect a political settlement between the Nationalists and the Communists. The cease-fire Marshall negotiated in January 1946 provided a respite to the Communist armies, which at that point were still inferior to the Nationalist forces. But the American dream that the two enemies would transfer their military struggle to the arena of parliamentary politics was naive.

In the summer of 1946 full-scale civil war erupted. The Truman administration provided open military and financial assistance to the Nationalists, and the Soviet Union covertly aided the Communists. In June 1949 the Communists invited U.S. Ambassador J. Leighton Stuart to visit Beijing. Mao did not intend to seek alignment with the West, but he may have been trying to keep communications open in preparation for a postrevolutionary relationship with the United States. Washington viewed the invitation with suspicion, perceiving Mao as committed to social revolution at home and to Soviet leadership in international affairs, and denied Stuart permission to go to Beijing.

There was no lost chance for a Chinese Communist tilt toward the West. But until early 1950 there was still the possibility of formal diplomatic ties that might have put Chinese and American embassies in each other's capital and helped avoid future miscommunication. Not long after Mao proclaimed the establishment of the People's Republic of China, on October 1, 1949, the United States began to prepare for recognition of the new Communist government, believing that its hold on power was irreversible. But pressure from congressional conservatives deterred the White House from immediately recognizing the PRC. Mao wanted to develop a working relationship with the United States, but under pressure from Stalin to prove his loyalty to the Soviet Union, he told his countrymen that China needed "to clean the courtyard before inviting guests."[3] He meant that China would have to eliminate the American presence and eradicate pro-American sentiments before it could deal successfully with its most dangerous enemy. Beginning in the fall of 1948 and culminating in the anti-American campaigns of the Korean War, Beijing applied pressure on U.S. diplomats, businesspersons, missionaries, and educators to force them out of China. The party compelled American-trained intellectuals to engage in self-criticism.

Mao reluctantly followed Stalin's lead in giving the North Korean leader Kim Il-song the go-ahead to reunify the Korean peninsula by force. When Washington decided to respond by defending South Korea under a UN mandate, Mao was surprised, as he was by President Harry S. Truman's order to interpose the Seventh Fleet in the Taiwan Strait to prevent China from invading Taiwan. Zhou Enlai immediately denounced the United States for interfering in Chinese domestic affairs.

Mao's priority had been to occupy Taiwan, not to encourage a war between North Korea and the United States. Now he faced American forces on the Korean peninsula. After General Douglas MacArthur's forces landed at Inchon on September 15, 1950, the U.S. Army rapidly approached the Chinese border. Mao would have accepted a cease-fire at the thirty-eighth parallel, the North-South division before the start of the war, but he was prepared to fight if the United States crossed that line. Because of miscommunication, Chinese efforts to maintain the secrecy of their deployments, and General MacArthur's confidence that China would back down before a display of strength, U.S. forces crossed the thirty-eighth parallel and moved toward the Chinese border.[4] When the U.S. forces were most vulnerable, China attacked. The Chinese People's Volunteers failed to drive American forces into the sea as Mao hoped, but they reversed the northward momentum of UN forces and pushed the Americans back 200 miles, to what became the armistice line. China had avoided the positioning of U.S. forces on its border and even a possible U.S. invasion, and it had established itself as a significant military power. But the confrontation in Korea eliminated any chance for diplomatic relations between Beijing and Washington.

In China and the United States images of the other as implacable enemies hardened. McCarthyism in the United States—a hunt for communists and their sympathizers in government, academia, and the media—destroyed the careers of many China specialists. In the 1952 presidential election Republicans charged that the Truman administration had "lost" China to the Communists. The rigid international alignments of the early Cold War seemed to leave little room for rapprochement with China in any case. The Eisenhower administration held to a hard-line foreign policy designed to split Beijing from Moscow. The strategy aimed to maintain a quarantine that would force Beijing to make demands on the Soviet Union that Moscow could not satisfy.[5]

U.S. containment of China employed military, diplomatic, and economic instruments. Militarily, the United States constructed an offshore line of alliances, like a floating chain-link fence along China's eastern and southern borders. Its central section was the U.S.-Japan security treaty of 1951. During World War II, President Roosevelt had envisioned the United States and China as postwar partners that would cooperate to prevent the resurgence of Japanese militarism. Now, under Truman and his successors, the roles were reversed: the United States and Japan became partners in containing China. The security treaty afforded the United States military bases throughout Japan, particularly on Okinawa, which remained under U.S. control until 1969. Japan followed the American lead in treating Chiang Kai-shek's Republic of China (ROC) on Taiwan as the legitimate government of China. With U.S. encouragement Japan gradually rebuilt its armed forces.

After signing the Korean armistice agreement in July 1953, the United States maintained substantial forces in South Korea. Equipped with theater and battlefield nuclear weapons, these forces held North Korea in check as part of a regionwide effort to contain Chinese influence in Asia. The ANZUS Treaty (1951), linking Australia, New Zealand, and the United States, refashioned World War II–era fears of Japan into an instrument of Cold War containment of China. In 1954 the United States assumed France's role as the supporter of anticommunist forces in Indochina after the Geneva conference temporarily divided Vietnam. Secretary of State John Foster Dulles brought Thailand, the Philippines, and Pakistan into the semicircle of containment via the Southeast Asia Treaty Organization (SEATO), which soon extended its protection to the U.S. client state in South Vietnam.

Containment was supplemented by isolation. The United States blocked China's entry into the United Nations and other international organizations, enabling Chiang Kai-shek's ROC to represent China. Washington avoided diplomatic contact with Beijing apart from intermittent, unproductive, partly secret ambassadorial meetings in Geneva and, later, in Warsaw. The European allies followed suit, except for Britain, which recognized the PRC in early 1950 because it needed the diplomatic tie to protect its colony in Hong Kong, and France, which established relations with China in 1964 in a Gaullist assertion of foreign policy independence.

A key component of Washington's strategy was to tighten the economic screws, denying China the opportunity to conduct normal trade, and saddling the USSR with the burden of assisting its ally's economic development. The United States cut off all trade during the Korean War and orchestrated an international embargo by way of a UN resolution. Washington stamped U.S. passports "not valid for travel to China." Goods imported to the United States from Hong Kong had to bear a "certificate of origin" to prove they had not come from China. Economic isolation was enforced partly through the Coordinating Committee for Multilateral Export Control (COCOM), a group of advanced industrial countries (NATO minus Iceland plus Japan), which had to approve exports of strategic goods to communist countries. The U.S.-led economic embargo of China imposed even tougher restrictions on trade with China than on that with other target countries, including the Soviet Union.

China developed a number of responses to U.S. containment. Most important, it consolidated cooperation with the Soviet Union (Chapter 3). During the 1950s the Sino-Soviet treaty and Soviet military and economic assistance to China made vital contributions to Chinese security and economic construction. Beijing also formulated diplomatic counter-strategies toward Third World countries (Chapter 6). In the aftermath of the Korean War, it first pursued "peaceful coexistence" with American allies in Asia. With the "spirit of Bandung," as this moderate policy was called, China tried to foster a more peaceful international environment in which to modernize its economy and weaken American encirclement. When this policy failed to ease its isolation, China adopted a more radical posture toward American power. It voiced diplomatic support for revolution in the Third World and aligned with anti-American Third World governments, including those of Indonesia and North Vietnam.

THE TAIWAN STRAIT CRISES, 1954 AND 1958, AND THE VIETNAM WAR

An enduring legacy of the Korean War was the Taiwan problem (Chapter 11). In the late 1940s the United States briefly considered supporting an independent Taiwan in order to deny the strategic island to the Communists, but backed off when it failed to locate an indigenous force that could stand up to Chiang Kai-shek. Once Korea spotlighted Taiwan's strategic importance to the defense of American interests in Asia, the United States resumed military and economic assistance to the Nationalist regime. In doing so, it stepped into the Chinese civil war as the guarantor of Taiwan's de facto independence, a position from which it has yet to extricate itself.[6]

It was here that containment hurt China most. The Seventh Fleet patrolled the Taiwan Strait. The U.S. Military Assistance Advisory Group (USMAAG) helped Chiang Kai-shek rebuild his demoralized army. From the offshore islands of Jinmen and Mazu (Quemoy and Matsu), U.S.-trained Nationalist commandos raided mainland coastal targets and collected intelligence. Remnant Nationalist troops that had taken refuge in northern Burma after the civil war carried out raids into Yunnan province. In December 1954 the United States and the ROC signed a mutual defense treaty. U.S. military support was matched by programs of economic and political assistance that revived Taiwan's economy and shored up the government. And the United States considered organizing a "Northeast Asia treaty organization," which would bring Taiwan into the U.S. treaty system and consolidate Taiwan's separation from the mainland.

Mao saw Taiwan drifting out of reach. To awaken the Americans and the Kuomintang (KMT) to the risk of their course, in 1954 China began to shell the smaller Nationalist-held islands closest to the mainland. In January 1955 Mao ordered Chinese forces to invade the Dazhen Islands. Chiang Kai-shek was compelled to evacuate the islands, and the PRC took them. In response to Chinese belligerence the U.S. Senate passed the Formosa resolution, giving the president permission to defend Jinmen and Mazu if he deemed an attack on them to be a prelude to an attack on Taiwan. Faced with a dangerous rise in U.S.-China tension, including an American threat to use nuclear weapons, China agreed to consultations with U.S. diplomats in Geneva. Chiang Kai-shek strengthened his garrisons on Jinmen and Mazu, but Washington did not conclude a regional security framework for Northeast Asia and left mention of Taiwan out of its security agreements with other countries.

Despite Chinese militancy the United States continued to develop relations with Taiwan. In 1957 Washington deployed on Taiwan Matador surface-to-surface missiles capable of carrying nuclear weapons and began construction of a major air base near Taichung, on central Taiwan, capable of handling B-52 strategic bombers. It suspended the talks at Geneva, having failed to secure a PRC renunciation of use of force against Taiwan. Developments in U.S.-Taiwan relations were making unification less likely, and Mao tried again to weaken the U.S.-Taiwan tie. In 1957 the Soviet Union had demonstrated that it was ahead of the Americans in missile technology by launching the first space satellite, called *Sputnik*. Mao believed that the Communist bloc had taken the strategic initiative over the West and should press its advantage (Chapter 3). The domestic atmosphere in China was supercharged with the exuberant fantasies of the Great Leap Forward that promised the conquest of nature and a shortcut to the communist utopia. An international crisis might help mobilize the masses to work harder and longer.[7]

In summer 1958 Beijing initiated the second Taiwan Strait crisis. The People's Liberation Army (PLA) renewed its shelling of the offshore islands. The United States provided naval escort for KMT shipping to Jinmen and warned Beijing that it might use nuclear weapons if the conflict escalated. Eight years earlier Mao had characterized atomic bombs as paper tigers,[8] but now Zhou Enlai announced China's willingness to negotiate with the United States to reduce tensions in the Taiwan area, and the United States agreed to reopen ambassadorial-level talks with China, this time in Warsaw. The PLA reduced its shelling of the offshore islands to a symbolic peppering every other day, a pattern that continued until the normalization of U.S.-China relations in 1979.

While defending Taiwan from Chinese attack, the Americans also vetoed Nationalist plans to invade the mainland. One such occasion came in 1962, when China was embroiled in its border crisis with India (Chapter 6) and Chiang Kai-shek believed the Communist regime was ready to collapse in the aftermath of the 1959–61 famine on the mainland. For the Americans the goal of the security treaty with Taiwan was not a "rollback" of Chinese communism, a strategy that had been considered and rejected. It was to use Taiwan in its effort to contain China. Through the Warsaw talks Washington informed Beijing that it would not support a KMT invasion of the mainland. In fact, once the second Taiwan Strait crisis had subsided, Washington urged Chiang Kai-shek to redeploy most of his offshore forces to Taiwan and accept the possible loss of the islands to the mainland. To Mao's relief, Chiang refused. For both men the offshore islands formed an issue separate from that of Taiwan because they had never been part of the Japanese empire and belonged administratively to Fujian province. In Chinese eyes they symbolized the connection between Taiwan and the mainland and the inevitability of China's eventual unification.

Although the Kennedy administration considered relaxing relations with China, a suitable opportunity never arose. China's denunciation of U.S.-Soviet détente, its 1962 border war with India, and its revolutionary rhetoric increased U.S. apprehension. The Kennedy administration supported India in the border war and in 1963 considered carrying out a preemptive attack on China's nuclear weapons facilities.[9] Most important, it decided to prop up the teetering South Vietnamese government, which it deemed at risk of becoming the first "domino" to fall to communism in Cold War Asia. The Kennedy administration sent advisers to aid South Vietnam's army. By 1964 the Johnson administration had all but taken over the war from South Vietnam, and soon over half a million U.S. troops were there.

Chinese leaders had been content with a divided Vietnam since the 1954 Geneva settlement so long as China's "strategic backyard" was free from foreign military influence (Chapter 6). But once the U.S. military occupied South Vietnam and reinforced its encirclement of China, the PRC dedicated itself to assisting North Vietnam's war against the United States. America's war in Vietnam had joined the Taiwan issue as an obstacle to improved U.S.-China relations.

CONSTRUCTING THE "COMMUNIQUÉ FRAMEWORK"

Sino-American rapprochement reflected changing security circumstances. For China the escalation of Sino-Soviet conflict in 1969 and the prospect of a Soviet nuclear attack raised the costs of its dual adversary policy and strategic isolation. At the same time it was becoming clear to Chairman Mao, Premier Zhou Enlai, and other Chinese leaders that the United States was losing the war in Vietnam and would have to withdraw its forces from Indochina, that it was on the retreat in Asia and on the defensive in the superpower balance of power. This created the opportunity for Beijing to align with the United States against the Soviet Union.

At the same time, the growing opposition in America to the war in Vietnam, and more broadly to high levels of defense spending and an activist foreign policy, undermined Washington's ability to maintain its two-and-a-half war strategy, which called for the capability simultaneously to fight a war with China and the Soviet Union. Washington had to prevent the Soviet Union from taking advantage of its defeat in Vietnam to expand throughout Asia. Moreover, by the end of the Johnson administration the United States had developed a more realistic assessment of China's limited economic and military capabilities. The Sino-Soviet border crisis revealed China's strategic vulnerability to Soviet power and suggested that Chinese leaders might be interested in reducing U.S.-China friction. By 1969 the Nixon administration had perceived an opportunity to improve relations with China to contain the spread of Soviet power.[10]

The result of these calculations on both sides was Richard M. Nixon's spectacular February 1972 visit to China, viewed in the United States on network television. After meeting Mao Zedong in his book-lined study, touring scenic spots with Zhou Enlai, and completing negotiations begun by National Security Adviser Henry Kissinger, Nixon exulted, "This was the week that changed the world." It was true. Just as Mao's 1950 trip to Moscow symbolized the addition of China to the Soviet bloc and a fundamental transformation of the strategic balance, Nixon's visit to China reflected China's alignment with the West against Moscow and an equally important transformation of the global balance of power. While the United States no longer had to prepare for war against China and could devote its resources to contending with Soviet power, the Soviet Union faced the coordinated actions of its two largest enemies. China's cooperation with the United States would frustrate Moscow's effort to capitalize on America's defeat in Vietnam.

Common strategic interests did not make cooperation easy. China and the United States had to find a way to work together without relinquishing their respective interests in Taiwan. The United States, satisfied with the status quo, sought strategic cooperation with China without sacrificing diplomatic, strategic, and economic relations with Taiwan. But the PRC had not abandoned its objective to end the civil war by defeating the KMT and unifying Taiwan with the mainland. Constantly hanging over the relationship was the danger that if the United States did not make the minimal compromises necessary to accommodate PRC interests, strategic cooperation would stagnate and perhaps even deteriorate, leaving each side exposed to Soviet power without the benefit of the other's assistance. China's size and its history of challenging the superpowers made credible its threat to allow U.S.-China relations to deteriorate.

Beijing demanded that the United States break relations with Taiwan, withdraw its troops from Taiwan, and abrogate the U.S.-ROC defense treaty. These issues were at the center of the secret negotiations that Henry Kissinger conducted with Zhou Enlai beginning in 1970. The negotiations culminated in the U.S.-China joint communiqué, signed by President Nixon and Premier Zhou Enlai in Shanghai on February 27, 1972. Despite Chinese efforts to pressure the United States to agree that Taiwan was part of China, in the Shanghai communiqué the United States made the ambiguous statement that it "acknowledge[d] that all Chinese on either side of the Taiwan Strait maintain that there is but one China and that Taiwan is a part of China." It did not state its own position on Taiwan's status. Despite Chinese opposition the United States also asserted its "interest in a peaceful settlement of the Taiwan question by the Chinese themselves," suggesting that there was a linkage between U.S. compromises and the mainland's not using force against Taiwan.

The Shanghai communiqué established the basis for U.S.-China strategic cooperation. But Beijing refused to establish formal U.S.-China diplomatic relations so long as Washington recognized the ROC. Concerned about Soviet missile deployments and expansion in the Third World, the Carter administration in 1978 met China's conditions for normalization. It agreed to recognize the PRC as "the sole legal government of China," to remove all U.S. troops from Taiwan, and to abrogate the U.S.-ROC defense treaty. But in the normalization communiqué, issued on December 15, 1978, the United States maintained its formal ambiguity on the international status of Taiwan. Rather than state its own policy, it merely "acknowledge[d] the Chinese position that there is but one China and Taiwan is part of China." In keeping with the American position in the Shanghai communiqué, it also asserted, "The United States continues to have an interest in the peaceful resolution of the Taiwan issue and expects that the Taiwan issue will be settled peacefully by the Chinese themselves." Despite vehement opposition from Deng Xiaoping, Washington maintained its right to sell defensive weapons to Taiwan.

Despite the euphoria surrounding the normalization of U.S.-China relations, Congress was alarmed by the Carter administration's treatment of Taiwan. Many members of Congress worried that Taiwan would not be adequately protected now that the United States had severed diplomatic and security relations. Congressional leaders were also irritated that the administration had negotiated the normalization agreement in secret. Congress asserted its authority by reworking a weaker administration proposal for relations with Taiwan into the Taiwan Relations Act (TRA) of April 1979. The TRA expressed U.S. determination to "consider any effort to determine the future of Taiwan by other than peaceful means . . . a threat to the peace and security of the Western Pacific area." It further required the United States to provide Taiwan such "defense articles and defense services . . . as may be necessary to enable Taiwan to maintain a sufficient self-defense capability," codifying in law the commitment to continued U.S. arms sales to Taiwan. The TRA affirmed that U.S. law would apply to Taiwan as it would to any sovereign state, even though the United States had withdrawn diplomatic recognition.

In order to minimize PRC suspicions of U.S. duplicity and build trust in a fragile relationship, Washington stopped treating Taiwan's representatives as official diplomats. White House officials were not allowed to meet in their offices representatives from Taiwan, senior Taiwan leaders were not allowed to visit the United States, and senior U.S. officials stopped visiting Taiwan. Rather than have an embassy in Taiwan, the TRA established the American Institute in Taiwan (AIT) as a nominally private but actually quasi-governmental institution to manage U.S. "nonofficial" relations with "the people of Taiwan," including economic and cultural matters. The staff of the AIT stepped down from the U.S. foreign service while holding their posts. Taiwan's office in the United States was called the Coordination Council for North American Affairs; it was not allowed to use the name Taiwan.

Chinese leaders had gone a long way toward achieving their objectives. They had normalized relation with the United States largely on their terms and had isolated Taiwan in international affairs. But Beijing regarded U.S. arms sales to Taiwan and defense commitments in the TRA as challenges to Chinese sovereignty and as symbols of an ongoing U.S. commitment to Taiwan's security that would embolden the KMT to resist unification proposals. It tolerated these conditions in order to achieve its immediate objective of establishing diplomatic relations with the United States in preparation for its February 1979 invasion of Vietnam (Chapter 6).

In 1981–82, however, China resumed the diplomatic offensive against U.S. arms sales to Taiwan, taking advantage of the Reagan administration's preoccupation with the Soviet threat and its interest in strengthening U.S.-China strategic cooperation. Beijing threatened to downgrade relations if the United States did not agree to end all arms sales to Taiwan within a specified period. The United States made many compromises, but resisted meeting all of China's demands. Once again Beijing achieved partial success. In the August 17, 1982, arms sales communiqué, Washington promised gradually to reduce the quantity, and not to improve the quality, of arms sold to Taiwan. These were important concessions, but the Reagan administration explicitly linked them to China's "fundamental policy" to strive for "peaceful resolution" of the Taiwan issue. It then maintained a high level of transfers to Taiwan while abiding by the letter of the agreement. Despite continued grumbling, by the end of 1983 China finally accommodated itself to high levels of U.S. arms sales to Taiwan, and relations stabilized. In January 1984 Premier Zhao Ziyang visited Washington. In April, President Reagan traveled to Beijing, making the first visit to China by an American president since President Gerald Ford's visit in 1975.

Normalization of diplomatic relations opened the way to the expansion of contacts in other fields. The United States granted China most-favored-nation trade status, and economic relations soon blossomed. The United States quickly became China's largest export market and a major source of investment for the Chinese economy. Cultural ties also grew. Tens of thousands of Chinese scholars came to study in the United States, constituting two-thirds of the Chinese studying abroad.

China and the United States enlarged their strategic relationship. During the Maoist era strategic cooperation was confined to onetime imports of dual-use items, such as jet engines from Great Britain, with U.S. encouragement, and an advanced computer from the United States. After normalization extensive security relations developed. In December 1980 the director of the Central Intelligence Agency, Stansfield Turner, secretly traveled to China to conclude an agreement for the United States to set up electronic intelligence facilities on Chinese territory to monitor Soviet missile tests.[11] Despite the Reagan administration's interest in expanding strategic cooperation, in 1981 China suspended military ties in response to U.S. arms sales to Taiwan. Following the August 17, 1982, communiqué the two sides reopened earlier discussions of an arms transfer program. Washington agreed to sell Beijing artillery equipment, antisubmarine torpedoes, artillery-locating radar, and advanced avionics packages. Following Premier Zhao Ziyang's 1984 visit to the United States, CIA Director William Casey secretly visited China to discuss cooperation in opposing the Soviet occupation of Afghanistan. Complementing arms transfers and intelligence cooperation were broad exchanges between the two militaries that contributed to a greater understanding of each other's institutions and operating procedures.

From 1972 to 1989 the United States and China cooperated in opposing the Soviet Union, while developing cultural, economic, and strategic relations. They continually negotiated their conflict of interest over Taiwan. Despite Chinese pressure, Washington maintained an informal security commitment and arms sales to Taiwan. Taiwan's continued ambiguous status in U.S.-China relations ensured that it would again disrupt these relations once the strategic basis for compromise eroded.

THE END OF THE COLD WAR, THE TIANANMEN INCIDENT, AND THE POLITICIZATION OF CHINA POLICY

Congressional intervention in U.S.-China relations in the case of the Taiwan Relations Act was not an aberration. It was part of a trend of congressional assertiveness in foreign policy that had started several years earlier and that would continue to complicate the American relationship with China. During the Cold War the principle of foreign policy bipartisanship decreed that "politics stops at the water's edge." With the exception of the sterile debate in the early 1950s over "who lost China,"

China policy enjoyed bipartisan support until 1979. But congressional deference on issues of foreign policy eroded under the impact of the Vietnam War and Watergate, both of which undermined trust in the president's word. The 1973 War Powers Resolution, limiting the president's ability to deploy troops into hostile situations, was an early sign of the new mood.

American policy toward China during the 1980s was not subjected to struggle between the executive and the legislative branches because of the broad consensus on the contribution U.S.-China cooperation made to the containment of the Soviet Union. Most Americans overlooked aspects of China that offended their values. Maoist totalitarianism created one of the most brutal governments in history, yet Americans rejoiced at the warm reception that Chairman Mao offered Richard Nixon. Deng Xiaoping's regime, although a great improvement over Mao's, remained a repressive government. Americans focused on positive trends in Chinese politics and economics, believing that the Chinese were moving toward American values.

The nearly simultaneous June 1989 Tiananmen incident and the end of the Cold War transformed the policy-making environment in the United States. The PRC's violent repression of the Chinese democracy movement, witnessed on television sets around the country, transformed Americans' understanding of the Chinese human rights situation. The ensuing collapse of the Warsaw Pact and of communist governments in Eastern Europe eliminated the strategic imperative for cooperation with China. Americans' perspective on China became more critical. What had been a liberalizing Chinese regime had overnight turned into an atavistic Communist dictatorship imprisoning the Chinese people. The broad national consensus on the importance of U.S.-China cooperation evaporated, and China policy suddenly became one of the most divisive issues in American foreign policy.

In these circumstances interest group politics assumed an increased importance in U.S. China policy. China's political system elicits opposition from human rights organizations, including Human Rights Watch/Asia and Amnesty International; its population policies have outraged the Right to Life movement; its inexpensive consumer goods exports lead to demands for protection from organized labor; its reliance on coal and megadams for energy worries environmental groups; its arms and technology exports anger arms control activists; its sovereignty over Tibet arouses protests from Tibetan expatriates and their American supporters; the film and software industries demand protection of their copyrights in the Chinese market. Indeed, China seems to attract the attention of more American interest groups than does any other country.

Congressional activism in foreign policy has combined with interest group attention to politicize China policy. Members of Congress sometimes vote for legislation or pressure the White House to adopt policies toward China that meet the interest of vocal constituencies. Small groups enhance their influence by "bundling" campaign contributions, which the campaign finance law otherwise limits to $1,000 per individual donor and $5,000 per group. In recent years the spectrum of congressional critics of U.S. policy toward China has run from Senator Jesse Helms on the right, through Republican moderates like Representative Ben Gilman, to human rights liberals on the Democratic left like Representative Tom Lantos and Senator Edward Kennedy. Congresswoman Nancy Pelosi, a California Democrat, found in human rights an issue that resonated with some of her Chinese-American constituents; Senator Claiborne Pell and former Representative Stephen Solarz, both Democrats, found support from Taiwanese-Americans for their defense of Taiwan's interests; Senator Alan Cranston, a Republican, championed Tibetan rights with support from the Hollywood entertainment industry. Members can demonstrate their competence on global issues and their support for an assertive anti-Communist foreign policy at little cost to their districts by taking positions critical of China.

The politicization of China policy increased after the Tiananmen incident.[12] American outrage at Chinese repression found its voice in Congress's opposition to President Bush's efforts to maintain cooperation with Beijing. The issue was joined over renewal of China's most-favored-nation status. Since China is a "non-market economy," under U.S. law MFN status has been extended only on an annual basis and subject to congressional review. This provision originated in the Jackson-Vanik amendment to the 1974 Trade Act, which was designed to pressure the USSR to allow free emigration of Soviet Jews. After China's MFN status was approved in 1980, it was routinely renewed until the year after Tiananmen. Between 1990 and 1994 the debate over MFN raged each spring, as members of Congress tried to amass the votes necessary to overturn the White House decision to extend China's MFN status unconditionally. Many in Congress sought to condition China's MFN (that is, normal) trade status on improvement in its human rights policies. In 1990, 1991, and 1992, President Bush vetoed legislation that would have enacted such a linkage. He paid a high political price for sending his national security adviser, Brent Scowcroft, on two secret missions to China in 1989, by meeting personally with Foreign Minister Qian Qichen in early 1991, by dispatching Secretary of State James A. Baker to Beijing in November of that year, and by holding a brief meeting with Premier Li Peng in New York in early 1992.

China's foreign policy-making environment also changed in 1989. Just as the United States no longer required strategic cooperation with China, with the end of the Sino-Soviet dispute China no longer needed to cooperate with the United States. The June 1989 democracy demonstrations and the fate of communism in Eastern Europe in 1989 convinced Chinese leaders that their political survival depended more on suppressing dissent than on maintaining good ties with the United States. Any Chinese leader who showed weakness in dealing with dissent became vulnerable to political attack. While the Tiananmen incident transformed American perceptions of China, it also transformed Chinese perceptions of the United States. American support for the Chinese democracy movement was now seen as part of a long-standing U.S. effort to overthrow the Chinese regime. China no longer viewed the United States as a strategic partner but as an ideological adversary. Even pro-reform leaders found it increasingly difficult to make concessions to the United States, particularly on human rights issues.

The more domestic politics replaced common interests as the basis for policy in both countries, the more difficult it became for the two sides to maintain cooperation. During the 1992 presidential campaign, Bill Clinton criticized George Bush for "coddling dictators" and promised to use trade relations to compel China to improve its human rights performance. Once in the White House, Clinton demanded that China improve its behavior or the United States would withdraw its MFN status. The policy failed because Chinese leaders cared more about political stability than MFN and because American business and employment interests would have been hurt by U.S. sanctions and Chinese retaliation. In 1994 the president abandoned linkage rather than apply sanctions. But throughout his first term, high-level meetings with Chinese leaders remained controversial, so Clinton was unable to arrange an exchange of formal state visits and bring President Jiang Zemin to the White House.

The politicization of relations has often compelled Chinese leaders to adopt positions that aggravate the PRC's poor reputation in the United States. For example, China did not allow Fang Lizhi, a dissident who sought political protection at the U.S. embassy in June 1989, to leave China until 1990, even though President Bush needed well-timed Chinese concessions to win domestic support for his efforts to maintain U.S.-China cooperation. Chinese diplomats tend to blame every U.S.-China conflict on American "hegemonism." Stating that "he who tied the knot should untie it," they have supplied fewer and fewer "stepping-down stools" *(xi-ataijie)* to ease the political problems of American presidents. Such diplomacy fuels domestic opposition in the United States toward the Chinese leadership and undermines the ability of U.S. policymakers to reach compromise solutions with China.

THE BILATERAL AGENDA

President Clinton's 1994 decision to delink U.S.-China trade from China's human rights policy and his 1996 adoption of a new policy of "strategic dialogue" represented an attempt to refocus U.S.-China negotiations on specific conflicting and common interests. The two countries confront a large agenda, and with domestic politics in each country influencing policy on even technical issues, maintaining cooperation remains a difficult process. Many of the details are sketched in the chapters that follow, and Chapter 13 offers some suggestions for policy. The focus here is on bilateral conflicts of interests and on their domestic political context.

Taiwan has forced itself back from the margin to the center of the U.S.-China relationship. This occurred not at Beijing's or Washington's initiative but at Taipei's. As Taiwan developed democracy, the wishes of its voters compelled its leaders to adopt "pragmatic diplomacy," challenging Beijing's efforts to isolate and delegitimize Taipei (Chapter 12). While Taiwan's leaders lobbied in capitals around the world for greater legitimacy, the end of the Cold War and the Tiananmen Square incident eroded support in the United States for adhering to the U.S.-China communiqués. At the same time respect for Taiwan's democratic reform generated pressure to treat Taiwan better.

In response to domestic political pressures, the Bush and Clinton administrations altered U.S. Taiwan policy. During the 1992 presidential election, in order to appeal to the voters of Texas, where F-16 military jets are manufactured, President Bush agreed to sell 150 of the jets to Taiwan, in violation of the 1982 U.S.-China communiqué. In 1994, under congressional pressure, the Clinton White House conducted a Taiwan policy review and decided to upgrade the protocol status accorded to Taiwan's officials and to receive Taiwan cabinet-level officials in U.S. government offices. In the face of additional congressional pressure, the State Department in 1995 issued a visa for President Lee Teng-hui of Taiwan to visit his alma mater, Cornell University.

These changes in U.S. policy were important to China because the United States has enormous influence over Taiwan's policy toward the mainland. Backsliding in the American position on Taiwan could create momentum in Taiwan for support for a formal declaration of Taiwan independence. China has stated that such a declaration would lead to war. But it made only limited protests against the F-16 decision and the 1994 Taiwan policy review. Chinese leaders believed that the U.S. policy shifts were minimal concessions to political pressures by administrations committed to honoring the historical understandings on Taiwan. But the visa for Lee Teng-hui suggested that the United States was ignoring Chinese interests. Coming just as Taiwan's presidential election was entering its final stage, it had the potential to encourage Taiwan's candidates to declare support for a sovereign Taiwan.

The 1996 Taiwan Strait crisis was the result of these events. By conducting military exercises near Taiwan, including live-fire missile tests less than fifteen miles from Taiwan's major ports, Beijing hoped to put a stop to one-sided American amendments of the ground rules for U.S.-Taiwan relations. It also aimed to reinforce its warning to the people of Taiwan that they would pay a high price for declaring independence. The immediate outcome of Chinese maneuvers was greater American sensitivity to the risks of mismanaging U.S.-Taiwan relations and greater attention on the part of the White House to managing U.S.-China relations. Over the long run Taiwan's reaction will also be important. Although the pro-independence Democratic Progressive Party lost support during the election, after the election Lee Teng-hui showed little interest in restraining his pragmatic diplomacy. China could initiate a new crisis if either Taiwan or the United States attempts to alter the status quo in the U.S.-Taiwan-China triangle.

A second prominent issue on the U.S.-China agenda is arms proliferation (Chapter 9). From the perspective of the United States, the concern is not with all Chinese arms sales but with certain transfers that Washington believes either upset regional power balances or contribute to the spread of technologies of mass destruction. U.S. officials fear that the sale of Chinese intermediate-range missiles to Pakistan, and the transfer of nuclear reactors and nuclear technology to Pakistan, Algeria, and Iran, may destabilize favorable regional power balances in the Middle East or undermine the fragile global nuclear nonproliferation regime. Washington also worries about China's alleged sale to Iran of the precursor chemical agents required to manufacture chemical weapons. From Reagan through Clinton presidents have pressured China to desist from such sales.

Chinese leaders consider the American position disingenuous. They point out that the United States is itself the world's largest arms exporter and that U.S. proliferation sometimes directly harms Chinese interests, as did the sale of F-16 fighter planes and other military hardware to Taiwan and the transfer of nuclear reprocessing technology to Japan. The Chinese argue that if U.S. weapons sales are a legitimate hard-currency export, so are their own. Nonetheless, in response to U.S. pressure, China has accommodated many U.S. demands. The PRC stopped supplying Silkworm missiles to Iran, broke its commitment to provide Syria with M-9 missiles, and suspended its nuclear energy cooperation agreement with Iran. China's nuclear energy program with Algeria complies with the inspection requirements of the International Atomic Energy Agency (IAEA).

The major exception to the record of Chinese cooperation has to do with Pakistan. China has a vital strategic interest in Pakistan, which confronts in India a power many times its size (Chapter 6). Should India, which has its own nuclear weapons capability, succeed in dominating Pakistan, it will have established hegemony throughout Southern Asia and could challenge Chinese border security. Moreover, China's transfer to Pakistan of the M-11 missile occurred on the heels of the U.S. decision to sell F-16s to Taiwan, suggesting that China is unwilling to exercise restraint in deference to U.S. requests when the United States refuses to exercise symmetrical restraint to honor Chinese interests. In 1996 a Chinese enterprise transferred to Pakistan magnetic rings that could be used in nuclear reprocessing. Despite U.S. charges, it was not clear that the sale formally violated any international arms control agreements or that the Chinese government was aware of the transfer. Washington decided not to impose sanctions, in return for a Chinese commitment to cease assistance to any nuclear reactors not under IAEA safeguards.

In February 1992 China told the United States that it would abide by Missile Technology Control Regime (MTCR) restrictions on missile exports. After the United States sold F-16s to Taiwan and China transferred M-11 missiles to Pakistan later that year, Washington and Beijing negotiated a new agreement. In 1994 Beijing agreed to abide by those aspects of the MTCR that govern the export of missiles. (It did not agree to abide by the regime's guidelines on the export of missile technologies.) While pressing China to honor these commitments, the United States has not invited Beijing to sign the agreement, because it wants to restrict Chinese access to the sophisticated dialogue on missile systems among the signatories. Complicating the management of the proliferation issue are laws enacted over White House opposition that require the president to impose sanctions on any country that violates the MTCR or the Nuclear Non-Proliferation Treaty (NPT), whether it is a signatory or not, or that sells "destabilizing" weaponry to Iran. This minimizes the White House's flexibility to negotiate compromise solutions to conflicts of interest, such as those concerning Pakistan.

Trade relations have created a third set of U.S.-China problems (Chapter 9). The arenas of conflict are diverse—negotiations on opening markets, on intellectual property rights protection, and on China's accession to the World Trade Organization. The United States is not the only government pressing China on these issues, which have become entangled with other concerns, including human rights and weapons proliferation. But the political engine of trade conflicts is the U.S. trade deficit with China. According to U.S. figures, it has grown from $68 million in 1983 to $33.8 billion in 1995.

The rising deficit is caused largely by forces that elude American or Chinese government control. Economists argue that the low savings rate in the United States rather than other countries' protectionism is the main cause of America's overall trade imbalance. Unlike Japan, which runs a trade deficit with all the industrialized countries and enjoys an overall trade surplus every year, China has a trade deficit with many countries, and its overall balance changes from year to year.[13] Its surplus with the United States in large part reflects a decision by entrepreneurs in Hong Kong, Taiwan, Japan, and South Korea to shift the production of consumer products to mainland China, where labor costs are lower. In doing this, the entrepreneurs also shifted to China much of their nations' trade surpluses with the United States. Adjusted for inflation, the size of the combined U.S. deficit with China, Taiwan, South Korea, Japan, Singapore, and Hong Kong was approximately the same in 1995 as it was in the late 1980s, suggesting that the growth of the bilateral deficit with China has had a small marginal impact on the U.S. trade balance and employment situation. Chinese exports to the United States have taken jobs directly from workers in other exporting countries, whose exports to the United States long ago eliminated most employment opportunities for Americans in such sectors as textiles, shoes, and low-cost electronics. U.S. products that compete well in international markets have done well in China. America is the largest exporter to China of civilian aircraft (Boeing), personal computers (AST, Compaq, and IBM), cellular telephones (Motorola), and other high-technology consumer goods, as well as of agricultural goods and fertilizer, and it is one of China's largest providers of industrial equipment.

Nonetheless, as China's trade surplus with the United States moved into second place in 1991, ahead of Taiwan's and behind Japan's (and sometimes into first place on a monthly basis in 1996), it drew increasing political attention. Constituencies hurt by Chinese competition—labor unions, textile and toy manufacturers—criticized China and asked for protection. Producers of intellectual property pressed the White House to adopt tough policies in negotiations over copyright protection. Beneficiaries of trade with China—including aircraft manufacturers, wheat and cotton producers, and fertilizer companies, on the export side, and consumer goods retailers, on the import side—pressed their viewpoints quietly in Washington without drawing public attention to themselves. As with proliferation and human rights, some members of Congress used the trade issue to challenge the president, increasing pressure on the White House to adopt a tough posture toward China.

U.S.-China trade cooperation is a central element of China's modernization strategy. For much of the post-Mao era, the United States has been China's largest market. Exports to the United States of low-technology, inexpensive consumer goods earn China the hard currency its needs to import the high technology necessary to modernize its economy and upgrade its defense capabilities. By contrast, trade with China represents a small portion of U.S. foreign trade, and the benefits are concentrated in certain sectors of the economy. A disruption of trade would affect some companies and regions severely, but would have only a small, temporary impact on the size and growth of the U.S. economy. America's economic bargaining power with China is high.

Beijing has made many compromises on trade issues. It has lowered trade barriers and taken steps to curtail piracy of intellectual property. Still, neither the trade imbalance nor the intellectual property rights conflict is susceptible to quick resolution; the trade deficit has continued to grow and Chinese copyright pirates have found new ways to evade the rules. U.S.-China trade crises reemerge periodically to threaten cooperative relations.

Finally, a broad sector of American opinion shows concern about the problem of human rights in China (Chapter 10). The problem encompasses such specific issues as political and religious prisoners, torture, repression in Tibet, the export of prison labor products, and the use of coercion in China's population-planning program. The Chinese government takes the position that these are internal affairs that brook no interference from foreign governments, organizations, or individuals. The American position, supported by most government officials as well as private citizens, is that there exist universal human rights norms and that their violation is a matter of international concern.

Since the Tiananmen incident Americans have given more attention to human rights in China than in any other country. This reflects China's size, its importance in world politics, the long history of Americans' contact with the Chinese people, and the enduring impact of the Tiananmen crackdown. Since 1994 the debate over linking MFN trade status to China's human rights violations has receded in importance. The widespread belief that the threat of sanctions had failed to change China's human rights policies but undermined U.S.-China economic and political cooperation led growing numbers of members of Congress to support the White House policy rather than conditionality legislation. But human rights remains on the agenda of U.S.-China discussions. The Jackson-Vanik amendment remains U.S. law, so Congress still has the authority to influence U.S.-China trade relations on human rights grounds. Should China adopt large-scale violent measures to repress democracy activists, especially in Hong Kong after 1997, China's MFN status could again be in jeopardy.

FRUSTRATIONS OF ASYMMETRY

Although concealed by the smoke of polemics, asymmetry of power defines Sino-American relations. China's power is growing, but America's remains incomparably greater. The United States has unrivaled ability to facilitate or frustrate China's ambitions to modernize its economy. Militarily, Washington can challenge core Chinese interests in Taiwan or Korea. China could not insulate its regional diplomacy from U.S.-China economic or military conflict. If relations deteriorated, Washington would look for support from its allies. Chinese access to markets and technology in Asia and throughout the world would be affected.

Almost as damaging to Chinese interests as heightened conflict with the United States would be American withdrawal from Asia. If America weakened its commitment to the region, China would have to confront security challenges without the benefit of an outside balancing power. Chinese policymakers think the PRC's rival in such a situation would likely be a resurgent and militarized Japan, a view shared to varying degrees in South Korea, Russia, the Philippines, and elsewhere in East Asia. The combination of Japanese wealth and technological prowess creates a formidable military potential (Chapter 5). Chinese leaders also have in mind the long-term possibility of a resurgent Russia, whose military technology, natural resources, and geographic and demographic size would make it an imposing enemy (Chapter 3). Barring an intensification of the U.S.-China conflict, Chinese leaders perceive the American presence in Asia as contributing to regional stability and Chinese security.

The U.S. stake in the relationship with China is not as great. The United States is not dependent on China for peace in the Americas, Europe, the former Soviet Union, or the Middle East. Its interests in cooperation with China involve regional stability and the construction of international regimes. Chinese cooperation is not essential to support the American position even in Asia, since other countries, including Japan, welcome the U.S. presence there and are likely to embrace it even more if China behaves in ways they consider aggressive.

Yet the asymmetry in power has not given Washington an unchallenged upper hand. The American economy benefits from access to the Chinese market. The development of effective international arms control, trade, and human rights regimes and the control of global pollution depend on Chinese cooperation. Stability in Asia and a reduced U.S. defense burden require that the United States and China not develop an adversarial relationship.

The potential for cooperation is substantial. Both countries favor political and economic stability in Russia, stability on the Korean peninsula and in Cambodia, protecting Pakistan's security, and safeguarding Inner Asia and the Middle East from Muslim fundamentalism. Both oppose aggressive nationalism in Japan. Globally they favor resolving world environmental problems and developing the world trading economy, although they disagree on the allocation of benefits and costs in these areas. At the bilateral level the United States has a long-stated and authentic interest in China's prosperity and stability. China in turn has no reason to favor economic or political turbulence in the United States. The two sides are positioned to profit from one another's prosperity. In the cultural and educational fields they have forged ties of cooperation that benefit both sides.

These common interests shape the relationship in many ways. There are extensive people-to-people ties in trade and investment, education, science and technology, and the arts. The two governments at working levels consult on matters of diplomatic strategy and policy toward third parties, such as North Korea. They have cooperated to protect the global environment. The U.S. government and private institutions assist the development of Chinese public health, medicine, and educational, political, legislative, and judicial institutions. China cooperates with American geologists studying plate tectonics and the causes of earthquakes, and with paleontologists examining fossils on Chinese territory. A quarter century of cooperation has created substantial interests in both countries that gain from stable relations and that encourage China and the United States to avoid unnecessary conflict.

Despite the benefits of stable relations, hard negotiations are required to resolve conflicts. America uses negotiations to try to move China closer to American goals. China seeks to define the boundaries beyond which it refuses to allow the United States to push. In the period of the strategic triangle, the PRC was able to check American power by taking advantage of the superpower rivalry. With the end of the Cold War, China has found America more difficult to manage.

The two sides are hampered in managing their relationship by the contrasting attributes of their political systems. Each system is a puzzle to members of the other. America's political structure is open to the diverse pressures of a democratic society; its foreign policy is buffeted by crosscurrents of ideology and pragmatism. Rhetoric and practice often conflict, policies change, promises are broken, and favors are not long remembered. China's authoritarian political structure produces a foreign policy that is generally patient and focused on strategic interests, although a weakening leadership increasingly strays from consistency (Chapter 8). Both peoples are nationalistic—Americans in a proactive way that promotes national values, Chinese in a reactive way that resents American interference. Yet in contrast to the situation at midcentury, the conflicts between the two nations do not inevitably threaten the vital security interests of either, and their many common interests are expressed in working-level contacts at both governmental and private levels.

A recent American policy study predicts that "the United States may be in for several decades of difficult and possibly costly dealings with China as an emerging great power."[14] Clashes are inevitable, but the two countries' fundamental interests pull them together more than they drive them apart. The outcome of their interactions will depend on whether the two governments draw on their respective traditions of foreign policy realism, or instead allow domestic politics to dominate over the pursuit of fundamental interests. If the U.S.-China Cold War of the 1950s and 1960s was a tragedy, painful but unavoidable, a new Cold War would be simply a needless and wasteful mistake.

5

DIFFICULT FRIENDS: JAPAN AND THE TWO KOREAS

F OR ALL OF Beijing's justified obsession with Russia and the United States, China may face more immediate challenges and opportunities from Japan and Korea in the decade ahead. At a time when Russia is in retreat and the United States, uncertain about its role in post–Cold War international politics, has reduced its military presence in Asia, Japan and the two Koreas are powerful nearby states with unpredictable trajectories. Japan is a vibrant society that continues to develop impressive economic and military capabilities. Although it has a small standing army and a subordinate role in the U.S.-Japan alliance, its 1994 military budget of nearly $45 billion was the second largest in the world. Its economy is also the world's second largest, and it possesses some of the world's most advanced technology. Its neighboring location in Asia means that Japanese actions inevitably affect Chinese interests.

The two Koreas do not have the great-power status of China or Japan, but neither are they passive participants in Northeast Asian politics. Not only does South Korea possess one of the most advanced economies in the world; in 1994 it also had the world's eighth-largest defense budget ($13 billion) and the sixth-largest standing army (600,000). Draconian communism has eroded North Korea's economic and military strength, yet Pyongyang is one of the least predictable governments in the world and retains the ability to unleash a devastating war on China's borders—there is no telling what the North Korean leadership will do to survive in the face of economic collapse and popular discontent. Even after the Cold War the Korean peninsula remains a site of great-power competition, including potential Sino-Japanese conflict.

Despite security concerns Japan and the Korean peninsula also present opportunities for Chinese interests. In 1994 Japan outranked all other nations in aid to China and stood behind only the United States and Hong Kong in investment there. It was China's third-most-important export market, and China was Japan's fifth-most-important export market. South Korea also ranked among China's top trading partners and sources of investment capital. In addition to the economic gains China gets from these ties, improved political relations with South Korea and Japan can contribute to its security by promoting regional stability and by offering China potential alignment partners, should relations with the United States and Russia deteriorate.

The long history shared by the three neighbors in Northeast Asia adds a level of complexity to the current situation. Korea, the smallest of the three, has at different times been colonized by both of the other two. Japan and Korea, borrowers of China's Confucian culture and writing system, have in some ways outdone their old master in economic and political development. So close culturally and geographically, each people views the others with an element of condescension. Bias and misperception color China's relations with these two nations more thickly than with more-distant countries.

China's management of these important bilateral relationships is further complicated by their enmeshment in the larger power structure of Northeast Asia. Chinese leaders see their bilateral relations with Japan and the two Koreas through the prism of each country's interactions with the two others, as well as in the context of U.S. and Russian policies in Northeast Asia. Japan and the two Koreas in turn shape their relations with China in light of their important ties with America, Russia, and each other. Not only is Northeast Asia the region most central to Chinese security interests, but it is also the most complex setting in which China must manage numerous and often conflicting policy objectives.

Japan: The Best and the Worst

Japan has always held a key place in China's foreign policy. In the 1930s Japan subjugated the Chinese people in a humiliating occupation, and it was not China but the United States that ultimately defeated the Japanese military. The U.S. occupation of Japan did not ease Chinese concerns. Chinese leaders watched with apprehension as the United States rehabilitated many Japanese wartime leaders and helped revive Japan's industrial economy. The February 1950 Sino-Soviet treaty focused on the Japanese threat as the cornerstone of security cooperation between Moscow and Beijing (Chapter 3). Despite Japan's minimal military capabilities and weak economy for much of the Cold War, U.S.-Japanese cooperation was the linchpin of America's effort to encircle and weaken the People's Republic of China.

Chinese Communist leaders spent the first twenty years of their rule trying to detach Japan from the U.S. alliance system. They persistently attacked the U.S.-Japan security alliance and the revival of Japanese "militarism" and attempted to work with the Japanese Socialist and Communist parties to create political pressure on the ruling Liberal Democratic Party (LDP) to improve diplomatic relations with China. China tried to manipulate Japanese war guilt, hoping that the Japanese people's desire to make restitution for the occupation of China would force the government to open diplomatic and economic relations with Beijing. Following the Korean War and the 1954 Geneva conference that ended the first Vietnam war, Beijing emphasized "peaceful coexistence" in Sino-Japanese relations. Premier Zhou Enlai pushed for the establishment of diplomatic relations, and Japan seemed ready to respond. But the United States compelled Japanese leaders to turn aside China's overtures. In 1957 Prime Minister Nobusuke Kishi of Japan adopted a hard-line China policy and paid the first state visit to Taiwan by a Japanese prime minister. The Japanese military also began training Nationalist soldiers. Sino-Japanese relations deteriorated as Chinese diplomacy hardened.

Beijing dangled before Japan the economic lure of the Chinese market, holding Sino-Japanese trade relations hostage to Japan's opening of diplomatic relations with Beijing. This led to Chinese policy gyrations.[1] During the mid-1950s, on the basis of a succession of private trade agreements and the support of both governments, trade gradually expanded.

China tried to use the accords to develop de facto diplomatic relations. In 1955 Tokyo agreed that Chinese trade representatives would have diplomatic privileges. In 1957 it granted Chinese agencies additional privileges, including the right to fly the PRC flag. But determined opposition from Taiwan and the United States compelled Tokyo to abandon the 1957 agreement. China retaliated by canceling all economic and cultural relations with Japan. Beginning in 1960, faced with the economic dislocations of the Great Leap Forward, China tried to develop unofficial "friendship trade" with Japan. It would trade only with Japanese companies it identified as "friendly"—those that did not oppose Sino-Japanese diplomatic relations and that opposed a two-China policy and the U.S.-Japan security treaty. By 1962 Beijing had identified 162 such enterprises. But friendship trade promoted neither Sino-Japanese trade nor friendship.

In 1962 Chinese leaders once again entered into semi-official trade relations to promote Sino-Japanese economic and political ties. On the basis of annual memorandums between Chinese government officials and leading officials of the LDP, trade expanded. During the mid-1960s Japan replaced the Soviet Union as China's number one trading partner. Tokyo also agreed that the two sides could establish official trade liaison offices in each other's country. But Beijing could not persuade Tokyo to establish diplomatic relations and break relations with Taiwan. In 1967 Prime Minister Eisaku Sato paid a state visit to Taiwan. These setbacks and the ideological fervor of the Cultural Revolution led to a decline in Sino-Japanese memorandum trade, to a renewed PRC emphasis on friendship trade, and to a decline in total trade.

Beijing's economic diplomacy had failed. Japan was too dependent on the United States for its security and economic growth to diverge from U.S. policy on such an important issue as China policy. When Japan finally decided to open relations with China, the impetus was not developments in China's Japan policy but in America's China policy. When Richard Nixon announced in July 1971 that Henry Kissinger had just visited Beijing and that the president planned to hold a summit there, Japan suffered "Nixon shock." Tokyo quickly made policy adjustments. In July 1972 Tokyo opened normalization negotiations with Beijing, and in September Prime Minister Kakuei Tanaka traveled to China, where he and Zhou Enlai issued a joint statement establishing diplomatic relations, which included Japan's agreement to sever diplomatic ties with Taiwan. Now Sino-Japanese trade expanded without diplomatic impediments.

Total trade tripled between 1972 and 1975; China became Japan's third-largest export market and the eighth-largest exporter to the Japanese market. Only in the final year of Mao's life, when radical ideologues experienced a burst of renewed authority and Chinese managers suspended relations with Japanese firms, did trade suffer a temporary decline.[2]

U.S.-China rapprochement also transformed Sino-Japanese security relations. China now saw the United States and Japan as counterweights to the Soviet Union, and regarded the American defense umbrella over Japan as a guarantee that Japan would not remilitarize in the face of the Soviet threat—above all, that it would not make nuclear weapons. The strategic importance Chinese leaders attached to the relationship was underscored in 1978. In August, as Soviet-Vietnamese cooperation reached new heights, the prospect loomed of a Vietnamese invasion of Cambodia. These Soviet moves also posed a threat to Japan, which depends on the sea-lanes for its energy supplies, much of its food, and most of its other international trade. In these circumstances Beijing and Tokyo finally reached agreement on a peace treaty ending the Sino-Japanese state of war dating back to World War II. The accord included a clause in which the two countries denounced "hegemony," Beijing's code word for Soviet expansionism and "encirclement" of China.

Throughout the 1980s common Sino-Japanese interests in the face of the Soviet threat provided the basis for frequent summitry, political consultations, and friendly diplomacy. Economic relations flourished. From 1977 to 1981 two-way trade tripled, reaching more than $10 billion. During much of the 1980s Japan was China's number two trade partner, second only to Hong Kong. In 1979 the two sides reached their first agreement on Japanese loans to China. The loans totaled fifty billion yen and assisted in the completion of six major construction projects in China. Altogether, from 1979 to 1989, Japanese low-interest loans to China amounted to over $17 billion.[3]

During the Cold War, Beijing and Tokyo pushed aside secondary conflicts of interest and underlying long-range concerns so that they could jointly counter the Soviet threat. Nonetheless, Chinese leaders did not forget the potential danger of resurgent Japanese militarism. Through the 1970s and 1980s, in the context of U.S.-Japanese security cooperation regarding the Soviet Union, Japan developed its military capabilities.[4] Defense spending increased along with the GNP. Much of the new spending went to the buildup and modernization of the Japanese navy, as

Tokyo sought to fulfill its commitment to the United States to undertake the defense of the sea-lanes within 1,000 nautical miles of the home islands.

Japan now boasts the largest surface fleet in the western Pacific. Almost all of its naval vessels have been built within the last fifteen years and are constructed and equipped with highly advanced technology. Japan, unlike China, possesses the technology to build, support, and manage aircraft carriers, the key element in power projection—although it has not so far chosen to do so. Indeed, it deployed aircraft carriers over fifty years ago during World War II. Tokyo has also modernized its air force. In 1976 Japan decided to coproduce with Mcdonnell-Douglas the American F-15 fighter jet. In the 1980s it agreed to codevelop and manufacture with the United States a cutting-edge military jet, dubbed the F-2. The F-2, based on the U.S. F-16, will be superior to any aircraft China can manufacture. Japan also developed some of the most advanced missile technology in the world, including missile guidance systems that were better than America's, and in the 1990s acquired advanced electronic warfare equipment, such as airborne warning and control system (AWACS) aircraft. Japan has developed all the elements of a nuclear weapons program except the assembly and testing of a nuclear device, so it would take only a matter of months for Tokyo to deploy a nuclear warhead on a long-range missile.

Meanwhile, Chinese defense spending continued to stagnate (Chapter 8), with the result that by the end of the 1980s Japan had achieved military superiority over China in all forms of weaponry, with the sole exception of nuclear weaponry, an exception Tokyo could rapidly eliminate. These Japanese successes occurred with minimal economic sacrifice. The Japanese defense budget stayed below the politically sensitive threshold of one percent of the GNP for most of this period, so Japanese gains have barely approximated Japanese spending and technological potential. During the 1970s and 1980s Japan also developed its economic presence in Asia. Its aid and investment have been determining factors in the economic growth of Thailand, Malaysia, Indonesia, and South Korea, fostering considerable influence in their decision making.

The growth of Japanese power caused apprehension in the Chinese elite, but the leadership remained largely silent until Beijing began to improve relations with Moscow.[5] In the mid-1980s China initiated a relentless campaign against support for "militarism" in the Japanese leadership. China joined South Korea and other Asian countries in criticizing Japanese politicians' statements and government-approved secondary school textbook revisions that so much as hinted at positive reappraisals of Japanese behavior during World War II. In 1987 Deng Xiaoping told a visiting Japanese delegation, "Frankly, China bears no responsibility for the historic conflicts in the history of Sino-Japanese relations. . . . Relations have developed, but we cannot be very satisfied with them. Japan can and should do more. It should appropriately resolve some unhappy incidents." The party ideologist Hu Qiaomu wrote, "We do not want to bring up the past, but things are going contrary to our wishes. Some people in Japan deliberately try to forget and change these unforgettable and unalterable historical facts. . . . Japan gives China the cold shoulder. China will not accept it quietly. It is Japan that will suffer in the end."[6]

China also carried out campaigns against even the slightest intimations that Japan was developing a "two-China" policy. China's concern about Japan's Taiwan policy is second only to its concern about America's Taiwan policy. Tokyo controlled Taiwan from 1895, when China ceded it to Japan after military defeat, until the end of World War II, and many people on Taiwan have favorable recollections of the Japanese occupation. Chinese leaders suspect Japan of having strategic objectives in regard to Taiwan. Just as Taiwan was an "unsinkable aircraft carrier" for the United States during the period of Sino-American confrontation, it could become a Japanese asset if Sino-Japanese relations deteriorate. Chinese leaders also suspect that the Taiwan leadership considers an alignment with Japan as a fallback position if the United States reconsiders its commitment to Taiwan's security.

In the mid-1980s Beijing adopted a belligerent posture following a 1986 Japanese court decision that a student dormitory owned by the Taiwan government remained the property of Taiwan despite the normalization of Sino-Japanese relations in 1972. Deng Xiaoping personally warned Japanese legislators that the court decision created a "very serious" problem for Sino-Japanese relations, the PRC Foreign Ministry threatened retaliation, and a Sino-Japanese media war erupted. The Foreign Ministry also tried to pressure the Japanese government to cancel the plans of private citizens to host an international meeting celebrating the hundredth anniversary of the birth of Chiang Kai-shek, insisting that the event was "tantamount to support for the creation of two Chinas."[7]

Beijing campaigned against increases in the Japanese defense budget. Polemics became especially harsh in 1987, when the defense budget increased to just over one percent of the Japanese GNP. One percent had been a threshold reflecting Japan's post–World War II commitment to abandon the use of force in diplomacy. Before the increase Foreign Minister Wu Xueqian expressed China's concern that once Japan's defense budget crossed the threshold, Tokyo would be on its way to becoming a major military power. *People's Daily* warned that after this break with tradition, "it is unavoidable that the second and third 'breaks' will follow, and that the state of affairs will get out of control."

China's shifting appraisal of the Japanese threat was reflected in PRC policy concerning the Soviet-Japanese dispute over the four islands Japan calls its Northern Territories. The southernmost islands of the Kuriles chain had been taken from Japan by the Soviet Union after World War II and are considered unreclaimed territory by the Japanese. The Northern Territories have natural resources, a predominantly Russian population, and a strategic location near Soviet naval ports. China supported Japan's position during the Cold War, contributing to the cohesiveness of the anti-Soviet coalition. But in early 1991, after the demise of the Soviet Union, it shifted to a neutral stance on the islands. The value of strategic cooperation with Japan had declined, and China was no longer inclined to support Tokyo's effort to recover lost territories. Not only would support for Japan's claim needlessly aggravate relations with Moscow, but Beijing also has no interest in seeing Japan actually recover the islands. On the contrary, in some respects the Russo-Japanese territorial dispute now complements Chinese interests. It focuses the attention of the Russians and the Japanese on each other, inhibits Russian-Japanese economic and political cooperation, and keeps Japan from fully concentrating on its worries about China.

In the aftermath of the 1989 Tiananmen incident, China halted its intense criticism of Japanese policies, despite Japan's participation in UN peacekeeping operations in Cambodia and its contribution to the allied effort in the 1991 Persian Gulf War, both of which represented a weakening of the taboo on deploying Japanese troops abroad. Faced with near global isolation and Western economic sanctions, Beijing was compelled to woo Japan to regain access to Japanese aid and loans and to drive a wedge in the West's isolation of China.[8] Chinese efforts paid off in 1990, when Japan took the lead among Group of Seven (G-7) countries in ending sanctions and reaching new agreements with China on generous loan and aid programs. Japan also rewarded Chinese silence by adopting a low profile on such issues as China's human rights abuses, its nuclear testing program, and its growing defense budget and by avoiding provocations regarding Taiwan. Stable diplomacy, growing economic cooperation, and the beginning of a security dialogue in 1993 suggested that Beijing and Tokyo had developed ways to manage a potentially explosive relationship.

But by 1995 the divisive issues resurfaced in Sino-Japanese relations.[9] With the development of multiparty politics in Japan following the collapse of LDP hegemony in 1994, China policy has become politicized. This is particularly true of the Taiwan issue. Taiwan's economic and political successes and growing Japan-Taiwan economic relations have created Japanese domestic interests opposed to accommodation of the mainland and the diplomatic isolation of Taiwan. After Lee Teng-hui visited Cornell University in March 1995, Japanese opposition politicians urged their government to grant Lee a visa to visit Kyoto University, his undergraduate institution, or to invite him or Taiwan's Vice Premier Hsu Lee-teh to attend the November 1995 APEC summit in Osaka. China warned that any such visits would place the relationship "in the greatest danger," and President Jiang Zemin promised to boycott the summit if either Taiwan leader attended the meeting.[10] Ultimately, Japan succumbed to Chinese pressure, and Taiwan was represented in Osaka by Koo Chen-fu, the head of its Straits Exchange Foundation.

The trend in Japanese politics was nonetheless clear. Throughout 1995, politicians from various parties in Japan called for enhanced Japanese-Taiwanese diplomatic contacts. Beijing criticized "pro-Taiwan forces" and warned the Japanese government to oppose any pro-Taiwan activities in Japan. When it seemed that a Japanese cabinet member might participate in a pro-Taiwan demonstration, Beijing made "solemn representations" with the Japanese Foreign Ministry.[11] During the 1996 Taiwan Strait crisis, hard-line members of the Liberal Democratic Party, reacting to China's military maneuvers, demanded that the Japanese government freeze its yen loans to China, compelling Japan to defer completion of a new agreement on yen loans. When asked about the prospect that Japan might freeze the loans, China's Foreign Ministry spokesman responded that China "would like to send a very clear and unmistakable message to the Japanese side, which is that the issue of Taiwan is purely an internal matter of China which brooks no foreign intervention or interference of any kind."[12] The "Taiwan lobby" is now embedded in

Japanese politics, and the Taiwan issue has added an element of uncertainty in Sino-Japanese relations.

The "China threat" has also emerged as an issue in Sino-Japanese relations, reflecting the changes in Japanese domestic politics as well as in Japan's post–Cold War strategic circumstances. Just as the end of the Cold War freed China to focus on Japanese capabilities, the demise of the Soviet threat has turned Japanese attention toward China's capabilities. There is opposition in Japan to Chinese nuclear tests, and in 1995 Tokyo retaliated against them by suspending its grant program to China. Chinese military exercises during the 1996 Taiwan Strait crisis heightened Japanese apprehension. The annual Japanese defense white paper now expresses direct concern about the modernization of China's nuclear, air, and naval forces, and treats China as a greater threat than Russia. The change in Japan's China policy is further reflected in the issue of human rights. Beginning in the mid-1990s Chinese violations undermined support for Japan's economic assistance program for China. Should China again use force against democracy activists, Japan's reaction might be more hostile than it was in 1989.

Shifts in Japanese policy since 1994 have brought on renewed counterattacks in China. Chinese media gave prominent coverage to the fiftieth anniversary of the end of World War II, featuring the atrocities of the Japanese occupation and warnings of the potential for revived militarism. For the first time since the 1970s, the Chinese media criticized Japan's military capabilities, including its nuclear program. It charged that Tokyo's defense buildup makes clear that Japan "harbors a strong desire to play a bigger military role in the world" and that it will "produce new instability" and "expand its sphere of influence through military means." One Chinese observer warned that the "situation in Japan is somewhat similar to that in pre-war Japan. What road will Japan take?—this question definitely cannot be ignored."[13]

Compounding Chinese concern about Japan's military program is the improvement in U.S.-Japan security cooperation. China has long accommodated itself to the U.S.-Japan alliance because of its role in inhibiting Japanese "militarism" and helping maintain stability in East Asia. But at the April 1996 U.S.-Japan summit, Washington and Tokyo adopted a joint action plan calling for greater Japanese military responsibility in the alliance, including for the first time responsibility in joint defense operations throughout Asia. This suggested to Chinese leaders that the alliance could promote rather than inhibit a Japanese defense buildup. Beijing floated the view that the agreement was a "dangerous signal" that Japan has been "brought into U.S. global strategy" and that it will "strengthen coordination with the actions of U.S. troops" in Asia. It "gives the feeling" that the two countries "work hand-in-hand to dominate the Asia-Pacific region."[14] The Chinese were especially disconcerted by U.S.-Japan discussions of deploying a theater missile defense (TMD) system in Japan. China has argued that an East Asian TMD would be "clearly aimed at China" and would "render ineffective" China's limited second-strike nuclear capability, enhancing Chinese vulnerability to U.S. military power and to a potential Japanese nuclear capability. It warned that it would reconsider its commitment to participating in a comprehensive test-ban treaty if such a system was deployed.[15]

China's hardened Japan policy reflects Beijing's concern about a renewed threat from its East Asian rival. Still, China's policymakers are mindful of Japan's economic importance. In the first six months of 1995, Japanese capital invested in China increased nearly 48 percent over the same period in 1994. Large Japanese firms, including Matsushita, NEC, and Toyota, began investing in large-scale manufacturing projects involving high-technology industries. In early 1996 Japan agreed to provide China with 580 billion yen in new loans for the period 1996–98, although it postponed formalization of the agreement in reaction to Chinese nuclear tests and tension in the Taiwan Strait.[16]

Beijing is also aware of the potential costs of heightened Sino-Japanese conflict. If Japan were fully to mobilize its economic and technological potential, China would have to divert considerably more of its scarce resources from economic development to military modernization, impeding its modernization and its ability to catch up with its great-power rivals. Sino-Japanese tension would destabilize Asian security and encourage the United States and Japan to enhance their cooperation in opposing China and to mobilize other Asian countries to distance themselves from Beijing.

Sino-Japanese relations continue highly sensitive and mutable. Chinese leaders often warmly welcome Japanese leaders and praise the two sides' success in developing economic and political ties. But Beijing is quick to criticize public Japanese statements suggesting support for a more activist defense policy or for a friendlier diplomatic posture toward Taiwan. It attacks Japan's nuclear weapons program and enhanced U.S.-Japan security cooperation. Most important, China continues to modernize its military capabilities (Chapter 8), despite Japanese apprehensions and the pressure this places on Tokyo to adopt countervailing military measures. But the alternative would be for China to accept permanent military and technological inferiority vis-à-vis Japan and the other great powers.

And additonal contentious issues loom on the horizon. One is the territorial dispute over the Diaoyutai/Senkaku Islands. The dispute has quietly existed since 1949, but in 1996 pressure from the Japanese legislature led Tokyo to reaffirm its claim publicly. Beijing responded by dispatching an oil-drilling vessel to the disputed waters and by warning Japan to avoid provocative actions. Later that year right-wing groups tried to reassert Japan's claim by building a lighthouse on the islands, further inflaming relations. Another source of friction is Japan's effort to obtain a permanent seat, with attendant veto power, on the UN Security Council. Chinese leaders worry that permanent Security Council membership would encourage Japanese military and political assertiveness. Beijing cannot look forward to the prospect of U.S.-Japanese cooperation on the Security Council. One Chinese report went so far as to assert, "It is absolutely impermissible to grant the veto to newly admitted permanent members."[17]

But there are encouraging signs as well. In 1996 the annual Sino-Japanese security dialogue broadened to include diplomats and defense officials. That same year the Japanese and Chinese foreign ministers agreed to hold talks on the economic development of the waters surrounding the disputed Diaoyutai/Senkaku Islands.[18] Such low-profile meetings may provide constructive ways to defuse mutual concerns about defense and foreign policies and minimize the risk of inadvertent conflict.

China and the Two Koreas

As in its policy toward Japan, Beijing views the Korean peninsula with security considerations uppermost in mind. But unlike Japan, the Koreas, either separately or as a united country, are too weak to challenge Chinese security on their own. China's main concern is that a great power might use Korean territory to threaten China. Korea lies right next to the Chinese industrial heartland of the northeast, their coastlines being separated by only a hundred miles. Moreover, Korea is almost as close to Japan as Taiwan is to southern China or Cuba to Florida.

Korea was the casus belli of the Sino-Japanese War of 1894–95, the costliest naval war in Chinese history, in which Japanese forces decimated the new Chinese navy. In the aftermath of the Russo-Japanese War of 1905, Japan used Korea as a base to expand its occupation of northeast China and to establish a puppet government in Manchuria. From 1937 to 1945 Japan launched its expansion into China from Korea. And in 1950, less than a year after its founding, the People's Republic of China was at war on the Korean peninsula with the United States.

The division of Korea at the thirty-eighth parallel under the 1953 armistice agreement accommodated China's security interests because the North Korean buffer state kept American military forces away from the Chinese border. For all the Chinese polemics against U.S. imperialism in Korea, China never subsequently encouraged Pyongyang to use military force to unify the peninsula.[19] On the contrary, China acted as a restraining influence on Pyongyang, much the way the United States helped maintain the status quo through its presence in South Korea. But beginning in the 1960s, with the escalation of the Sino-Soviet conflict, Moscow tried to displace Chinese influence in Pyongyang in order to strengthen its encirclement of China. In the mid-1980s the North Korean leadership allowed the Soviet Union broader access to airspace and ports in return for increased Soviet military assistance, including MiG-23s. But despite their growing enmity the Soviet Union and China shared an interest in stability on the Korean peninsula, so their competition for influence did not compel Chinese leaders to support North Korea's militant unification policies. Nor could China afford to improve relations with South Korea. Such a betrayal of North Korea would have given Moscow the opportunity it sought to become North Korea's sole strategic benefactor.

Sino-Soviet competition for North Korea's allegiance froze the Korean peninsula into competing blocs. On one side stood China, the Soviet Union, and North Korea; on the other, the United States, Japan, and South Korea. These dynamics ended when the Soviet Union sought to end the Cold War by reducing aid to former allies, including North Korea, and reaching out to former adversaries, including South Korea.[20] In 1990 the Soviet Union established diplomatic relations with South Korea and informed North Korea that henceforth all trade would be conducted with hard currency. China became North Korea's sole security guarantor and aid provider, as well as its sole supplier of subsidized oil. This transformation freed China to follow the Soviet Union in opening relations with South Korea, which was quick to respond, for it was engaged in a long-term diplomatic strategy—labeled *Nordpolitik*—to isolate North Korea. In 1988 China and the Soviet Union attended the Seoul Olympics, despite North Korean protests. In 1991 Moscow and Beijing refused to veto South Korean admission into the United Nations, forcing North Korea to agree to dual representation. In 1992 Beijing and Seoul established diplomatic relations.

Post–Cold War relations between China and South Korea focused on economic and security interests. South Korea, deficient in energy resources, buys coal and oil from China, which also supplies it inexpensive cotton textiles and other basic consumer goods. China imports large quantities of South Korean consumer electronics, including televisions and VCR machines. In 1995 the two-way trade between South Korea and China increased by nearly 45 percent over the 1994 trade, reaching nearly $17 billion, as China became South Korea's fourth-largest trade partner and South Korea became China's fifth-largest trade partner. With the recent increases in South Korean labor costs, China has attracted much South Korean direct investment: by 1995 China had become South Korea's largest target for such investment.[21] One of the better-known South Korean participants in this trend is Daewoo, which assembles televisions and refrigerators in Fujian province. Other South Korean firms have concentrated investment in Shandong province, which lies directly across the Yellow Sea from South Korea. Should current trends continue, Beijing will develop influence over the South Korean economy and Seoul will develop a strong interest in stable political relations with China.

China and South Korea also share views on important regional security issues, especially those having to do with Japan. Leaders in both countries have vivid memories of the Japanese occupation and remain wary of Japanese intentions. Seoul is as vocal as Beijing in its criticism of Japan's alleged militarism and its "whitewashing" of its imperial history. South Korea shares China's apprehension over the recent consolidation of U.S.-Japan defense relations. While some countries in Asia see Chinese power as a potential threat, South Korea to some extent welcomes it as a balance against its closer and potentially more powerful Japanese neighbor. In 1996 Beijing quietly expressed its sympathy for Seoul when it supported South Korea in its territorial dispute with Japan over Tokdo/Takeshima Island.[22]

China's relationship with North Korea is complex but also beneficial. The North Korean regime is dependent on China for its economic survival. China's discounted oil shipments make a vital contribution to the continued operation of many North Korean industries. Emergency food assistance from China prevents widespread famine in North Korea. In the harsh 1995–96 winter China shipped emergency clothing supplies. North Korea is also dependent on China for its strategic survival. North Korea once enjoyed military superiority over South Korea. But while Pyongyang pursued an economic development strategy of self-reliance that thwarted economic growth, Seoul adopted an export-based development strategy that transformed South Korea into one of the most advanced economies in the world. The North-South economic reversal transformed the balance of power, and by the 1980s North Korea confronted South Korean military superiority. China is North Korea's only ally.

Augmenting China's monopoly on foreign influence in North Korea is Pyongyang's self-imposed diplomatic isolation. For nearly fifty years the reclusive North Korean leadership denied its people any information about the outside world, while destroying its own economy, immiserating its society, and depriving its people of political freedom. Should Pyongyang develop extensive foreign economic or political relations with other countries, it would shatter the myths of North Korean economic success and of the wisdom of the North Korean Workers' Party, threatening the regime with social unrest and the prospect of rapid collapse.

China cannot ignore the potential for North Korean troublemaking and the possibility of war on the peninsula. In 1983 North Korean leaders had almost the entire South Korean cabinet assassinated when it was visiting Rangoon. Whereas Chinese leaders worked closely with Kim Il-sung, they have little confidence in the leadership or diplomatic skills of Kim's successors, including his son, Kim Jong-il. Chinese–North Korean diplomacy is characterized by Chinese contempt for the North Korean leadership and Pyongyang's resentment at Beijing's effort to impose its "revisionism." North Korea's effort to develop nuclear weapons is alarming and destabilizing. The introduction of nuclear weapons onto the Korean peninsula might persuade South Korea and/or Japan to develop nuclear weapons. China thus joins many nations, including the United States, in opposing North Korea's acquisition of nuclear weapons. China also shares international concern about the regional implications of a North Korean collapse. Such a "crash landing" might lead North Korean leaders to start a war in order to mobilize support. South Korean leaders fear that rapid unification would impose an intolerable economic burden on them, including a mass migration of refugees to the south.

China has the best chance of any regional power to influence Pyongyang. Beijing has brought North Korean leaders to see its modern, cosmopolitan cities, underscoring the benefits of reform and the disadvantages of ideological isolation and backwardness. It cooperates with Washington's effort to persuade North Korea to abandon its nuclear weapons program, going so far as to warn Pyongyang that it would support United Nations economic sanctions by halting its oil exports to North Korea.[23] China consistently draws American praise for having "concerns similar" to America's and for playing a "helpful supportive role" in the effort to contain nuclear proliferation in North Korea.[24] In 1994 it encouraged Pyongyang to reach agreement with Washington on nuclear controls, and it subsequently encouraged North Korea to fulfill its commitments. China's improving relationship with South Korea has also brought pressure to bear on Pyongyang.

Nonetheless, China's interests are not identical with those of its neighbors. Despite U.S.-China cooperation in restraining North Korea's nuclear program, Beijing has been reluctant to put excessive pressure on the North Korean leadership, for fear that Pyongyang might respond with aggressive and even violent behavior. Japan and South Korea have similar fears. Chinese leaders therefore hesitated to support Washington's efforts to impose a UN-sanctioned economic blockade on North Korea.

China has no interest in Korean unification, which would draw Seoul into a common border with China's massive population and formidable ground forces. This would undermine Seoul's positive assessment of Chinese power while reducing its suspicion of Japanese power. With Seoul no longer reliant on China to check North Korean recklessness, its strategic orientation might shift away from China. Moreover, it could substitute inexpensive North Korean labor for Chinese labor in its manufacturing industries. China, like other great powers, would rather have a border region composed of many small neighbors than a single, large neighbor.

China does not want to see the Pyongyang regime implode and understands that North Korean economic reform is a prerequisite to regional stability, but it shares with South Korea an apprehension over Japanese efforts to improve economic relations with North Korea. Beijing knows that if North Korea opened its economy to foreign trade, Japan would be well positioned to establish economic and political influence in Pyongyang. It also knows that the North Korean leadership resents its dependency on China. Like any small country bordering a large one, North Korea would like to emerge from China's shadow by developing relations with other great powers. Only its dire domestic predicament stands in the way of Japanese–North Korean cooperation, Japanese political influence on China's border, and heightened Sino-Japanese competition.

China's strategic position on the Korean peninsula is better today than at any other time in the last hundred years. Nonetheless, Korea is one of the least stable regions in the world. It is the focal point of competition involving the four great powers in Asia; it is divided into two states that remain locked in a struggle for control over the peninsula; and it is vulnerable to the unpredictable behavior of North Korea. As Chinese leaders ponder the future of the Korean peninsula, they cannot but be concerned that the status quo could rapidly deteriorate.

A FRAGILE BALANCE

Northeast Asia is the most complex of that continent's regions. The four great powers are all critical players there, bringing with them conflicts of interests, competitive alignments and alliances, and bitter historical rivalries. Their relations are fluid and unpredictable. North Korea and South Korea are autonomous actors with interests that are not always compatible with those of their great-power allies or with the maintenance of regional stability. Cold War diplomacy, in which friends and enemies were constant and the foreign policies of allies had a common purpose, was straightforward, compared with contemporary regional diplomacy, even if more dangerous.

Multipolarity creates conditions in which the security dilemma is particularly acute. Because intentions are never clear and always subject to change, one nation's reaction to another's policy can have unintended and destabilizing consequences for other bilateral relationships. Northeast Asia is full of possible unintended conflicts. Should North Korea's domestic instability and fear of South Korea drive it to acquire nuclear weapons, Japan may feel compelled to do the same. This would encourage China to hasten its own defense modernization, further undermining Japanese security and leading to a Sino-Japanese arms race. U.S. military assistance to Taiwan could lead China to purchase additional weaponry from Russia, giving rise to Japanese fears of Sino-Soviet strategic cooperation. Or enhanced U.S.-Taiwan cooperation could lead to renewed tension in the Taiwan Strait and to Japanese apprehension over Chinese militancy. In both cases, Japan might react by increasing its defense spending, leading to an arms race with China, or by strengthening its defense cooperation with the United States, promoting regional polarization into antagonistic blocs.

Any uncertainty in U.S. policy would be highly destabilizing. Chinese leaders perceive the U.S. naval presence in the western Pacific, the U.S.-Japan alliance, and U.S. troops in South Korea as positive factors in the Northeast Asian balance of power. They understand that the American presence reassures Japanese leaders that they do not have to take unilateral military measures to achieve security. Current U.S. policy contributes to Chinese and Japanese security simultaneously. If America's credibility as an Asian power were to diminish, Japan would be likely to expand its military power in order to protect its interests throughout Asia. This would prompt China to augment its military power, contributing to a Sino-Japanese arms race.

This scenario could be triggered by American hesitation during a crisis on the Korean peninsula or in the Taiwan Strait. U.S. military withdrawal following the unification of Korea by South Korea could create the perception that the United States was making a strategic retrenchment in Northeast Asia. A crisis in U.S.-Japanese relations, arising from politicized economic conflicts or popular resentment in either country at the costs of cooperation, could be the catalyst leading to American military withdrawal from Japan. A significant decline in the U.S. defense budget or in its naval presence in the western Pacific would call into question America's commitment to the regional balance of power. All of these developments would cast doubt on the future of the U.S.-Japan alliance and thus affect foreign policies throughout Asia.

A common element in these scenarios is the prospect of escalated conflict between China and Japan. Given the size of these two powers, their potential capabilities, their proximity to each other, and their historical animosity, this would be a costly conflict that could rival the Cold War. Sino-Japanese competition would polarize all of Asia, affecting great-power alignments, developments on the Korean peninsula, and the stability of Indochina and the rest of Southeast Asia.

6

NEIGHBORS
TO THE SOUTH

I N STRATEGY AS in real estate, location is the primary determinant of
value. The countries located to the south and west of China are important for China's security either because they abut its borders and
claimed territorial seas or because they are involved in regional politics
with countries that border China or can challenge its vital interests. On
land China is touched by Vietnam and Laos, which, with Cambodia,
make up the countries of Indochina, and by Burma, India, Pakistan, and
Afghanistan, as well as by the Himalayan states of Bhutan and Nepal.
Thailand does not border China, but is located in its political shadow on
mainland Southeast Asia. China's strategic and territorial interests in the
South China Sea meet those of the maritime states of Southeast Asia—
Malaysia, Singapore, Indonesia, Brunei, and the Philippines.

Southeast and South Asia are separate regions, each characterized
by its own strategic dynamics. Southeast Asia itself is divided into two
distinct strategic regions—Indochina and the ASEAN states.[1] When another great power dominates either Southeast Asia or South Asia, its presence threatens China. And when the same power simultaneously has a
strong presence in Northeast Asia, China is for practical purposes strate-

gically encircled. It is a measure of China's vulnerability that it faced just this situation three times in this century—during the Pacific war against Japan, in the 1950s and 1960s when America and its allies dominated Northeast and Southeast Asia, and in the 1970s and 1980s when the Soviet Union established a strong presence in Northeast Asia, Indochina, and South Asia. China has broken all three encirclements. Its current policies in these regions aim to keep a similar situation from arising again.

INDOCHINA AND CHINESE SECURITY

Southeast Asia is a cosmopolitan trading region and a meeting place of cultures, religions, languages, and ethnic groups. The region has a distinctive colonial history, a complex political map, and a record of internecine conflicts. The colonial powers of the past—Britain, Holland, France, and Spain—were drawn there by the lure of territory and trade. The powers of today—the United States, Russia, Japan, and China—are likewise subject to the pull of this rich and strategically located part of the world, although they seek not colonies but economic, political, and cultural influence.

Indochina has been the focus of the most intense great-power conflict in Southeast Asia. No outside power has a larger stake there than does China. Geography forces China to see the region much as America sees Latin America or Russia sees Eastern Europe. Although Chinese leaders have no wish to take over Indochina and its problems, Beijing cannot feel secure when the local governments are more friendly to its adversaries than to it. China has no formal equivalent of the Monroe Doctrine, by which Washington objected to any other power's military intervention in the Western hemisphere, but its policy has in effect sought to exclude other powers from Indochina. Other powers have, however, intervened there to contain Chinese influence. China's struggle to remove them has been long—and successful only recently.

When the Chinese Communists came to power in 1949, France had reclaimed its Indochina colonies from their Japanese occupiers. The French military was at war in Indochina and, with American assistance, suppressed Ho Chi Minh's Vietnamese Communist movement. This movement had been an ideological ally of the Chinese Communist Party since the 1925 founding of the Vietnamese Communist Youth League. The Indochinese Communist Party received military assistance and other aid from the Chinese Communists as soon as PLA forces reached southern China at the conclusion of the civil war in late 1949.[2] China supported the Vietnamese Communists partly to aid the spread of communism and the unification of Vietnam. But its central purpose was to eradicate the Western presence from its strategic backyard. Chinese priorities were clear when the two sets of goals came into conflict at the 1954 Geneva conference, called to make peace after the Vietnamese Communists defeated French forces in the Battle of Dienbienphu. Representing China, Premier Zhou Enlai joined the Russians in pressing the Vietnamese Communists to accept the partition of the country into northern and southern states.[3] North Vietnam later accused China of having sold it out at Geneva. For the rest of the decade China advised Hanoi to focus on domestic priorities rather than on unification, even as Saigon proceeded to decimate the Communists in South Vietnam.

China's strategic assessment of Indochina evolved with the changing policies of the great powers. Through 1962 China was content with the status quo. Communist parties were not in charge in every country, but the region was free from foreign military influence. But in that year the Kennedy administration prepared to send American troops to Laos to help right-wing military leaders prevent a victory by Communist forces. At the height of the crisis, Beijing warned that it would fight U.S. troops in Laos rather than allow an American occupation. The crisis abated when the Lao Communists halted their offensive and the United States compelled the right-wing leadership to participate in a coalition government that included Communists.

The civil war in Vietnam was less manageable. As the American military presence in South Vietnam increased in 1964–65 and it appeared that U.S. troops might approach the Chinese border, Beijing supplied North Vietnam with military and economic assistance. By 1969 over 320,000 Chinese troops had participated in the war as engineers and antiaircraft artillery forces.[4] In 1970, after pro-U.S. leaders in Cambodia overthrew the neutral government of Prince Sihanouk and the United States extended its military activities into Cambodia, Beijing supported Vietnamese-Cambodian cooperation against the United States. Despite the worsening Sino-Soviet conflict and the first tentative steps toward a U.S.-China rapprochement, Chinese leaders would not tolerate any U.S. military presence in Indochina.

But Beijing's strategic objectives remained distinct from Hanoi's. In a 1965 polemic called "Long Live the Victory of People's War," the Chinese minister of defense, Lin Biao, advised the North Vietnamese to fight a protracted war relying on their own resources.[5] This strategy would have limited Hanoi's need for advanced weaponry and minimized its dependence on Soviet assistance. It would have also reduced the risk of U.S.-China hostilities over Vietnam. These goals were more important to China than Vietnamese unification. Although Hanoi ignored China's advice, Beijing was compelled to continue supporting North Vietnam so as not to give Moscow a free hand in Indochina. China's primary contribution to Hanoi's war effort was its deterrence of American escalation of the war. But after Henry Kissinger's secret visit to China in 1971, America was confident that Chinese leaders would not undermine U.S.-China cooperation to defend North Vietnamese interests. Washington was then free to escalate the air war over North Vietnam. Chinese leaders even expressed sympathy for U.S. efforts to avoid a humiliating defeat in Vietnam. After unification Hanoi charged that the U.S.-China rapprochement was another Chinese sellout of Vietnamese interests.

In 1972, despite Chinese perfidy, North Vietnamese soldiers, relying on Soviet military assistance, forced America to withdraw from South Vietnam, and in 1975 they overran the South. After unifying Vietnam, Hanoi continued to challenge Chinese interests. Between 1975 and 1978 it accepted significant Soviet aid for its first postwar five-year economic plan and Soviet security support against China.[6] In mid-1978 it expelled over 200,000 ethnic Chinese, eliminating a suspected security risk, and in November it signed a security treaty with Moscow. These measures were part of Hanoi's strategy for contending with Chinese power while preparing to overthrow the belligerent, pro-Chinese regime in neighboring Cambodia.

China tried at first to mediate the Vietnam-Cambodia conflict and moderate Cambodia's domestic and foreign policies so as not to alarm Vietnam and encourage Soviet-Vietnamese cooperation. But Pol Pot was uncontrollable, presiding over a ruthless regime that took an estimated one million Cambodian lives. Ultimately, China decided to protect Pol Pot as a strategic asset, rather than reconcile itself to Soviet and Vietnamese domination of Indochina. In mid-1978 China expressed its resistance to Vietnam's alignment with the Soviet Union, its expulsion of the ethnic Chinese, and its preparations for war against Cambodia by terminating its economic-aid program for Vietnam and by openly aligning itself with the Khmer Rouge. Beijing warned Hanoi that, if it invaded Cambodia, it would face Chinese retaliation. With Soviet backing, Hanoi in December 1978 retaliated against Pol Pot's virulent anti-Vietnamese paranoia and aggressive military activities along the Vietnamese-Cambodian border by invading Cambodia and setting up a pro-Vietnamese government there. In expectation of the invasion China had made the compromises necessary for normalized relations with the United States (Chapter 4). In early 1979 it punished Hanoi with a three-week invasion intended to "teach Vietnam a lesson," namely, that China follows through on its warnings and is prepared to use force to protect its interests.

In this short war the PLA disappointed its leaders and surprised the rest of the world with a weak performance against a smaller neighbor. Nonetheless, the invasion achieved important results. By making credible a threat of a second Chinese invasion, Beijing emboldened Thailand and the other ASEAN countries to oppose the Vietnamese occupation of Cambodia rather than accommodate the expansion of Soviet and Vietnamese power. ASEAN subsequently made a major contribution to organizing the global diplomatic and economic isolation of Vietnam. The Chinese invasion also compelled Hanoi to deploy 300,000 troops on its northern border through the 1980s, preventing it from concentrating its resources on defeating the Khmer Rouge. At the same time Vietnam maintained up to 200,000 troops in Cambodia to protect its client government. Just as Beijing had relied on Vietnamese troops from 1949 to 1975 to eliminate the Western presence from Indochina, so Beijing now used Cambodian troops to oppose Soviet-Vietnamese cooperation in Indochina. Thailand, facing Hanoi's troops directly across its border with Cambodia, allowed China to ship supplies to the Khmer Rouge across its territory. Beijing and Bangkok even had tacit American support for their assistance to Pol Pot. Washington, just as eager as Beijing to roll back Soviet influence in Southeast Asia, was content to allow its regional security partners to carry the strategic and economic burden.

Still, the Vietnamese occupation of Cambodia marked a major setback for Chinese security. After the invasion Hanoi granted the Soviet Union access to military bases in northern and southern Vietnam. The Soviet Union based twenty to twenty-five warships as well as medium-range Badger bombers at former U.S. bases at Cam Ranh Bay and Danang. This vastly improved its ability to threaten Chinese territory, to patrol China's southern coastal waters, and to gain access to the South

China Sea, the Strait of Malacca, and other strategic straits necessary for its navy to move from bases in the Soviet Far East to the Indian Ocean and beyond.[7] Moreover, in the late 1970s Vietnam consolidated its hold over Laos, so Moscow's influence spread to all of Indochina. China's strategic backyard had become a Soviet sphere of influence.

Beijing used the war in Cambodia to bleed Vietnam and its Soviet patron economically, militarily, and diplomatically. Throughout the 1980s China cited Soviet support for the Vietnamese occupation of Cambodia as one of the "three obstacles" to improved relations with Moscow. China's deployments along the Sino-Vietnamese border and its military assistance to the Khmer Rouge led to the decay of the Vietnamese economy and placed a burden on the declining Soviet economy.

This strategy succeeded. In 1988 Moscow failed to support Vietnam in its naval clashes with China over the disputed Spratly Islands; in 1989 it agreed to discuss directly with Beijing a resolution of the Cambodian war, thus going behind Vietnam's back; and in 1990 it sharply reduced its aid to Vietnam. In 1990, lacking Soviet support and with its economy in shambles, Vietnam withdrew all its troops from Cambodia and agreed that the Vietnamese-installed government of Cambodia be replaced by a government elected under United Nations auspices. In 1991 the warring Cambodian factions signed in Paris the Comprehensive Political Settlement of the Cambodian Conflict, opening the way to Sino-Vietnamese détente. At a November 1991 summit of Chinese and Vietnamese premiers and party secretaries in Beijing, the two countries declared their relations normalized.[8]

Without directly engaging any of the great powers, China had at last seen its goals in Indochina realized. One by one the French, the Americans, and finally the Russians were ousted, leaving China the most influential outside force in a weakened, divided Indochina. The historic Vietnamese struggle for independence from China moved into a new phase. Trying to compensate for the loss of Soviet support to balance Chinese power, Hanoi has endeavored to diversify its foreign policy relationships. In January 1995 Hanoi resolved long-standing issues with Washington over the Americans missing in action and established normal diplomatic relations. Later that year Vietnam joined ASEAN, seeking security through membership in a regional institution. It has also sought to develop economic relations with all the major economic powers in Asia.

Sino-Vietnamese disputes are now limited to territorial conflicts involving the demarcation of the Tonkin Gulf and sovereignty over the small Paracel and Spratly Islands in the South China Sea. The island conflict has the most potential for escalation. Needing Chinese assistance to achieve unification, Hanoi recognized China's sovereignty over all of the islands. But after the American withdrawal from Vietnam, Hanoi announced that the Paracels and the Spratlys belonged to Vietnam. In 1974 PRC naval forces seized all of the Paracel Islands occupied by Saigon's forces. The Vietnamese and Chinese navies clashed in the region in 1988 when Chinese forces ousted Vietnamese troops from some of the Spratlys. In 1992 China reached an agreement with the U.S. Crestone Energy Corporation to drill for oil in disputed waters. Vietnam reached a similar agreement with Mobil.

But the dominant trend in Sino-Vietnamese relations is grudging Vietnamese accommodation to Chinese power. Now that China has restored its political influence in Cambodia and Laos, and that Hanoi has lost its great-power support, Vietnam's security depends on Chinese forbearance. China can also be economically helpful. Vietnam's recovering economy requires inexpensive Chinese agricultural and light-manufacturing goods to raise living standards. Chinese traders sell fruit and vegetables and clothing to Vietnamese villagers throughout northern Vietnam. Trade in 1995 doubled over the previous year, reaching approximately $1 billion. With the opening of the Sino-Vietnamese rail link in February 1996, trade and other such contacts should continue to grow.

Cambodia and Laos are now free to develop foreign policies independent of Vietnamese dictates. Both have turned to Beijing to balance Hanoi's power. After Sino-Vietnamese normalization, China normalized relations with Laos and signed a border agreement. Border trade between southern China and Laos has been booming, and China has given Laos economic assistance. Beijing established diplomatic relations with the Cambodian coalition regime even though former Vietnamese allies are influential in it. Chinese and Cambodian leaders meet frequently, and economic relations are developing. Beijing has turned its back on the remnant forces of the Khmer Rouge, its former ally.

Beijing seeks neither control over Indochina nor bases there for its military forces. Its interests are served when Indochina is divided and free of outside military influence. As long as Vietnam does not lend its territory to a great power, its animosity is only an annoyance.

BEYOND INDOCHINA:
THE SEARCH FOR INFLUENCE

Compared with China's stake in Indochina and its influence over the region, its relationships with the other states of Southeast Asia are less intense. One reason for this is that, with the exception of Burma, none of the non-Indochinese states border China. This geographic fact and China's limited power projection capacity constrain its ability to exercise influence in the region. But China cannot disregard regional trends. Rather, it must use what limited resources it has to promote its interests.

After the end of the Korean War, the Eisenhower administration constructed a Southeast Asian alliance system aimed at containing Chinese influence (Chapter 4). The Southeast Asia Treaty Organization (SEATO) included formal U.S. treaty relations with the Philippines and Thailand, as well as with Pakistan in South Asia. The United States constructed military bases in these countries. To counter U.S. encirclement and charges that China was an expansionist state bent on spreading revolution, Beijing adopted a moderate diplomacy stressing common interests between China and "national bourgeois governments." On the basis of a 1954 agreement between Chinese and Indian leaders, Beijing affirmed that its foreign policy rested on the Five Principles of Peaceful Coexistence. This trend culminated at the 1955 Afro-Asian conference of twenty-nine countries at Bandung, Indonesia, where Premier Zhou Enlai delivered a widely praised speech offering to improve relations even with the U.S. allies Thailand and the Philippines and to open negotiations with the United States over the Taiwan issue.

The Bandung phase of Chinese diplomacy persuaded many Third World leaders that China's Communist leadership was neither aggressive nor subversive. Nonetheless, Beijing failed to weaken the U.S. alliance system. The United States was simply too powerful for its smaller allies to adopt independent policies toward China. Moreover, Washington consolidated its encirclement by strengthening military ties with Taiwan. Beginning in 1958 China adopted a more aggressive posture toward Third World countries aligned with the United States, stressing ties with revolutionary movements. With the escalation of the Sino-Soviet dispute and the ideological fervor of the Cultural Revolution in the mid-1960s, Chinese diplomacy placed Beijing at the forefront of Third World revolutionaries in their struggle against superpower imperialism.

The escalation of American involvement in the Vietnam War and the deterioration of Sino-Soviet relations pushed Beijing to develop an "anti-imperialist" strategic partnership with Indonesia.[9] In the early 1960s it cultivated relations with Indonesia's anti-Western president, Sukarno, and with the Indonesian Communist Party. In 1964, as U.S. troops poured into South Vietnam, Beijing promoted the "Beijing-Hanoi-Jakarta axis." But this strategy collapsed in 1965 when the Indonesian Communist Party tried to oust the military from the government. The military leadership survived the attempt, wrested control of the government from Sukarno, and proceeded to massacre the rank and file of the Communist Party while anti-Chinese rioting spread throughout society. Beijing also tried to use support for revolution to pressure U.S. allies in Southeast Asia to distance themselves from American policy. Bangkok received special attention. As Thai support for American involvement in the war grew, Beijing increased its diplomatic support for the Thai Communist Party, threatening to foment civil war in Thailand.[10]

Beyond its focus on Bangkok and Jakarta, Beijing gave little attention to the other non-Indochinese countries of Southeast Asia. Lacking economic and military influence over these states, it used ties with Communist parties as an instrument of diplomacy.[11] Chinese diplomacy criticized the Philippines for housing American naval and air bases and gave symbolic support to insurgencies there, but placed a low priority on influencing Manila. It adopted a similar posture toward Malaysia, going so far as basically to ignore anti-Chinese riots there in 1969. Outside of Indochina, China had friendly relations only with Burma, whose geographic location on Chinese borders and self-imposed strategic isolation compelled it to accommodate Chinese interests. It was one of the few countries that consistently supported Chinese foreign policy positions throughout the Cold War.

China's support for revolution and its ties to the illegal Communist parties in Southeast Asia created an obstacle to its cooperation with the ASEAN states. Despite its revolutionary posture, after it ended financial and arms support to the Communist White Flag insurgency in Burma in 1955, China gave these Communist parties only rhetorical support and access to radio broadcast facilities on Chinese territory. Yet even such limited assistance alarmed the newly independent Southeast Asian governments, which were preoccupied with establishing political stability. In the 1970s, when Beijing tried to enlist the aid of these countries against Soviet hegemonism, Chinese leaders insisted that they did not "export revolution." But only in the 1980s, after Beijing shut down the radio operations and after economic modernization in these countries sapped the revolutionary ardor of Communist movements, did the issue become irrelevant to China's role in the region.

A second obstacle to cooperation was China's policies toward the overseas Chinese.[12] The ethnically Chinese residents of Southeast Asia have traditionally exercised disproportionate influence in these countries' commercial sectors, including the rice trade, banking, and finance. In recent years they have been at the forefront of the modern manufacturing sector and dominate many export industries. Many host governments viewed their ethnic Chinese citizens as potential "fifth columns," which might use their economic influence in the interests of Chinese foreign policy. They adopted laws prohibiting Chinese from entering sensitive professions. Regional mistrust also stemmed from a history of political instability involving the ethnic Chinese. Local Chinese were influential in both the Malay and the Indonesian Communist parties. Anti-Chinese riots in Indonesia in 1959 and 1965–66 led China to send ships with the demand that persecuted Chinese be allowed to return to the motherland.

To alleviate regional suspicions China in 1954 declared that Chinese no longer had the option of dual citizenship and encouraged local Chinese to adopt the citizenship of the host country. In 1955 it signed with Indonesia an agreement formalizing this policy. China has also tried to prevent local ethnic conflicts from disrupting cooperative relations. It avoided conflict over race riots in Indonesia (1959) and Malaysia (1969) and ignored the violent anti-Chinese polices of Cambodia's Khmer Rouge government from 1975 to 1978. On the other hand, China adopted forceful measures against anti-ethnic Chinese policies when the host government also adopted security policies antithetical to Chinese interests, as in Indonesia in 1965–66 and Vietnam in 1978.

Since Chinese migration to Southeast Asia virtually ended in 1940–41, when Japanese forces occupied the Chinese coast, nearly all Chinese living in Southeast Asia today were born in the host countries. They have gradually integrated themselves into developing local economies, and rising standards of living throughout these societies have eased resentment on the part of indigenous populations. The importance of the overseas Chinese issue in PRC diplomacy has diminished.

As the obstacles to cooperative relations between China and the

ASEAN countries receded, common interests emerged. Toward the end of the Vietnam War many Southeast Asian countries followed the U.S. lead in aligning themselves with Beijing, which became an important counterweight to Soviet power and Vietnamese aspirations. In 1974 Malaysia established diplomatic relations with China; Thailand and the Philippines quickly followed. As Soviet-Vietnamese cooperation flowered in the late 1970s and 1980s and after Vietnamese forces invaded Cambodia in December 1978, Beijing collaborated with the ASEAN countries to resist Soviet and Vietnamese influence. Common security interests provided China the opportunity to overcome a legacy of mistrust and establish a pattern of cooperation with ASEAN states that lasted until Vietnam withdrew from Cambodia. In 1990 Indonesia, which had broken diplomatic relations with China in 1965, finally restored them. The normalization of Sino-Indonesian relations freed Singapore, traditionally deferential to Jakarta on China policy, to recognize the PRC.

With the end of the Cold War, China's strategic importance to the non-Indochina states again diminished. The collapse of Soviet power and the Vietnamese defeat in Cambodia removed the necessity for the ASEAN countries to cooperate with China. China now wields considerably less influence in the region than does America or Japan. It is unable to project military power into the southern reaches of the South China Sea. With no aircraft carriers, China's navy is vulnerable to aerial attack when it ventures far from shore. A single carrier, which China is unlikely to acquire before 2010, will be insufficient for it to maintain a continued military presence in distant waters (Chapter 8). China is thus far weaker in the coastal waters of the ASEAN countries than the United States, which deploys the formidable Seventh Fleet in the western Pacific and has access to port facilities throughout the region, including Indonesia, Malaysia, Thailand, and Singapore. Indeed, the PLA Navy is vulnerable to attack from the land-based air forces of Indonesia, Singapore, and Thailand, which possess U.S. F-16s, and of Malaysia, which has purchased advanced aircraft from Russia, Great Britain, and the United States. Only the Philippines and tiny Brunei are vulnerable to Chinese power.

China also lacks economic influence in the region. It is a minor trading partner of the ASEAN states because they have similar export structures, competing with one another to sell light-industrial manufactures.[13] In 1994 China was Indonesia's sixth-largest export market, Thailand's tenth-largest, Malaysia's eleventh-largest, and Singapore's twelfth-largest.

The Chinese market plays an insignificant role in these countries' economic growth. Nor, with the exception of Singapore, have the ASEAN countries invested heavily in China. Instead, they are economically dependent on the United States and Japan, which are the major export markets for the region and the major investors in the local economies.

Compounding China's weakness in the region is the positive attitude of local leaders toward the American presence. Even Vietnam prefers to see the United States remain a major actor rather than allow either China or Japan to assume regional leadership. The local powers also believe that the U.S. presence minimizes friction among each other. A regional arms buildup among the ASEAN countries has already developed, as these countries can now afford to spend more on defense and to focus their security concerns on external threats rather than internal instability. Most local leaders believe that without the U.S. presence, this relatively modest rise could evolve into an arms race driven by mutual insecurity. Chinese leaders can thus no longer do what they did in their Cold War diplomacy against the Soviet Union—take advantage of regional strategic cleavages or great-power threats to develop strategic partnerships.

Because of China's limited importance to the maritime states of Southeast Asia, the primary determinant of their relations with China is relations among themselves. Indonesia lies at the core of regional politics in both location and size. Its population is the fourth largest in the world, at nearly 200 million. Jakarta aspires to regional leadership and expects deference on regional issues from its smaller neighbors. It views China as an obstacle to its leadership and, with the exception of the Philippines, is the loudest critic of the China threat, even though it is also the most powerful of the ASEAN countries and the one farthest from the Chinese mainland. It was the ASEAN country most reluctant to normalize diplomatic relations with China. Indonesian leaders were also willing to cooperate with Vietnam despite its occupation of Cambodia, reflecting common Indonesian-Vietnamese interests in restraining Chinese influence.

Malaysia tends to treat Beijing cautiously. Because its population includes a Chinese minority of about 40 percent, which is excluded from political power by the ethnically Malay dominant political party, it believes it has no choice but to avoid confrontation with Beijing over the ethnic Chinese issue. Malaysia is also attracted to the opportunities presented by the Chinese economy. In the mid-1980s a leaked government policy paper described Malaysia's China policy as involving "vigilance [combined] with commercial opportunism."[14] Despite the territorial dispute over the Spratly Islands, China and Malaysia have become cooperative, with expanding trade and friendly political ties. The two sides also cooperate against U.S. efforts to open rapidly the markets of Asia's developing countries.

Singapore, as an ethnically Chinese state with a stable government, has none of the ethnic or political apprehensions of its larger neighbors. On the other hand, this small island state sandwiched between Malaysia and Indonesia is perhaps the local power most interested in encouraging outside powers to participate in the regional balance. The lack of diplomatic relations with China in the 1970s and 1980s notwithstanding, Singapore was thus one of the first ASEAN states to develop cooperative economic and political ties with Beijing after the U.S. withdrawal from Vietnam in 1975. In the 1990s it has been the least vocal about the "China threat," instead emphasizing that regional stability requires accommodation of Chinese interests. For its part, China respects Singapore's combination of authoritarian government and economic development and frequently solicits the advice of its leaders.

China's relations with the Philippines are the most tenuous in the region. During the Cold War there was active summitry as China and the Marcos leadership had similar views of the Soviet Union and the Vietnamese occupation of Cambodia. Since the end of the Cold War, though, common interests have receded, and the conflict over the Spratly Islands has dominated the bilateral agenda. In response to the 1995 Mischief Reef incident (described below), Manila raised the alarm over the "China threat," trying to call international attention to the Chinese challenge to a small Southeast Asian country. But because the Philippine state lacks support from the United States, Japan, and its neighbors for a confrontational stance, it also tried to defuse tensions with China by opening a dialogue and considering joint economic activities in disputed waters.

China's relationship with Brunei is the least developed of all its regional ties. A tiny nation on the island of Borneo, Brunei does not possess sufficient economic or strategic importance to warrant sustained Chinese attention. The only point of direct contact between the two nations is their dispute over the Spratly Islands. But their negotiations on this issue tend to take place in multilateral settings, which minimize the conflict's importance to the bilateral relationship.

In contrast to its relations with distant states, Beijing's interactions with nearby Thailand and Myanmar (formerly Burma) are intense. China has developed greater influence in Thailand than in any other ASEAN country. When the United States withdrew from Indochina, Thailand was quick to establish diplomatic relations with China. Shortly thereafter, Beijing became a strategic asset to Bangkok when Vietnamese troops invaded Cambodia and reached the Thai border in 1979. Thailand allowed Chinese equipment to pass through its territory to the Cambodian resistance. Relations continued to flourish after the 1991 Cambodian peace agreement. China and Thailand have maintained a close military relationship. Thailand buys Chinese tanks, armored personnel carriers, antiaircraft guns, and frigates, and the two countries participate in frequent summitry and exchanges between military leaders. Living under the shadow of the Chinese army, Bangkok is determined to avoid unnecessary tensions.

China's relations with Myanmar, not a member of ASEAN, are also close. Throughout the Cold War, Myanmar pursued a neutral foreign policy with a pro-China tilt. Unimportant to the other great powers and sharing a long border with China, Rangoon has had little choice but to avoid conflict with China. This situation continued after the ascension to power of the State Law and Order Restoration Council (SLORC) in 1988. China has been the dominant supplier of weaponry to Myanmar, intent on maintaining stability on its southern border by helping the SLORC defeat domestic insurgencies. Economic relations have expanded with the SLORC leadership's attempt to adopt the Chinese model of carrying out economic reform without political reform. A major component of this strategy has been cooperation with Chinese merchants in bordering provinces. During the 1990s trade between Myanmar and southwest China boomed.

With the exception of Thailand and Myanmar, the states of non-Indochina Southeast Asia have not fallen under the influence of Chinese diplomacy. China's status as a second-rank great power in the region could lead to considerable instability, especially if it seeks a status in Southeast Asia equal to that of Japan or the United States. On the other hand, China has little reason to disrupt regional stability for secondary interests. The countries least susceptible to Chinese influence—Malaysia, Singapore, Indonesia, Brunei, and the Philippines—are also the Asian countries farthest from the Chinese mainland and of least strategic importance to its regional security.

Recognizing that China is sympathetic to regional stability, regional

CHINESE CLAIMS IN
THE SOUTH CHINA SEA,
1995

EAST

CHINA

SEA

Shanghai

Yangtze R.

C H I N A

Senkaku

Ryukyu

Xun R.

Xi R. Guangzhou

Macao Hong Kong

TAIWAN

Gulf of Tonkin

Hainan

V I E T N A M

L A O S

S O U T H

*Xisha
(Paracel)
Islands*

Luzon

C H I N A

CAMBODIA

S E A

PHILIPPINES

Cebu

*Nansha
(Spratly)
Islands*

Palawan

Minda

BRUNEI

M A L A Y S I A

*Natuna
Islands*

M A L A Y S I A

CELEBES

I N D O N E S I A

leaders seek to consolidate cooperative diplomacy by institutionalizing Chinese participation in regional dialogues. A central focus of this effort has been the establishment of the ASEAN Regional Forum (ARF), which aims to develop a permanent regionwide security dialogue to avoid any unintended escalation of conflicts. Beijing, however, fears that Washington or Tokyo could manipulate ARF so as to isolate China. When it first joined the ARF, as well as the forum on Asia Pacific Economic Cooperation (APEC), China used its influence to prevent these institutions from becoming too active. In recent years, however, Chinese leaders have grown more skilled at multilateral diplomacy, aware that the PRC can use membership in regional institutions to promote its political and economic interests. This trend bodes well for the development of China's participation in consensual approaches to resolving regional conflicts.

The largest obstacle to closer relations between China and maritime Southeast Asia remains a variety of territorial conflicts in the South China Sea. China, Taiwan, and Vietnam claim sovereignty over the Paracel Islands, a small chain in the northern part of that sea. The more troublesome conflict concerns the Spratly Islands, located in its southern reaches. In addition to China, the claimants to the Spratlys are Taiwan, Vietnam, Malaysia, the Philippines, and Brunei. It is uncertain whether China also claims economic zone in the vicinity of the Natuna Islands, which are claimed by Indonesia. Chinese leaders have yet to clear up this ambiguity.

During the Qing dynasty, long before the other claimant states were founded, China declared the Paracel and Spratly Islands part of its sovereign territory. The map on page 114 reflects PRC claims through 1995. Other countries complained that this line was imprecise and suggested that China claimed the entire sea within the line as territorial waters, including control over sea-lanes, fishing grounds, and underwater resources. In response, and to comply with the provisions of the law of the sea, China undertook a detailed survey of the islands and in 1996 issued precise figures delimiting its claim to each of the Paracel Islands and the twelve-mile territorial zone surrounding each. This move did not quiet criticism. The specificity of China's claim aroused new objections because it became evident that China did, in fact, claim all of the Paracels. The surveys did not clarify its claims in the Spratlys.

Meanwhile, the other states had lodged their claims in the 1970s, citing other principles. Because occupation is the strongest basis for legitimating a claim, land grabbing has escalated as the claimants have tried to increase the number of islands on which they have national markers. All the claimants have occupied some of the disputed islands. Although China expelled Vietnamese troops from their posts in the Paracel Islands in 1974, Vietnam still occupies the greatest number of Spratly islands, Taiwan occupies one of the largest islands in the chain, and Malaysia has been developing tourist accommodations and an airstrip on one island. China, Taiwan, and Vietnam claim the entire Spratly archipelago, which extends their territorial boundaries to the coastal waters of Malaysia, Brunei, and the Philippines.[15]

The legal issues surrounding the islands are complex and ambiguous. But ultimately the Spratly Islands are not a legal issue but a security issue. Because of China's size and strategic potential, its claim to the entire Spratly archipelago challenges the security of Vietnam, Malaysia, Brunei, and the Philippines. In 1988 it fought a naval battle with Vietnam for control of some of the islands. In 1995, after the Philippines protested Chinese construction of a reconnaissance station on Mischief Reef, Beijing sent naval vessels into the vicinity of the reef. As long as Beijing claims the entire archipelago and shows a willingness to use force to defend its claim, the other claimants will regard China as a potential security threat and China will face difficulty in developing stable relations with these countries.

Natural resources are probably not the major factor in China's decision to claim the Spratly archipelago. Surveys indicate that the oil fields in the outlying areas are not especially large and that the geological structure of the deposits will make for expensive drilling. These technical and economic obstacles combine with the distance of the region from China to render exploitation difficult and expensive. Moreover, with the exception of extensive natural gas exploration near the Natuna Islands, international oil companies have shown minimal interest in developing the southern area of the South China Sea. On the other hand, China is actively drilling in more-promising oil fields in Xinjiang province and is constructing pipelines to connect these fields to the Chinese interior. That the South China Sea is a prosperous fishing area also seems to be an inadequate explanation for China's uncompromising position on an issue of such strategic importance to neighboring countries.

A second reason sometimes suggested for Beijing's interest in the Spratly Islands is that the sea-lanes running through the archipelago are vital to the trade that passes between Europe and the Middle East and East Asia. But China has not claimed that the South China Sea is an internal sea, and it has never protested the passage of other countries' naval vessels through the region. It thus lacks a legal basis for interfering in commercial shipping and naval activities there. The islands are too small to support logistical facilities, such as landing fields for advanced aircraft or bases for naval vessels, and many of the islands are underwater much of the year. The irony of the Spratlys is that possession of them does not augment power projection, but that power projection capability is needed to defend occupation of the islands. For the foreseeable future China will not have such capabilities.

The interest that best explains Beijing's unyielding stand on the South China Sea is one that motivates its policies in several regions: its interest in territorial integrity and its concern over the political ramifications of any compromise of sovereignty. The territory now defined as China is the product of a long history, first of imperial expansion and later of clashes with other countries to define borders (Chapter 2). The claim to the Spratlys is part of this history. Chinese governments have claimed them without interruption since the Qing dynasty. Contemporary Chinese leaders used maps in grade school during the Republican era that included the Spratlys as Chinese territory. Retreat in the face of other countries' claims would threaten China's credibility on other territorial issues.

Any concession on such an issue would require a leadership in Beijing strong enough to defend it against political adversaries. Under Chairman Mao, China made territorial concessions to Afghanistan, Pakistan, Nepal, and Burma, offered a compromise solution to the Sino-Indian border dispute, acknowledged that Mongolia was an independent country, and yielded some points to reach a border agreement with Mongolia. In the absence of a leader with Mao's authority, it will be difficult for Beijing, as well as for the other governments with similarly weak leaderships, to compromise their positions in the Spratly dispute anytime soon.

China has proposed that the claimants shelve the dispute and conduct joint economic activities in the disputed regions. But the other countries fear that joint exploration would legitimate China's claim and encourage it to strengthen its presence in the area. China has also proposed bilateral discussion of territorial disputes with each of the other claimants. These have hesitated to negotiate individually with China and have proposed multilateral negotiations involving all sides. China suspects that such a framework would allow the smaller countries to promote a common position against it. As long as the issue remains unsettled, local governments will remain anxious about Chinese strategic intentions and

China will confront an impediment to its efforts to consolidate cooperation in Southeast Asia.

CHINA AND SOUTH ASIA

The hinge of China's policy in South Asia for over thirty years has been its security relationship with Pakistan. This alignment joins two countries that for different but parallel reasons oppose India's aspiration to regional dominance. For Pakistan the stake is national survival; for China it is the need to check a major power that abuts Chinese territory and has the ability to challenge Chinese borders and destabilize Chinese rule in Tibet. The goal of Chinese policy since the collapse of the ephemeral Sino-Indian friendship of the 1950s has been to hem in Indian power. The end of the Cold War has not changed it fundamentally.

At the time of their founding in 1948 and 1949, respectively, the new Indian and Chinese governments celebrated a rhetoric of postcolonial brotherhood. But an undemarcated border of some 2,500 miles in mountainous terrain proved a barrier to amity. India grounded its claim on historical lines drawn between the British colonial authorities in India and British-dominated Tibetan leaders. China rejected these agreements as an illegal legacy of imperialism, pointing out that Tibet was not a sovereign state. In 1956–57, without consulting India, China constructed a strategic highway linking Xinjiang and Tibet across the Aksai Chin plateau in Ladakh, an area India claimed. China soon stated that it had a right to about 40,000 square miles of territory that India considered its own. Border clashes between the two countries broke out in the mid-1950s.

In 1959 the conflict took on the triangular implications that have shaped it since. The Soviet Union had invested considerable resources in friendship with both Beijing and New Delhi. Following a border clash in October 1959, China proposed a summit with India to resolve the conflict. Chinese leaders were ready to trade PRC acceptance of the historical McMahon line in the eastern sector for Indian acquiescence to Chinese control over the strategically vital Aksai Chin. But Prime Minister Jawaharlal Nehru demanded that the Chinese withdraw from Aksai Chin as a precondition for negotiations. Chinese suspicion increased when the Kremlin opted in 1959 for an evenhanded policy that made little distinction between China, the Soviet Union's socialist "comrade-in-arms" and formal treaty ally, and "bourgeois nationalist" India and then, beginning in 1961, increased its diplomatic and military support to India as the Sino-Soviet split came out into the open.[16]

Spurred by patriotic fervor among his people, and convinced that the Chinese would not go to war over barren territory, Nehru adopted an assertive policy of forward patrolling along the eastern sector of the border. After repeated Chinese warnings that Indian troops must return to their previous positions, on October 20, 1962, the PLA launched a vigorous attack down the Himalayan ridge lines against an Indian army that was inadequately prepared and poorly led. After inflicting a rapid, decisive defeat on the Indians, China declared a unilateral cease-fire, and the PLA withdrew to the preexisting areas of control along the McMahon line.

India intensified its economic and security relationship with the Soviet Union, which looked upon India as its major Asian ally in both the Sino-Soviet and the Soviet-American conflicts. Soon Moscow was supplying roughly three-quarters of India's imported military equipment. During the 1971 South Asia crisis, when East Pakistan broke away from Pakistan to form a new state called Bangladesh, New Delhi and Moscow signed the Soviet-Indian Treaty of Peace, Friendship, and Cooperation, encouraging India actively to support the East Pakistan secession movement. Beijing saw India lending itself to the construction of a Soviet-supported hostile arc around China while simultaneously expanding its power in Southern Asia at the expense of China's regional ally Pakistan. Sino-Indian-Soviet relations thus became a secondary triangle in the great-power relations of the 1970s.

China took initiatives to counter Soviet and Indian strategy. In 1963 it signed a border agreement with Pakistan. During Indo-Pakistani wars of 1965 and 1971, an informal alliance between China and Pakistan took shape.[17] The alignment threatened Indian security by opening the possibility of a two-front war, although this did not materialize, and by bringing Chinese assistance to Pakistan's clandestine nuclear weapons program.[18] Pakistan, in return, served as Henry Kissinger's bridge to China. In 1970–71 its president, Yahya Khan, relayed secret messages between Kissinger and Zhou Enlai, and Kissinger used the cover of a diplomatic visit to Islamabad to slip off to Beijing for his secret 1971 meetings with Mao and Zhou.

Throughout the 1970s and early 1980s China also pursued an active diplomacy vis-à-vis the smaller states of South Asia, including Nepal, Bhutan, Sri Lanka, and Bangladesh, trying to use them to balance India's power.[19] But by the end of the 1980s it was clear that India had established dominance over these countries. It has militarily intervened in Sri Lankan affairs and now dominates its domestic and foreign policies, and it has used its economic influence in Nepal and Bhutan and its strategic dominance over Bangladesh, which it almost completely surrounds, to compel them to tilt toward India. Pakistan was China's sole remaining strategic partner in Southern Asia.

In the early 1980s China supplied Pakistan with designs for nuclear weapons and for nuclear-reprocessing equipment. In the 1990s China sought to provide Pakistan with medium-range ballistic missiles (Chapter 8). These transfer programs aimed to guarantee Pakistan's strategic independence from India, which has its own nuclear weapons program. During the last decade of the Cold War, a shared interest among Pakistan, China, and the United States in opposing the Soviet intervention in Afghanistan contributed to the strengthened relations among these states at the same time that India and the Soviet Union deepened their long-standing economic, political, and military ties.

Not until the Soviet Union signaled to New Delhi its determination to normalize relations with China in 1984–85 did India have an incentive to improve relations with Beijing. In October 1985 Premier Zhao Ziyang and Prime Minister Rajiv Gandhi met at the United Nations and agreed on the need to upgrade Sino-Indian contacts to the highest political level. In 1986 border talks under way since 1981 finally produced agreement on general principles for boundary demarcation, as well as China's acceptance of India's insistence on a sector-by-sector approach to the issues. But the two sides were unable to reach agreements on the territories in dispute.[20]

The liquidation of the Soviet military intervention in Afghanistan accelerated the normalization of Sino-Soviet relations and made more space for the improvement of Sino-Indian ties. China no longer feared Soviet-Indian collusion in Southern Asia, and India could no longer count on Soviet assistance in its conflict with China. Meanwhile, the Indian defense buildup after the 1962 border war had made the Indian military a match for the PLA on the Himalayan front. India's military now possesses a large force of advanced Russian fighter jets, including MiG-27s, MiG-29s, and French Mirage 2000s, and deploys a significant number of Soviet anti-aircraft missiles. Although India has not tested nuclear-tipped missiles, it has exploded a nuclear device, deployed short-range missiles, and started a program to develop intercontinental ballistic missiles. With a credible shield against the remote possibility of a Chinese conventional attack, India has the confidence that it can negotiate with Beijing on equal terms. China's anxiety about Tibet reinforced its desire to improve relations with New Delhi.

In December 1988 Prime Minister Rajiv Gandhi traveled to Beijing for a summit meeting. Gandhi reiterated India's recognition of Chinese sovereignty over Tibet and its policy of not interfering in China's internal affairs. The two sides agreed to establish a joint working group on border issues. Although the border remains unsettled, primarily owing to a lack of political will in India to accept Chinese occupation of the Aksai Chin plateau, the de facto line of control has emerged as a stable boundary. The two countries have signed a series of agreements in the fields of economic cooperation, agriculture, trade, science and technology, civil aviation, cultural and educational exchange, and communications. In November 1996, Jiang Zemin made the first visit to India by a Chinese head of state. During the visit, India and China signed an agreement limiting military exercises in border regions and committing the two sides to troop and weapons reduction along the border.

The collapse of the Soviet Union gave China and India a common interest in opposing American dominance in world forums like the United Nations and in counteracting U.S. human rights diplomacy. It has allowed the two countries to negotiate border conflicts and conduct leadership exchanges. But the thaw did not end their competition. China's role in the rivalry between India and Pakistan remains the fault line in the subcontinent.

If Beijing were to sacrifice its relationship with Pakistan in the hope of improving its relationship with India, it would lead to China's exclusion from the region except on terms dictated by New Delhi. This would strengthen India's regional position at China's expense and allow India to focus its military resources on the Sino-Indian border. In order to maintain Pakistan as a regional counterweight, Beijing has supplied Islamabad with advanced weapons systems, nuclear technology, and missiles. China's improving relationship with India makes Chinese military assistance to Pakistan even more important. Beijing must reassure Pakistan that Sino-Indian rapprochement will not threaten Pakistani security and require Pakistan to accommodate itself to Indian power.

In all four regions around its periphery—Inner Asia, Northeast Asia, Southeast Asia, and South Asia—China is more secure today than at any other time since the establishment of the PRC. This is so not because its raw power resources have increased to the point where it can dominate its neighbors. Indeed, South Korea, Indonesia, India, and others have expanded their economies and upgraded their armaments at about the same rate as China. Rather, Chinese influence has risen because of changes in the relations between China and the other three great powers in Asia.

For now at least, the United States, Japan, and Russia have not tried to mobilize other regional actors to contain or threaten China. For all the complexity of diplomacy in each region of Asia and each region's critical impact on Chinese interests, the key to regional security for China continues to lie in its relations with the other great powers. So long as relations among the four great powers remain balanced in such a way that each enjoys a measure of influence in every part of Asia, China will neither face a major threat from its neighbors nor pose a major threat to them.

7

POLICY-MAKING

THE MOST IMPORTANT foreign policy-making institution in the People's Republic of China has no formal status and may not survive the succession to Deng Xiaoping: the post of preeminent leader. So far this position has been occupied by only two men, Mao Zedong and Deng Xiaoping. The existence of a preeminent leader has given Chinese foreign policy some of its operational characteristics—consistency of strategic vision, the ability to enforce sacrifices upon certain institutions and individuals, and the ability dramatically to change course without negotiating with other domestic power centers. And the leaders' understanding of the world shaped the substance of China's search for security—its attentiveness to balance of power, its willingness to go it alone without allies, and its fearlessness in the use of force.

For foreigners, negotiating with Beijing under Mao and Deng had advantages and disadvantages. The considerations that shaped policy either were in plain sight in the leader's speeches and the official newspaper or were so private that intelligence agencies could not discover them. From demonstrators in the streets to diplomats in conference rooms, the nation maintained unanimity behind a seemingly rigid ideology. But an

André Malraux, a Henry Kissinger, or an Edgar Snow might be ushered into Mao's or Deng's presence to hear disquisitions marked by candor and flexibility. An enemy like Nixon could be received as a friend, or a friend like Khrushchev as an enemy. China's diplomats presented poker faces of discipline and secrecy during negotiations. But in the presence of the great leader or his authorized representative, under Mao normally Premier Zhou Enlai, everything might be negotiable. Even so, any policy changes would be cloaked in public claims of doctrinal consistency. Any agreement reached could be relied on.[1]

At its best, China's authoritarian political system could produce a foreign policy that was strategic and disciplined, whereas confusion and inconsistency often characterize foreign policy in a democratic system like the United States. Issues that were technical and minor tended to be relegated down the chain of command, where they were subject to indecision or reversal. Those that came before the political system when the supreme leader was weak were fought over or postponed.

Compared to Mao, Deng Xiaoping built a larger bureaucratic apparatus for policy-making and ceded more power to experts, as was probably unavoidable when China's increased involvement in the world raised a host of new specialized issues. Yet Deng retained control of grand strategy until near the end of his life. When he ceded authority to a collective headed by Jiang Zemin, central power seemed to weaken. Foreign negotiators increasingly find China speaking with many voices, as military and economic bureaucracies gain more influence over policy but fail to coordinate with one another.

THE SUPREME LEADER AND POLITICAL FACTIONS

China's formal government structure provides for no post of supreme leader.[2] Reflecting a Communist tradition that goes back to Marx and Lenin, the constitution says that "all power in the People's Republic of China belongs to the people." This means that sovereignty is theoretically concentrated in the institution that represents the people, the National People's Congress (NPC). There is neither separation of powers nor federalism. Instead, the NPC appoints the premier, who heads a cabinet (State Council) and whose job is to execute policy set down by the NPC. The NPC also appoints the officials of the judicial branch and itself retains the power to interpret and supervise implementation of the constitution—or, for that matter, to amend or replace it. Territorial power is delegated from the central government down to the provinces, cities, and counties.

Also recognized in the formal structure is the leadership of the state apparatus by the Chinese Communist Party. This means that the party decides on major policies and personnel decisions and hands these over to the government to implement. The party also has a constitution, which makes its highest organ the Central Committee. The Central Committee's powers are exercised on a routine basis by the Political Bureau (Politburo), consisting of twenty-odd top leaders, and by the Politburo's Standing Committee of five to ten members, which meets still more often. Mao headed the party as chairman. After his death that post was abolished to honor him, and the highest party official was called the general secretary.

In keeping with the Leninist tradition that the people have no conflicts of interest among themselves, power is monistic by design. Both functional power and territorial power are delegated from the center. Except in some recent cases at the village level, elections do not foster competition but allow the masses to coronate leaders chosen by the party. Under the nomenklatura system, the party appoints personnel throughout the government, army, economy, and the cultural and educational establishments. Likewise, financial allocations are made from the top down.

In practice, the structure calls forth a supreme leader. As commands go downward, disputes flow upward. Because of the lack of horizontal institutions like courts and legislatures that have real power, problems can be resolved only where vertical bureaucratic lines meet. For disputes between villages, this may be the office of the township party secretary; for disputes between industrial departments, it may be the office of the provincial party secretary. The three large bureaucracies—party, state, and army—send their biggest problems to Zhongnanhai, the complex of central party offices in the heart of Beijing. If in America all politics is local because issues find their ultimate resolution through the election process, in China all politics is court politics. If the "Center" is not to freeze in institutional deadlock or break down in personal rivalries, it needs a final arbiter.

In Mao and Deng the system managed to produce the dominant figures it needed to function. They enforced their decisions on other leaders with a mix of power resources. Official position was one. Mao was head of state, a mainly ceremonial post he relinquished in 1959 to Liu Shaoqi. He was also chairman of the Chinese Communist Party, a position that allowed him to control personnel appointments not only in the party itself but throughout society and the economy; the chairmanship also gave him control of information and ideology through the party Propaganda Department.

But Mao's most important positional source of power was the chairmanship of the Central Military Commission, a job he gripped tightly throughout the power struggles of the turbulent 1950s, the Cultural Revolution of the 1960s, and the presuccession crises of the 1970s. In the provinces this office enabled Mao to dictate the course of the Cultural Revolution through the military. In the capital, through the central guard corps and the Beijing garrison, he controlled the physical security of his rivals in the central leadership. With this trump card Mao stood down his top military officers' opposition to the Cultural Revolution in 1967 and prevented his comrade-in-arms Lin Biao from conducting a coup against him in 1971. Upon Mao's death in 1976, allies of Deng Xiaoping gained control of the Beijing guard corps and garrison. They arrested Mao's radical followers (the so-called Gang of Four, who included Mao's wife), as the first step in passing power to Deng. In 1989 Deng mobilized Beijing and provincial forces to suppress democracy demonstrators in Beijing who were backed by a leading party faction. Whether Deng's successor, Jiang Zemin, can keep power will depend above all on his ability to command backing from the generals.

But official position is neither sufficient nor necessary to guarantee power in China. Despite his high offices, Mao found himself so marginalized by his colleagues in the early 1960s that he had to mobilize the mass movement called the Great Proletarian Cultural Revolution to fight his way back to power. The highest post Deng Xiaoping held during his supremacy was chairman of the Central Military Commission. After he relinquished that position in 1989, he was listed solely as honorary chairman of the Chinese Bridge Association.

Other sources of power for the ultimate arbiter are informal. In a country with a tradition of emperorship and a large peasant population, the top leader's godlike image has been an important resource of legitimacy for the party-state. Mao's authority reflected not only his long history in the party—he was present at the creation in 1921 and led the Long March in 1934–35—but his reputation as the leader of the revolution, founder of the army, and creator of China's form of Marxism-Leninism. During the great famine of 1959–61, when China sustained an estimated 30 million deaths chiefly because of Mao's misguided economic policies, the CCP managed to hold on to power partly because of Mao's status as a demigod. The dying peasants believed that Mao could do no wrong and would rescue them. Precisely when he caused the regime's greatest crisis, his colleagues could least afford to purge him.[3] Similarly, when Mao's intraparty victims came back to power after his death, to consolidate their own power as his heirs they felt it necessary to say that Mao's "contributions to the Chinese revolution far outweigh[ed] his mistakes." By reaffirming in words many of the practices they abandoned in practice, they preserved their title to Mao's hand-me-down charisma.[4]

The endless game of maintaining supremacy also depended on attributes of character. Mao's deviousness, willpower, and ruthlessness seemed to cow even the former bandits and warriors who made up his circle of intraparty rivals.[5] Deng's style was more consultative. After the 1989 Beijing massacre, he allowed foreign policy to move in a hard-line direction to placate critics who argued that his domestic reforms and economic open door had generated domestic discontent and given the United States an opening to subvert the regime. His power came mainly from his prestige and personal connections throughout the party, army, and bureaucracy dating back to the earliest years of the Communist movement.

The paradox of the PRC's political structure is repeated throughout the system. The supposedly efficient, technocratic bureaucracy is broadly laced with intricate networks of personal power. Communist China's government is highly bureaucratic, with millions of officeholders operating at four levels of party and government and across a dozen or so bureaucratic "systems," which are in turn divided into scores of ministries, commissions, and departments with branches reaching down the system to every level. The system runs on tons of paper. Until recently, even telephones were used relatively rarely, although cadres attended many meetings. Government was suffused with formal etiquette and acute status consciousness.

Yet many a bureaucratic office, high or low, is a mini-Zhongnanhai that has one person in supreme authority, usually the party secretary. With unchecked power the secretary controls personnel, ideology, finance, housing, health, vacations, and as much as he wishes of his subordinates' personal lives and private thoughts. During periods of political upheaval, citizens have been loath to use the channels supposedly available to them to circumvent the party secretary's power—letters to the editor, appeals to higher levels, petitions to top leaders—because such channels nearly

always fail. Many Chinese have called their own system "feudal"; Western scholars have labeled it "neotraditional."

Personal power generates political factions.[6] Just as at the top of the
system, so too at levels below, factional leaders' power resources include
institutional position, personal connections, attractive or fearsome attributes of character, and the ability to define the unit's ideological or-
thodoxy. Some factions dwell in the top leader's court and draw power
from access to him; others center in the military, the bureaucracy, or regional governments and root their influence in the bureaucratic resources
they command. They take shape through networks of people who have
connections *(guanxi)* based on long association and personal trust. Senior leaders contend for power by adopting ideological and policy positions that serve the needs of their power bases. Some stress ideological
purity; others, the practical needs of their institutions. When the supreme
leader is vigorous, the factions fight for his ear. When he is weak or
chooses not to intervene, other senior leaders try to take control over policy.

Foreign policy is not usually the central issue in Chinese factional conflicts. It is a realm unfamiliar to most of the senior Communist leaders,
and one that affects their power interests less than domestic issues. Despite factionalism, a confident and healthy supreme leader can have his
way on many foreign policy issues, imposing his style and strategy across
a range of decisions.[7] Most of Mao's senior colleagues at first opposed in-
tervening in the Korean War, but they united quickly behind his determination to do so. Mao's choice to break with the Soviet Union in the early
1960s faced hardly any dissent at top levels of the leadership. The chairman was personally responsible for launching the two 1950s Taiwan
Strait crises and for the policy of rapprochement with the United States.

Similarly, Deng Xiaoping decided on China's open-door policy in the
late 1970s, normalization of relations with the United States in 1979, the
1979 incursion into Vietnam, rapprochement with the Soviet Union in
the 1980s, the "one country, two systems" policy for the reunification of
Hong Kong and Taiwan, and the agreement with Great Britain on the return of Hong Kong to China. PRC foreign policies may not always have
been correct, but under Mao and Deng they were usually the product of
a coherent vision and were carried out with discipline.

On the other hand, every major factional struggle has drawn foreign
policy issues into its vortex. Mao's early conflicts with party rivals over
revolutionary strategy all involved the question of how closely to follow

orders from the Soviet-dominated Communist International (Comintern). The first major power struggle after 1949 led to the purge and death in 1954 of a top leader, Gao Gang, who had tried to cultivate close relations with Stalin independently of Mao. Mao's purge of Peng Dehuai in 1959 was based partly on the charge that Peng wanted closer relations with Moscow. As a count against Peng this may have been unjustified, but it sent a message to other colleagues who doubted the wisdom of the Sino-Soviet split and of the divergence from the Soviet development model that helped fuel it. When Mao purged Liu Shaoqi and other orthodox party leaders in the Cultural Revolution, he accused them not only of domestic deviations but of conciliatory foreign policies as well. The power struggle between Mao and Lin Biao in 1970–71 embroiled Lin in resistance to Mao's opening to the United States, and after Lin's death he was charged, justly or not, with favoring capitulation to the Soviet Union.

When the leader was weak, factional struggles might not only refer to foreign policies but affect them as well. When Mao was incapacitated late in his life, the court faction led by his wife attacked their rivals for their association with U.S.-China rapprochement and with China's conciliatory Taiwan policy, forcing a temporary hard-line phase in policy toward the United States. Even after the radicals were defeated, the power struggle between Deng Xiaoping and the politician he later ousted from power, Hua Guofeng, froze policy toward the United States for a time. Not until 1978 did Deng establish the preeminence needed to make compromises over Taiwan and normalize relations with the United States. Setbacks to Deng's power after the 1989 Tiananmen incident were associated with hardening policies on U.S.-China trade, arms transfers, human rights, and Hong Kong, among other areas. Deng's illness in 1995–96 seemed to contribute to the hardening of PRC policies toward Taiwan, human rights, trade, and other issues.

Paramount leadership and political factionalism are the two faces of personal power. Deng Xiaoping may turn out to have been the last Chinese leader with enough authority to dominate the factions and impose consistency on the major elements of Chinese foreign policy.

THE APPARATUS

In Mao's era, the foreign policy apparatus was rudimentary. Major decisions were made by Mao, often in private, and implemented by a small staff under Zhou Enlai, Mao's premier and sometime foreign minister. During the Cultural Revolution, Mao disbanded the few foreign policy institutes China had, called home all but one of its ambassadors, and sent most of the foreign policy establishment to the countryside to be reeducated by the peasants. After receiving a phone call or written instruction from Mao, Zhou frequently handled even small details of policy personally. He negotiated all the arrangements for the 1971 visit to China of an American Ping-Pong team that opened the way for Henry Kissinger and later for Richard Nixon. Even on his deathbed, Zhou continued his diplomatic work, receiving a Romanian delegation and holding discussions on policy toward Taiwan. Deng Xiaoping restored and built up the foreign policy apparatus to deal with the growing complexity of the issues China faced as he steered it into a deeper engagement with the world. As institutions grew more complex, a larger part of the process came to be conducted in routine ways, in regularly scheduled meetings with institutionalized procedures.[8]

At the level of policy-making under the supreme leader stands the Politburo of the Chinese Communist Party. The Politburo is the organ best able to coordinate policy across a spectrum of bureaucracies that do not otherwise communicate easily. Its members normally include the top two or three officials of the party, government, and military bureaucracies as well as some of the most powerful provincial leaders. The top leader is often a Politburo member, but for many years of their respective reigns Mao and Deng did not attend meetings. Although top military leaders often sit on the Politburo, it seldom scrutinizes military affairs. When the military is loyal to the top leader and the leader is vigorous, civil-military coordination functions through him. When these conditions do not apply, the military carries out its duties with little civilian scrutiny (Chapter 8).

The Politburo is also the level at which foreign policy decisions are most likely to become linked to domestic policy decisions. It was at this level that policymakers dealt with such issues as the negative impact of the Great Leap Forward on relations with the Soviet Union (Chapter 3), and the need to relax domestic ideology in order to implement Deng Xiaoping's open-door economic policy (Chapter 9). The Politburo closely guides sensitive negotiations. When the United States and China were negotiating the agenda for Richard Nixon's visit to China in 1972, the Politburo issued the negotiating instructions for Chinese diplomats. In 1995, when the Clinton administration allowed Taiwan's leader Lee Teng-hui to visit the United States, a meeting of the Politburo decided on China's response, which included military exercises in the East China Sea and Taiwan Strait, the withdrawal of the Chinese ambassador to the United States, and the suspension of high-level U.S.-China diplomatic and military contacts.

Below the Politburo, the central Party Secretariat houses a general office and four departments that set policy for specific aspects of foreign and domestic affairs. The Propaganda Department governs the propaganda apparatus at home and abroad, which includes the media, the educational sector, and the cultural establishment. The United Front Work Department oversees policy related to nongovernmental people and groups in Taiwan, Hong Kong, and overseas Chinese circles, as well as relations with the intellectuals, national minorities, and the religious communities at home and abroad. The International Liaison Department manages party-to-party relations with political parties abroad, which was a central element of Chinese foreign policy during the years of high Maoism. The Organization Department is in charge of personnel matters. At one time the Central Committee included the Central Investigation Department, which was responsible for state security, but its functions are said to have have been taken over by the Ministry of State Security, an organ that performs many of the functions of America's CIA and FBI.

Also working under the central party apparatus are ten or more ad hoc leading groups that are supposed to coordinate policy on particular issues within the parameters set by the supreme leader and the Politburo. They include the Taiwan Work Leading Group, the Hong Kong and Macao Affairs Leading Group, and the Leading Group on Overseas Propaganda. The Foreign Affairs Leading Group, usually chaired by the premier, is the coordinating institution (or "mouth") for the whole foreign affairs bureaucratic "system." Its other members include the foreign minister, the minister of foreign trade and economic cooperation, the minister of defense, the senior military officer on the Central Military Commission, and selected deputy ministers. In some ways the Foreign Affairs Leading Group resembles the National Security Council in the United States. But unlike the NSC, it is only one of many organs at the central level with interests in foreign policy. Its influence depends on the personal power of its head and the use to which he wants to put it.

In the State Council (cabinet) the Foreign Affairs Office, under the premier, coordinates the work of the many state agencies involved in foreign affairs. These include four ministries. The Ministry of Foreign Affairs manages diplomacy and staffs embassies and consulates overseas. The Ministry of Foreign Trade and Economic Cooperation (MOFTEC) concentrates on trade issues, such as conflicts regarding protection of intellectual property rights and accusations of Chinese protectionism, and policy toward multilateral economic institutions, including APEC and the World Trade Organization. The Ministry of Defense represents the military establishment in the cabinet and in dealings with foreigners. The Ministry of State Security handles border control, diplomatic security, espionage, and counterespionage.

Other cabinet-level ministries and commissions conduct negotiations on specific issues. The Ministry of Finance, for example, has been China's primary representative to the International Monetary Fund. The Ministry of Public Security handles police functions relating to foreigners, from crime solving to fire safety and traffic control. The State Commission on Science and Technology controls allocation of foreign currency among civilian and military industries for importing advanced technology. The State Education Commission administers the policy of sending students abroad. The Ministry of Culture has a Department of Cultural Relations with Foreign Countries. Below the cabinet other government agencies that have foreign policy roles include the Bank of China, the customs administration, the travel and tourism administration, the aviation administration, and the foreign experts bureau (which recruits foreign teachers, engineers, and other specialists).

The outer ring of the Chinese foreign policy establishment consists of research institutes. The Chinese Academy of Social Sciences has numerous area studies institutes studying all parts of the world from the angles of politics, economics, history, religion, and culture. In addition, there are over twenty think tanks in Beijing devoted to analyzing international affairs. Specialized think tanks serve the Ministry of Defense, the Foreign Ministry, the State Council, the Communist Party's Military Affairs Committee, and the General Staff of the PLA. Each provincial government runs a social sciences academy that includes international relations in its field of studies. The governments of Shanghai, Guangzhou, Xiamen, Harbin, and other major cities have also established foreign policy think tanks.[9]

Think tank staff are often sent to Chinese embassies abroad. They visit foreign universities and institutes to give lectures and conduct interviews, spend time abroad as visiting scholars, and attend academic conferences. The analysts prepare reports for their government agencies, informing the Chinese leadership of the latest thinking among foreign officials and experts on policies toward China and issues affecting Chinese security. Many of these research organizations also provide periodic reports to the Politburo.

The Chinese government posts around the world a third large staff consisting of journalists, who prepare reports on the same subjects as embassy personnel and think tanks. Most Chinese journalists work for the official New China News Agency, the China News Service, or a government or party newspaper like *People's Daily*. Most are party members. Abroad as at home, reporters write not only for publication but also for classified, "internal" news bulletins that circulate among high-ranking officials of the party and government. In most foreign countries reporters are allowed to base themselves more widely and travel more freely than diplomats.

Like all major powers, China has a sophisticated covert intelligence system. By definition, it is a secret institution about which we know little. But apparently the Chinese security agencies focus on technological information. They develop relationships with some Chinese going abroad for long-term visits or permanent residence, expecting that some will develop careers in fields dealing with national security or sensitive technology and will one day provide classified information to the Chinese government. Most of the few cases in which the United States, Japan, and other countries have apprehended Chinese spies involved efforts to transfer sensitive information on advanced technologies with potential military use.

THE GLOBAL AGENDA

Although China is not a global power, it has a global agenda. While senior policymakers tend to Chinese relations with the great powers and neighbors that can threaten Chinese security, professional diplomats spend much of their time working on issues below the level of grand strategy.

One major Chinese goal with global implications is to deny Taiwan wider diplomatic recognition and membership in international organizations. China seeks to maintain diplomatic relations with every country, no matter how poor or remote, to prevent it from recognizing the

Republic of China (Chapters 11–12). This requires a detailed knowledge of the politics and diplomatic priorities of countries in Africa, Latin America, Oceania, and the Middle East that otherwise have little influence over Chinese interests. In cultivating favor with such countries, China dispenses economic aid (Chapter 9), provides sympathetic help in the UN Security Council and other multilateral forums, and bestows prestige on Third World governments. In a busy program of high-level state visits, Beijing extends its trademark hospitality to leaders from many small states and dispatches top PRC leaders on frequent trips to out-of-the-way countries.

A second goal that engages Chinese diplomats throughout the world is the effort to shape the emerging system of international treaties and agreements that increasingly constrain the autonomy of states in areas as diverse as arms exports, arms control, human rights, the environment, air and sea navigation, and international economic relations. We show in the next three chapters that as China has become more involved in the world, it has fallen under attack for violating many of these international regimes. One purpose of its diplomacy is to gain more influence in shaping them.

China can do so partly by influencing smaller countries that participate in shaping such systems of international rules. Many states hold rotating seats in the UN Security Council, the UN Commission on Human Rights, and other UN agencies and attend international conferences like those sponsored by the United Nations on the environment in Rio de Janeiro in 1992, on human rights in Vienna in 1993, and on women's issues in Beijing in 1995. Specialized intergovernmental organizations often include nearly all countries and give each member one vote regardless of size. Some multilateral treaties are negotiated by near-consensus. Even rich countries' clubs, like the World Trade Organization and the World Bank, include certain countries that on some issues identify themselves more with China than with the United States, Europe, or Japan.

Just in those areas where China is most often criticized—weapons proliferation, interference with free trade, violation of intellectual property rights, and human rights abuses—it shares an interest with other developing countries in altering or resisting norms that serve the interests of dominant, advanced states. As the largest country and the only Third World permanent member of the UN Security Council, China sees itself as a natural leader of the non-West and the nonrich. This position of leadership serves Chinese interests but must be cultivated country by country.

Although its diplomacy is omnidirectional, China does not invest equal diplomatic resources everywhere. It expends special efforts in centers of influence in each region. In Europe, one of these is Germany, a country China long viewed as a barrier to the expansion of Soviet influence, and which it now sees as a forceful economic rival of the United States and a balance against American influence over European China policy. China also fostered a close relationship with France because of Paris's independence of Washington. France was the first American ally other than Britain to recognize the PRC, which it did as early as 1964.

In the Middle East, China's largest embassy has long been in Egypt, the region's largest country in population and one of its most influential. Beijing also focused much attention on strategic Iran (Chapter 3). In Latin America, it has maintained close ties with Mexico, Brazil, and Chile. In Africa, it devoted disproportionate resources to the frontline states against South Africa. Since the end of apartheid Beijing has developed friendly ties with Johannesburg, seeking to woo it away from diplomatic relations with Taipei.[10]

BUREAUCRATIC POLITICS AND LEADERSHIP SUCCESSION

China is interacting more with the outside world at all levels of government at the same time that the center has lost its formerly absolute control over bureaucratic agencies and local authorities. Although the Foreign Ministry is China's designated negotiator on most international issues, it is a weak bureaucratic actor, unable to guarantee that its commitments for action within China will be implemented, because it lacks the economic resources and bureaucratic authority to enforce them in the absence of direct intervention by the preeminent leader. Arms sales provide an example, discussed in Chapter 8: within broad guidelines established by the top leader, Chinese generals have the power to decide whether certain weapons should be exported to certain countries. Likewise, Chinese diplomats made commitments to uphold intellectual property rights but did not control the localities where factories that are pirating Western CDs and software are operating (Chapter 9).

The central party and state foreign policy organs are increasingly unable to monopolize decisions that relate to foreign policy. Educational, banking, police, and military authorities at all levels frequently make decisions that affect foreign interests and that may expand into central-level issues. On the other hand, Chinese policy continues to be strategic and disciplined in areas where the leadership enjoys consensus and powerful bureaucratic actors support the policy. Examples include policies toward foreign human rights pressure, Taiwan and Hong Kong, and minority independence movements in Xinjiang, Inner Mongolia, and Tibet.

The post-Deng era is likely to see a continued diminution of the preeminent leader's authority. Many leaders in China's successor generation joined the party only in the 1950s. Since they have pursued careers in one bureaucracy, they have not developed personal networks throughout the system. None of them has the revolutionary legitimacy of either Mao Zedong or Deng Xiaoping. Central civilian leaders are likely to have less control over the military than did Mao and Deng.

Rising military influence on foreign policy could complicate China's external relations in several ways. The military may be less inclined to comply with obligations under arms control treaties and to take on new obligations in response to U.S. and Western pressure. Under military influence policy may harden in regard to prodemocracy dissidents, Tibetan, Moslem, and Mongol nationalists, Hong Kong political activists, and Taiwan independence forces. Rising tensions in these areas could increase regional apprehensions and make management of U.S.-China relations more difficult. The military may also be more assertive in conflicts with neighbors over such issues as territorial rights in the South China Sea.

In the absence of either an institutionalized succession process or a leader who consolidates preeminent informal power, a state of chronic succession crisis could come to characterize Chinese politics. Should this scenario occur, China will become an increasingly difficult player in world affairs.

8

MILITARY POWER
AND FOREIGN POLICY

C HINA'S STRATEGIC VULNERABILITY has not deterred it from using
force in its foreign policy. The People's Liberation Army fought
against American forces in Korea in 1950–53, against India in 1962,
against the Soviet Union at several points on the border in 1969, against
South Vietnam in naval battles in the South China Sea over the Paracel
Islands in 1974, against Vietnam on land in 1979, and over the Spratly
Islands in 1988. China bombarded the offshore islands in the Taiwan
Strait crises of 1954–55 and 1958 and conducted demonstrative naval and
missile exercises in 1995–96 to deter Taiwan independence. It also provided significant assistance to the Vietnamese Communists and deployed
troops in North Vietnam during Hanoi's war against the United States.

China's use of force, however, was narrower in ambit than that of
the other major powers in Asia. The United States and the former Soviet
Union have employed force far from their borders and have armed allies
to protect economic interests and political clients across the globe. European powers have done the same. Even Japan, despite its "peace constitution" and its limited power projection capability, has developed the

capability to defend distant sea-lanes crucial to its worldwide commerce, and engaged in a policy of regional security stabilization by supplying base facilities and in other ways cooperating with the American military.

By contrast, China's purpose in using force was always the near-in defense of home territory and deterrence of invasion. Its military doctrine was tagged by Mao Zedong as "people's war." In the early years of the post-Mao era, Deng Xiaoping revised the label to read "people's war under modern conditions." Both terms described a strategy to maintain control with thin resources over a vast territory, to protect national borders characterized by difficult mountain terrain, long coastlines, and sometimes inhospitable populations, to confront numerous rival states directly at the border, and, if necessary, to retreat to the interior to fight a protracted war. China's strategy emphasized continental defense. It required large, low-technology armed forces to suppress unrest at home and to resist incursions; a coastal air and naval force to meet seaborne threats a slight distance offshore; and a minimal second-strike nuclear deterrent against superpower nuclear blackmail.

This chapter and the next two consider how China uses, and responds to the use of, each of the three kinds of influence in international politics: military, economic, and ideological.[1] On each of the three dimensions of power, China's greater involvement in the world has brought both more power and more vulnerability. Chapter 9 shows that China is more penetrated by foreign economic influence than in the past but that economic modernization has enhanced its ability to influence others. Chapter 10 describes how the Chinese government has been placed on the ideological defensive and how it is working to recruit other countries to support its own vision of human rights.

There is similar ambiguity in the contribution of rising military capability to national security. Economic development under Deng Xiaoping has enabled China's military to upgrade its equipment and training. Threats to Chinese territory have receded. But a revolution in military technology has ushered in an era in which America enjoys unchallenged supremacy, and Japan possesses the technology to develop similar capabilities. Russia is weak now, but has the resources and human capital to recover. Even the smaller ASEAN neighbors are modernizing their militaries from formidable economic and technological bases. As China races to modernize, it risks stimulating its neighbors to accelerate their own pace of advance, potentially widening rather than narrowing the gap between China's security needs and its military capabilities.

PEOPLE'S WAR

The People's Liberation Army (PLA) began as a guerrilla force fighting to overthrow the Kuomintang (KMT, Nationalist) government in a revolutionary war. (Today the term People's Liberation Army covers all branches of the Chinese military, including the People's Liberation Army Navy, PLAN, and the People's Liberation Army Air Force, PLAAF.) In the civil war of the 1940s the PLA grew into a conventional military that expelled the KMT from mainland China by a combination of mobile and positional warfare. In Korea it fought the American military to a stalemate in a classic clash of ground forces.

China's commander in Korea, Peng Dehuai, returned home as defense minister to continue building the PLA as a conventional force able to complete such tasks as the suppression of armed opposition, the occupation of Tibet, and a planned amphibious assault on Taiwan. He also had to consider the possibility of another war with the United States, whose troops were stationed in South Korea, in Japan, on Taiwan, and throughout Southeast Asia. After a period of Soviet-inspired modernization, Peng's ambitions fell victim to Mao Zedong's economic and political vision. As Mao shifted China into the Great Leap Forward, he attacked professionalism in all sectors of society, including the military. Mao feared that a professional military would develop a narrow bureaucratic mission, escaping the authority of the party and of Mao himself. Mao revived the revolutionary strategy of people's war, insisting that men rather than weapons decide wars. When he purged Peng Dehuai for openly criticizing the Great Leap Forward, he replaced him as minister of defense with Lin Biao, a commander personally loyal to Mao and committed to the ideological mobilization of the troops and the interpenetration of military and civilian life.

During Mao's rule the PLA devoted its best energies to internal problems. In the 1950s it battled remnant KMT troops and local militias in the southwest and northwest, took Hainan Island, participated in violent political campaigns to wipe out the landlord class and suppress counterrevolutionaries, and occupied Tibet. During the Great Leap Forward the PLA-controlled militia guarded the railway stations to prevent peasants from fleeing famine-stricken rural areas. In the early 1960s Mao dispatched military officers to take over many government offices and state-owned enterprises. During the Cultural Revolution he ordered regional military commanders to choose sides among rival "red guard" and "rebel" groups. As the Cultural Revolution ended, he placed the military in charge of local administration through organs called revolutionary committees.

The military's defense mission did not disappear after the Korean War. China's greatest external challengers remained the United States and the Nationalist Party on Taiwan, which might invade along the southeast coast with air assaults and amphibious landings. In the 1960s China's strategic situation was exacerbated by conflict with the Soviet Union, which was capable of invading from the northeast with infantry preceded by bombers and led by tanks and battlefield missiles. In either case, if invasion came, Chinese defenders intended to trade space for time, "lure the enemy deep," and prevail by mobilizing popular resistance and engaging in close combat over a long period of time.

Chinese propaganda sometimes pictured people's war as a romantic reprise of revolutionary guerrilla combat, in which lightly armed peasant militiamen would shoot enemy airplanes from the sky. Sometimes it was portrayed as a version of the Red Army's Long March or the early phase of the civil war, with the regular army living among the people, like "fish in the water," marching across the landscape paying for what they ate and bivouacking with friendly peasants, avoiding the enemy when he was strong and attacking him when he was dispersed. Making a virtue of necessity, the undereducated and underbudgeted Chinese military learned simple techniques, which emphasized the ability to operate flexibly in small groups without regular contact with the command structure. Soldiers took constant ideological training to prepare them to overcome hardship, live among civilians, and guide civilian resistance. The model soldier Lei Feng supposedly darned his own socks, grew his own food, and intensified his battle readiness by committing Mao's works to memory.

After the 1969 border clashes with the Soviet Union, the government mobilized urban dwellers and military garrisons to "dig tunnels deep and store grain everywhere" for civil defense against a potential Soviet nuclear attack. Military experts who later saw the tunnels concluded they would have been of little use against a nuclear attack, but it is not clear if Chinese planners knew this. In any case, the structures conveyed the seriousness with which Beijing took the threat and a message of determination to survive, both to the Soviets and to the Chinese people.

China also built nuclear weapons and ballistic missiles, which compensated to some extent for its stagnation in conventional military capabilities.[2] Although the Chinese nuclear force was small, the Chinese bomb concerned Soviet and American leaders. In 1963 President John F. Kennedy instructed Assistant Secretary of State Averell Harriman to probe Soviet attitudes toward a possible U.S. preventive strike against China's nuclear facilities. The strike was never undertaken, and China exploded its first nuclear device in 1964. In 1970 it was the turn of the Soviet Union to ask the Nixon administration how it would respond to a Soviet attack on Chinese facilities.[3] This strike also never occurred. In the end China's costly nuclear effort paid dividends. Nuclear weapons bolstered Chinese leaders' confidence in 1969 when China and the Soviet Union clashed on the border and in 1979 when China invaded Vietnam. Because China is a member of the "nuclear club," its great-power status is enhanced and other nations pay close attention to its interests.

Chinese propaganda lauded the PLA as a "Great Wall of steel." This Great Wall had relatively little behind it—Chinese conventional capabilities declined during the 1960s and 1970s—but the PLA seems to have persuaded potential enemies that China could not be conquered. People's war might not have been a successful strategy for fighting an invasion, but in conjunction with nuclear weapons and China's vast territory it was an adequate strategy for deterring one.

THE PLA IN POLITICS

Although Mao insisted that "the party controls the gun," the PLA was in fact a self-contained organization that intersected the Chinese Communist Party hierarchy only at the top. There Mao, as chairman of both the party and the Central Military Commission (CMC), melded civilian and military power in one person. Nominally a party organ, the CMC ran the military without reporting to anyone below Mao. Deng Xiaoping's reforms did not alter this structure. The civilian party-state exerted no control over the military except in the person of the leader at the top of both hierarchies—at first Deng himself and later his successor, President and Party Secretary Jiang Zemin.[4] There is even some question whether Jiang, despite his formal authority, has been able to exercise full authority over senior military officers.

The political commissar system within the armed forces indoctrinated the troops in the leader's thought, but the commissariat had no solid horizontal link to the civilian party or state apparatus. The Ministry of Defense was a powerless façade that represented the CMC in the State Council and to foreign visitors. The military had its own structure of party branches and cells, which ran parallel to the civilian party rather than subsidiary to it. Indeed, the party-in-the-army was the main part of the Chinese Communist Party organization until 1949. After 1949 it still considered itself senior to the civilian party organization, and ideologically purer as well.

At the highest levels, the Maoist regime was thus not a model of civilian or party control over the military, as it has often been depicted, but a quasi-military regime. Senior military officers occupied posts in top party organs like the Central Committee and the Politburo and participated in the factional politics of the party center. Mao's decisions to purge Minister of Defense Peng Dehuai and later another general, Luo Ruiqing, and to promote Lin Biao to the post of minister of defense reflected his concern about the power struggle in the party rather than their qualifications as military leaders. In the Ninth Central Committee of the Communist Party (April 1969), 45 percent of the members were active PLA officers, showing that China at this time had come close to having a military- rather than a party-led government. In effect the Chinese political elite was a civil-military fusion, with the military taking part in policy decisions of all kinds.[5]

Beneath the Central Military Commission were the central PLA departments, including Political Affairs, General Staff, and Rear Services (logistics). The operational forces were divided among military regions—first thirteen, then eleven under Mao, seven today—each equipped to fight independently. China lacked the communications and transport capabilities to manage a centralized military system. Nor could it conduct combined, coordinated warfare across the national map. Since invasion might come from any quarter or several quarters at once, each region had to be prepared to meet it largely on its own.

The military regions also shouldered responsibilities for internal security within their geographic areas. The garrisons came into play whenever major urban disturbances broke out. In the countryside in the 1960s each military region organized rural dwellers through the commune system into a vast militia, encompassing perhaps one-quarter of China's population. The militia was divided into three levels—ordinary, basic, and armed—and given simple training, often with wooden rifles, by militia departments staffed by PLA officers. Although it was ostensibly trained for use against foreign invasion, its primary role was in internal security.

As part of his decentralized vision of China's defense, Mao ordered each military region to make itself virtually self-sufficient in food, clothing, vehicles, and all but the most sophisticated arms. The troops ran farms to grow their own food and factories to produce spare parts and clothing. To maintain the fish-and-water relationship with the local people, military manpower assisted peasants in the harvest and donated time to engineering and construction projects in the civilian economy. At the level of the central government, during the 1960s the military-industrial complex consisted of eight ministries of machine building, managing or producing nuclear facilities, aviation, electronics, shipbuilding, ordnances, and ballistic missiles. Like the PLA itself, these ministries were represented in the civilian government's State Council but operated independently, with their own budgets and economic plans, answering only to the CMC.[6]

At his death Mao bequeathed a military that was large and armed with nuclear weapons and that had deterred aggression on China's territory. Yet his PLA was more a domestic and border force composed of large infantry units than a modern military. Its success in conventional warfare in Korea had depended more on size and motivation than on tactical sophistication or advanced weaponry. The PLA triumphed against India in 1962 because the Indian military had not prepared for war, although it had provoked the clash with its forward deployments. And in 1969, in limited engagements with the Soviet military, the PLA suffered defeats. Inferior conventional weaponry undermined Beijing's ability to compete with the Soviet Union for influence in Hanoi during the Vietnam War. Lack of power projection meant that China did not even try to defend its claim to the disputed Spratly Islands in the South China Sea until late 1988, when its navy engaged much weaker Vietnamese forces. Most important, China's vulnerability to Soviet power in the 1970s and 1980s compelled Beijing to compromise on Taiwan in order to develop cooperative relations with the United States.

Rhetoric to the contrary notwithstanding, people's war plus nuclear weapons was a strategy that reflected weakness. Had the worst ever come to pass—Soviet or American invasion—the PLA's prospects would have been dim. At best, the PLA would have had to cede extensive territory to the invader and fight a costly protracted war with an uncertain outcome. More likely, the invader would not have fallen into China's trap, opting instead to make limited incursions along the length of the border and aerial attacks on China's industrial centers, leaving the PLA with few retaliatory options. That the superpowers did not invade China was a tribute more to the Soviet and American fear of fighting China while simultaneously risking war with each other and, in later years, to China's nuclear deterrent than to the fighting prowess of the PLA or the wisdom of its strategy.

THE PLA AFTER MAO—"LOCAL, LIMITED WAR"

Richard Nixon's 1972 visit to China ended the prospect of war with the United States and supplied China with a more effective deterrent to a Soviet attack than the PLA itself could provide. In 1970 the Nixon administration had expressed its opposition to the Soviet proposal to bomb Chinese nuclear installations, and in February 1979 Washington warned Moscow against retaliating when the PLA invaded Vietnam. When the 1980s in turn brought a decline in Soviet power and an easing of Sino-Soviet tensions, Chinese strategists ceased to consider world war "inevitable." They began officially to anticipate "a considerable period of peace."

Accordingly, the Central Military Commission declared in 1985 that the most likely military contingency was no longer "early, major, and nuclear war" but rather "local, limited war."[7] Chinese borders remained potentially troublesome, tensions continued with India and Vietnam, and the Korean peninsula was unstable, but an invasion by the great powers was no longer likely. The PLA now moved from preparing for immediate large-scale war to developing the resources necessary to compete militarily in the next century.

The Chinese view of security in the coming decade is not complacent. China's ability to defend its territory from a land invasion is greater today than at any time in the previous 150 years. But the PLA lacks both power projection capabilities and a nuclear deterrent that is secure for the long term. Strategic planners must prepare for the possibility of a revitalized Russia that possesses a formidable nuclear force and may try to restore its military presence in Inner Asia; for a fully armed Japan with sophisticated conventional and strategic weaponry, power projection capabilities, and considerable economic power; and for hostile relations with the United States. The United States has the ability to pose either a direct threat to Chinese security or an indirect threat by forging an anti-

China coalition that includes Japan and other Asian states. Such scenarios may seem far removed from American intentions and unlikely in post–Cold War international politics, but they cannot be ignored by Chinese planners who are aware of American might and of the potential for renewed great-power conflict.

Nor can China be confident that relations with its smaller neighbors will remain stable. Tension in the Taiwan Strait may persist for years, sparking periodic crises. A unified Korea possessing nuclear weapons could prove a less cooperative neighbor than the two halves of a divided Korea that are focused on each other and compete for Chinese favor. Vietnam is in constant search of a great-power ally to help it offset Chinese influence. China's relationship with India has improved, but disagreement over Pakistan and unresolved border issues could cause renewed tension. Its Inner Asian borders require surveillance against separatists. Finally, its territorial disputes with the ASEAN countries in the South China Sea could give rise to heightened conflict.

To deal with this uncertain strategic environment, Deng Xiaoping sought a smaller, more sophisticated PLA. In 1984 half a million railway troops were transferred to the Ministry of Railways, and the People's Armed Police (PAP) was established as a separate unit for internal security. In 1985 China announced that it would demobilize one million men, reducing its forces from 4.2 to 3.2 million, and it reclassified some military employees as "nonmilitary cadres." Older, less educated soldiers were sent to jobs in civilian government offices. The average age of the senior officers corps plummeted. In 1988 Deng reduced Mao's eleven military regions to seven, each comprising three or four provinces and facing one or more major strategic rivals. He downsized the militia, creating a semiprofessional regular reserve force numbering about one million.[8] Ineffective civil defense activities came to a halt. In 1988 the military reintroduced ranks, which had been abolished as part of Mao's pattern of egalitarianism. Now that officers were expected to have specialized educations, various service institutes assumed importance in the training of senior officers. In 1985, in order to facilitate combined warfare, the National Defense University was established to provide integrated training for officers from the various services.

The PLA developed enhanced maneuverability and conducted larger, more sophisticated training exercises. During the mid-1990s it conducted training operations under simulated nuclear warfare conditions, missile exercises in the East China Sea, and combined naval and air operations simulating an attack on Taiwan's offshore islands. At the forefront of the trend are the Marine Corps, reestablished in 1980 after twenty-three years; "fist units," similar to U.S. special forces and Israeli commandoes for conducting raids and special operations; and division-size "rapid reaction forces" designed to operate like U.S. Marines and the Eighty-second Airborne Division in high-impact operations utilizing high-technology equipment. These units boast China's most-disciplined and best-trained soldiers. They have also been given first access to modern battlefield weaponry, including antitank and surface-to-air missiles.

While the PLA concentrated on preparation for war, the PAP became the first line of defense against civil unrest. It has been given more manpower, special equipment, and better training. Nonetheless, the PLA often shares responsibility with the PAP for managing various internal security issues, such as independence activism in Tibet, and main force troops, local garrisons, and militia reserves deployed throughout the country remain available to back up the PAP.

THE DEFENSE BUDGET

Downsizing and improved training were relatively inexpensive ways to improve the PLA's performance. But Chinese leaders no longer subscribe to Mao's dictum that war is decided by men and not weapons. Preferring to follow his advice that "power grows out of the barrel of a gun," they have increased defense spending in order to modernize the PLA's hardware.

Most of the PLA continues to be equipped with old-fashioned, Chinese-made, Soviet-style tanks and planes. Specialists on the Chinese military have described the PLA as the world's largest military museum and as a junkyard army. Its new-generation fighter planes have been called the "most highly perfected obsolete aircraft in the world." Although the PLA Air Force is one of the world's largest, most of its planes are based on 1950s and 1960s technology, and over 90 percent are obsolete. Moreover, its size is shrinking as China takes the oldest planes out of service. The air force lacks the organizational and communications capabilities to coordinate with the other service arms in combat. Chinese pilots have limited time in the air, limited experience flying independent of ground control, and minimal experience flying over water. These weaknesses compromise the PRC's capabilities to operate beyond China's borders. Although the PLA Air Force might participate in offensive operations against Taiwan or elsewhere close to home, its main objective is to help defend Chinese cities from attack.[9] The navy is similarly outdated and restricted to conducting operations near the coast.

The extent of the PLA's backwardness was revealed to Chinese leaders during the 1991 Persian Gulf War.[10] They saw on CNN that the armies of the United States and its allies had widened their lead not only over China's but over all armies based on Soviet equipment and doctrine. They noted the ability of smart bombs to hit specific buildings and the sophistication of America's logistical capability, based on vast transport assets as well as on deep industrial resources, computerized planning capacity, and the financial wherewithal to stockpile spare parts and equipment throughout the world. Above all, Chinese defense planners were struck by real-time integrated electronic command of the battlefield—the so-called C^4I, or command, control, computers, communication, and intelligence. It enabled planes, ships, tanks, and infantry to execute a battle plan coordinated by central commanders using real-time information from every part of the battlefield.

To remedy its deficiencies, the PLA needed money. Deng Xiaoping's fast-growth economic policies provided enhanced resources for military modernization, but they were not unlimited. Upon taking power, Deng immediately raised the military budget above the level of the Mao years, setting a new high in 1979 to cover the Vietnam incursion (Chapter 6). He then diminished expenditures for ten years during the 1980s in order to channel resources into the civilian industrial economy, aiming to provide a basis of "comprehensive national strength" for national defense. The PLA did not strongly object to the temporary stringency. Apparently Deng persuaded the generals to wait for economic modernization to provide an improved technological and financial base for military modernization before demanding a greater share of the state budget.

Defense funds increased again after 1989, first to cover the costs of the military's role in suppressing the Tiananmen demonstrations and then in recognition of the PLA's deficiencies in hardware. But in dollar terms defense expenditures remained virtually steady into the 1990s. Indeed, if corrected for inflation, the announced defense budget fell, and even more dramatically if measured as a share of GNP. In 1994, official budget figures were in the range of U.S. $6 billion per year, a miserly sum compared with the U.S. defense budget of $282 billion, the Japanese of $42 billion, or even the Taiwanese of $11 billion.[11]

However, specialists consider each year's official Chinese figures to be understated by a factor of two to four or more.[12] Unlike other countries' defense figures, the official Chinese numbers leave out most military research and development and weapons acquisition, both of which are placed instead in the accounts of ostensibly civilian agencies. Under Deng's economic reforms erstwhile military enterprises have been allowed to produce goods for the civilian market. Although some of these enterprises enhance the military budget, their overall contribution remains unclear. In addition, State Council organs operate defense industries and the profits they earn do not necessarily contribute to the PLA's budget.

Including off-budget funds, Chinese military expenditures still remain, by most estimates, well under American, Russian, or Japanese figures in absolute terms or on a per capita basis. On the other hand, given the low cost of manpower, food, housing, uniforms, and domestically produced equipment, China's defense dollar buys more than that of other armies, raising defense expenditures' value in terms of "purchasing-power parity." Even in these terms, however, China's defense spending is much less than that of Japan or the United States. Adjusted for inflation and assessed as a share of the national budget, it may actually have declined from the early 1980s through the mid-1990s.

PLA HARDWARE

Estimates of defense spending are useful for evaluating a country's commitment to expanding its military power. By this measure China does not have the intention to destabilize Asia. More important, though, spending levels do not indicate capabilities. Capabilities are determined in part by the quality of the equipment a country possesses. China has done much window-shopping abroad, learning the state of the world's advanced weaponry so as to make effective use of its restricted resources. Foreign purchases have been in limited quantities, primarily serving to acquire technology for domestic production. During the Reagan administration the United States participated in the modernization of Chinese defensive weaponry, supplying artillery equipment, antisubmarine torpedoes, radar equipment, and avionics packages for an advanced fighter plane. After the Tiananmen incident the United States canceled such programs and, with other Western countries, curtailed exports to China of military-related equipment and technology. Searching for an alternative supplier, China turned to Moscow. Among other items, Beijing has bought Su-27 aircraft, Il-76 transport aircraft, SA-10 surface-to-air missiles, and Kilo-class attack submarines.[13] With the exception of the Su-27s, most such purchases serve technology-transfer objectives. Thus far, Russian arms transfers have had limited ability to augment Chinese power beyond coastal waters.

At home Beijing has invested in the production of a number of air-craft. China has been upgrading the F-8 interceptor as the F-8II. How-ever, the domestic aviation industry could not satisfy PLA Air Force demands, and China thus turned to the United States for assistance. The Reagan administration agreed to provide advanced avionics packages for the F-8II, but this program was suspended after the Tiananmen incident. The F-8II was then manufactured by means of domestic technologies and first deployed in 1992. But it is equipped with outdated weapons systems and powered by an inefficient engine. It is the equivalent of a 1960s U.S. F-4. The F-10 fighter, based on the avionics and radar from the Israeli Lavi, is the focus of PRC efforts to produce a multirole aircraft. Current estimates are that it will attain operational capability in 2005, yet it re-mains to be seen whether Chinese enterprises can develop such an ad-vanced aircraft. Development of the FB-7 interdictor/strike aircraft continues. The first prototypes were built in 1988, but the aircraft still does not have a power plant. In 1975 China acquired the production rights for fifty Rolls-Royce Spey engines. Britain supplied China with al-most fully assembled engines. After over twenty years, though, the en-gines were still not installed in operational aircraft. The Spey engine is no longer produced, and spare engines are not available. China is now considering a Russian engine for the FB-7.[14] China's domestic enterprises will not be able to produce world-class aircraft until well into the twenty-first century.

China in the early 1990s acquired from Russia twenty-six advanced Su-27 fighter planes and has agreed to purchase an additional twenty-four. It has also entered into a licensed-production agreement with Rus-sia to manufacture Su-27s. The decision to use hard currency to buy a large number of aircraft suggests that China is looking for a "quick fix" to offset declining capabilities vis-à-vis Taiwan following Taiwan's ac-quisition of advanced U.S. and French aircraft and its domestic produc-tion of an indigenous defense fighter (Chapter 12). China has deployed the first squadron of Su-27s within range of Taiwan. The Su-27 could also help consolidate China's strategic advantage over Vietnam for clashes at sea or on land. In similar ways a large number of Su-27s could improve China's strategic posture toward India and a unified Korea. Less clear is the implication of licensed production for China's ability to manufacture world-class military aircraft. Details of the agreement remain unclear. Given China's primitive manufacturing facilities, the PRC's role will consist primarily of assembling kits imported from Russia. The Su-27 licensed-production agreement will make only a limited contribution to the development of a high-technology military manufacturing base.

In the meantime the PLA Air Force not only cannot defend its own ground and naval forces from attack; it cannot provide air support in Chinese coastal waters. True power projection requires aircraft carriers. Without them, when the navy moves beyond the range of its land-based aircraft, it will be vulnerable to attacks from the land-based aircraft of smaller powers near the theater of operations. Similarly, Chinese forces occupying disputed territories in distant waters would not have around-the-clock air support to defend against the aircraft of closer rivals. But there is no more challenging task in modern warfare than manufacturing and operating an aircraft carrier. It is the most expensive of all military hardware, requiring the construction not only of the carrier but of a fleet of up to eight support ships. Aircraft that can land on and take off from a tiny airstrip on the open seas at night must have the most advanced avionics and power plants. To manage cooperation among the ships in the task force on the open seas and to coordinate the comings and goings of numerous aircraft on a small space requires sophisticated systems engineering and logistical capabilities.

China could master these technologies, as it has mastered others. But by the time it did so, contending militaries would have advanced as well. Experts caution that the earliest China could have an aircraft carrier is the year 2010.[15] China's carrier would be less than half the size of a current U.S. carrier and would have less capable aircraft—vertical/short takeoff and landing (VSTOL) aircraft rather than high-performance jets comparable to U.S. carrier-based aircraft. Nor would a single carrier be sufficient. The U.S. Navy needs three carriers in its fleet to keep one on location at all times. Given China's less efficient logistics and maintenance operations, its navy might need four or five carriers to keep one on location. If China acquired its first carrier in 2010, it would not get its third until about 2020. U.S. forces in the Pacific and the land-based air forces of the ASEAN countries would not be standing still, so there is no guarantee that Chinese aircraft carriers would significantly improve the force-on-force balance with potential adversaries. Overseas purchase does not seem to be a way out of this dilemma, even if a foreign supplier could be identified. The price of even one carrier task force equipped with the necessary aircraft and technologies is beyond China's reach.

Whether China decides to undertake the formidable task of aircraft carrier construction will depend on many things, including funding and technology development. But it will also hinge on the assessment of its defense priorities. The 1996 Taiwan Strait crisis reaffirmed that the PLA Navy and Air Force are not yet able to dominate waters 100 miles from the Chinese coast. That two American aircraft carriers deployed 200 miles from the Chinese coast could challenge Chinese forces underscores that coastal-water defense is a more pressing priority for the PLA Navy than acquisition of aircraft carriers for power projection into the South China Sea. Indeed, recent PLA acquisitions suggest an emphasis on "green water" capability entailing an operational range of 400–600 miles. Should China decide to build aircraft carriers, it might set back the PLA's efforts to respond to more pressing needs, while contributing to an arms buildup on the part of its more developed neighbors, including Japan and the United States, and to a regional arms race it might lose.

An additional urgent hardware need is to upgrade nuclear and missile capabilities to maintain deterrence against a first strike.[16] China's nuclear strategy is to rely on what specialists call "minimal deterrence"—that is, the possession of sufficient nuclear resources to survive an enemy's first strike and retaliate against the adversary's high-value targets, such as major population centers. Beijing has tested missiles that can reach Moscow and Los Angeles. Through concealment of its relatively few missiles—in caves, for example—and missile mobility, Beijing has kept adversaries guessing about whether a first strike could completely disarm its retaliatory capability. But since its commercial satellite-launch rockets have experienced numerous failures, observers think the missiles it uses for nuclear deterrence may also be plagued by problems. Accuracy has long been a problem for Chinese missiles. Further development of U.S. antimissile technology and talk of deploying U.S. theater missile-defense systems in Japan call into doubt the long-term viability of China's second-strike capability.

Beijing cannot afford to allow its nuclear and missile technologies to stagnate. Since its first missile launch, in 1966, China has built a series of new missiles, each with improved range and accuracy. Until 1996,

China resisted American pressure to join other powers in an immediate moratorium on nuclear testing, while trying to develop a smaller nuclear warhead that would improve the accuracy of its long-range missiles and open the way to multiple-warhead devices. In 1982 China successfully tested its first submarine-launched ballistic missile (SLBM). However, only one submarine built for this missile entered service, and it has encountered problems of reliability. The submarine force would have to be enlarged before the PRC could count on SLBMs to guarantee its second-strike capability.[17]

Arms Trade, Weapons Proliferation, and Disarmament

Besides using weapons against enemies, a country can export them in order to earn money and to develop influence in other countries. Smaller powers like France, Germany, and Israel depend on arms exports to maintain defense industries. For major powers like the United States and Russia, arms sales are at once important sources of income to help maintain peacetime military production and tools of influence over arms-importing countries.

Under Mao, China supplied military assistance free to friendly regimes in North Vietnam, North Korea, Albania, Pakistan, and Tanzania. These countries were among China's few allies, and they could not afford to pay for Chinese weaponry. Countries that could afford to buy Chinese weapons tended to shun the PRC, wary of its reputation for spreading revolution and sensitive to American disapproval.

As China became a participant in the global economy under Deng Xiaoping, arms sales grew.[18] Military leaders created eight arms export companies. Some of these companies are supervised by the PLA General Staff Department under the Central Military Commission, such as China Poly Group. Others are under the Commission of Science and Technology of the State Council, such as NORINCO, and operate under the personal protection of top leaders. These enterprises often enjoy even more leeway than other foreign trade companies under the reform of the foreign trade system. Arms sales hit a peak of $3 billion in 1988, when China sold weapons to both sides in the Iran-Iraq war. After the war ended, sales declined to less than $1 billion by 1993, far below the over $10 billion of 1993 U.S. exports. Compared with that of major arms suppliers like the United States, France, and the Soviet Union, the value of Chinese exports is modest. Moreover, because they are defense industries, their revenue is managed by the State Council rather than by the military.

China's primary weapons exports include field artillery, anti-aircraft artillery, including rocket launchers and short-range missiles, armored personnel carriers, tanks, and a limited number of naval vessels. China enjoys a comparative advantage in the international arms market in that its technology is often appropriate for Third World situations and its prices are lower than those of the advanced industrial countries. For close neighbors Thailand, Pakistan, and Burma, arms sales at friendship prices reinforce broader security relations. Of these three countries, Thailand has been the most active arms buyer, acquiring Chinese trucks, artillery, tanks, and frigates.

For the most part, China has been one seller among many in the international bazaar in conventional weapons. But its transfers of nuclear technology and certain types of missiles have attracted global concern. In the early 1980s China provided Algeria with a nuclear reactor. Profit was apparently the motive, since China had no strong strategic or economic ties with Algeria. The sale was criticized by the United States, but China defended it as falling within International Atomic Energy Agency safeguards and went ahead with it. In 1988 China delivered internationally proscribed CSS-2 ballistic missiles to Saudi Arabia. The deal was profitable for the PLA and helped persuade Saudi Arabia to break relations with Taiwan. But the missiles also could have destabilized the balance of power in the Middle East. Given the fragility of peace there and the destructive potential of the missiles, the delivery prompted the Reagan administration to impose sanctions on certain technology exports to China. Chinese leaders moved to limit the damage by assuring the United States that they would not supply Saudi Arabia with nuclear warheads for the missiles.

Since the end of the Cold War, China's record on arms transfers and nuclear reactor exports has been relatively clean. In the early 1990s China was negotiating to sell M-9 missiles to Syria, but canceled the agreement in 1992 after lengthy negotiations with the United States. In 1992, following the U.S. decision to sell F-16s to Taiwan, Beijing undertook to help Iran develop a nuclear reactor. In response to complaints from the United States and its allies that China was helping a terrorist state go nuclear, China announced in 1995 that it would suspend the agreement. The one glaring exception to China's accommodation of U.S. interests is its long-term program of assistance to the Pakistani nuclear weapons program. Because Pakistan is its sole ally in South Asia, Beijing has an interest in protecting its security against greater Indian power (Chapter 6). Over the years China has supplied Pakistan with a nuclear reactor, numerous nuclear weapons components, and specialist assistance. In 1992, to render the Pakistani deterrent more credible, China shipped the nuclear-capable middle-range M-11 missile to Pakistan. Beijing has resisted American pressure to terminate its nuclear and missile assistance to Islamabad. Chinese foreign affairs specialists point out that PRC policy toward Pakistan is similar to U.S. policy toward Israel. Instead of assuming direct responsibility for the defense of Israel, Washington looked the other way when Israel developed a nuclear deterrent. So too, China provided the most practical form of defense assistance to Pakistan within its means. Chinese analysts also argue that Pakistan's U.S.-provided F-16 aircraft are more formidable instruments for the delivery of both conventional and nuclear weapons onto Indian territory.

China has been more cautious than its image as a rogue arms exporter would suggest. Nonetheless, it has refused to commit itself to various arms control agreements, creating uncertainty about its intentions. Arms exports are one of the few options that China has for retaliating against American policies that challenge its interests. The transfer of M-11 missiles to Pakistan and the agreement to help Iran build a nuclear reactor both followed the 1992 U.S. decision to sell 150 F-16s to Taiwan. It is useful to have the United States worry that China might open its stockpiles to Third World countries. This is one reason Beijing refuses to commit to abide fully by the Missile Technology Control Regime, the agreement among the major producers of missiles controlling the export of certain categories of missiles. When U.S. diplomats raise the issue of Chinese missile proliferation, PRC diplomats raise the issue of U.S. proliferation of advanced weaponry on Taiwan.

Beijing's policies on other arms control agreements also reflect national security concerns.[19] In a 1995 white paper on arms control and disarmament, its first on this subject, China reiterated its long-standing position that it will disarm completely of nuclear weapons when the two superpowers do so themselves.[20] But China has refused to enter into nuclear arms reduction talks. Even a 50 percent reduction in the nuclear stockpiles of Russia and the United States would maintain their overwhelming strategic superiority and leave unaffected their ability to threaten China with massive destruction. Not until both of these powers reduce their stockpiles to China's level could Beijing become an equal partner in the negotiations. In July 1996, Chinese leaders announced a moratorium on nuclear testing. They have endorsed the comprehensive nuclear test ban and have committed the PRC to signing an agreement, but they have also warned that China would reconsider its commitment to the treaty if the United States were to deploy a theater missile-defense system in Asia that undermined China's second-strike deterrent capability. Unlike the United States, China has committed itself to a policy of no-first-use of nuclear weapons. This policy reflects Chinese strategic circumstances. Beijing would have to use nuclear weapons only against the United States or Russia, whose conventional forces are superior to China's, but in so doing it would undoubtedly incur massive nuclear retaliation, societal destruction, and military defeat; it thus has no incentive to use nuclear weapons first.

China has entered into confidence-building measures with a number of states on its periphery, especially Russia and the Central Asian states. Such measures increase military transparency by sharing information about military capabilities and troop movements. In Northeast and Southeast Asia, however, China has resisted U.S.-backed efforts to increase transparency. This may reflect its relative military weakness in these regions. In a modern version of the Empty Fortress stratagem, Chinese leaders may wish to allow their capability to appear more threatening than it is. This may be appropriate policy for contending with the great powers, but it undermines the confidence of China's smaller neighbors. The risk of this posture is that other countries may gird themselves against a threat that does not exist and thus undermine Chinese security.

China is often charged with exporting dual-use technology and materials—materials that have both civilian and military uses. In 1996 a Chinese corporation sold ring magnets used for uranium enrichment to Pakistan. Reports of Chinese exports of dual-use chemicals raise concern about proliferation of proscribed chemical weaponry. But in contrast to missile sales and nuclear energy agreements with Libya and Pakistan, some dual-use exports may not be the outcome of central government decisions. The May 1996 Clinton administration decision to refrain from sanctions in retaliation against the transfer of ring magnets to Pakistan reflected its understanding that Beijing has only limited ability to regulate the behavior of the numerous and scattered firms that produce dual-use technologies. A comprehensive export-control system is difficult to develop. The U.S. government employs numerous scientists and engineers to evaluate the dual-use potential of a profusion of civilian technologies, has a finely graded regulatory system reflecting the scientific subtleties of such technologies, and enforces the regulations with an effective licensing and sanctioning system. The Chinese government lacks both the expertise and the resources to impose such a system. The weakening of centralized authority in China has reduced the government's ability to control the international proliferation of dangerous materials and technologies to irresponsible states.

The PLA, Chinese Security, and World Order in the Twenty-first Century

The PLA has made progress since the end of the Mao era in the training of soldiers and the management of troops, thus enhancing joint-warfare capability. Downsizing and a renewed focus on war fighting has enabled the PLA to become a professional military capable of far more effective operations than it was in 1979, when it fared so poorly against Vietnamese troops. But these improvements in its capabilities have occurred mainly in the land forces. A modern air force and navy will require more funding and advanced technology than the PLA currently possesses. In this respect the PLA still has a long way to go before it catches up to the capabilities of many of its neighbors in East Asia. In many important areas, including those of advanced aircraft engines, avionics and communications technologies, it continues to fall behind advanced world levels.

This complex pattern of PLA modernization has implications for Chinese security. On the one hand, mainland China is more secure from invasion than at any other time in the last 150 years. On the other hand, its military remains the most backward among the great-power armies in East Asia. This undermines China's ability to develop alliances and influence adversaries beyond the mainland. China remains vulnerable to military challenges in its coastal waters, unable to win an air war against Taiwan, and unable to project power to defend its territorial claims to the Spratly Islands. Military modernization must advance further before it can fulfill the demands placed on it by policymakers.

For the foreseeable future China will lack the resources to compete as a military equal with the other great powers, much less establish regional domination or become a global superpower. But China could play

the role of the spoiler, creating sufficient disruptions to cause chronic security concerns among its neighbors and to prevent the consolidation of
stable regional and global orders. Beijing has preserved its options to export destabilizing weaponry, suggesting that it could cause trouble if it
becomes dissatisfied with U.S. policies or with a regional order that does
not incorporate Chinese interests. In addition, it lacks the ability adequately to control its own export of dangerous dual-use equipment and
technologies.

Engaging China in arms control negotiations and confidence-
building measures may offer the best approach for contending with these
issues. Agreements that reflect Chinese interests as well as the interests
of the other great powers will give China a stake in maintaining the regional order. Such agreements can also provide the basis for multilateral
sanctions against destabilizing Chinese policies. Through multilateral institutions China's more advanced collaborators can provide technical assistance to help China develop a more effective export-control system.
Negotiation combined with deterrence offers the most productive way to
channel Chinese military behavior toward constructive objectives.

9

DILEMMAS OF OPENING: FOREIGN ECONOMIC RELATIONS

I N THE EARLY nineteenth century the expanding world market appeared at China's borders in the form of English ships trading opium for tea. In a series of wars foreigners forced China to open itself to trade, investment, and the mission movement. By the end of the century Chinese leaders concluded that economic backwardness was the chief cause of their country's military weakness. How to modernize for wealth and power while preserving national independence became the leading issue in Chinese politics. The Chinese debated whether to modernize by integrating with the world economy or by seeking self-reliance.

Both autarky and integration found advocates. The attraction of autarky was that China could rely on its own resources to develop, avoid dependence on foreign capital and markets, and retain cultural purity. The argument for integration was that it would allow faster development and give China a better chance to catch up with the technology of the West. Autarky would preserve China behind a Great Wall, but it might not be strong enough to protect the country. Integration would dismantle the Wall, but without any assurance that China would then be able to resist outside pressures.

The choice was constrained by the world economy and China's strategic situation. A post–World War I world trade boom allowed China to develop foreign trade. Protectionist trends in the 1930s stimulated the Chinese to think about self-reliant development. After 1949 China was able for a time to borrow capital and technology from the Soviet Union. But Mao Zedong's decision simultaneously to confront the Western and Soviet camps left China in the 1960s with no alternative to autarky. By the time Deng Xiaoping came to power, Mao had already reopened channels to the West. Deng was able to make the decision to seek Western trade and investment to accelerate growth.

Foreign economic policy is always closely linked with domestic economics and politics. Mao's self-reliant development model was based on capital accumulated by repressing living standards and political freedoms. Deng's open-door policy brought in foreign capital and trade, but at the cost of greater vulnerability to Western influence not only in the economy but in culture and politics.

Deng's reforms encountered opposition, but in time they gained wide support. With each new step of reform imports surged, foreign exchange tightened, inflationary pressures mounted, and conservatives complained about the loss of cultural and ideological discipline. In response Deng decreed retrenchments in 1979, 1986, and 1988. Each retrenchment reduced inflation and tightened discipline, but slowed growth and provoked protests from pro-reform officials in the regions and bureaucracies that profited most from the open door. Each retrenchment soon gave way to a new phase of reform and accelerated growth that benefited wider circles of the population.

The 1989 democracy movement was sparked in part by public opposition to the inflation and corruption associated with the open-door policy. But the policy survived the suppression of the movement and gained new momentum in 1992 when Deng Xiaoping made a symbolic tour of the southern open zones to reaffirm his commitment to reform and opening.

China is not unique in the fact that its economic integration into the world has ambiguous implications for security, making the country at once stronger and more vulnerable to outside influence. But the issues are sharper for poor than for rich countries, for exporters of labor and importers of capital and technology, and for those that joined the world trading system late and that have as yet little influence over its rules. There are still sectors of Chinese society and the bureaucracy whose members view themselves as losers from that decision.[1] Their influence over policy is receding, but their voices are still heard. The farther the benefits of integration spread in Chinese society, the less realistic is the option of a return to autarky. But the open-door policy remains controversial because the decision for integration was so recent and so contested.

TRADE REFORM

Deng Xiaoping's open-door reforms began with trade. Under Mao, China practiced radical import substitution.[2] Mao's planners treated foreign trade as a residual activity, a way to get rid of the leftovers of the domestic economy and acquire those few necessities still not produced at home. China exported just a sufficient amount of agricultural products, minerals, and fuels that happened to be in surplus to cover the costs of machinery, equipment, and steel that had to be imported for the industrialization drive. Limited virtually to the Soviet bloc, China's foreign trade passed its high point of $4.38 billion in 1959 and then dropped to a low of $2.66 billion in 1962 before rebounding slightly as China shipped textiles, foodstuffs, and metal ores to the Soviet Union to repay its debts for development help. In this period China ranked with Singapore in the value of its exports.

As relations with the West thawed in the early 1970s, China climbed back into the lower-middle ranks of world trading nations. In 1973 China made its largest overseas purchases since the period of Soviet aid, importing industrial plants from the United States, Japan, and Europe. By 1976, the last year of Mao's life, foreign trade had risen to $13.4 billion, with Japan and Hong Kong the leading partners.[3] China still accepted no foreign loans or investments.

Shortly before Mao's death, Deng Xiaoping, then serving as deputy premier, advocated limited changes in trade policy. He did not break with Mao's slogans but reinterpreted them, arguing, "By self-reliance we mean that a country should mainly rely on the strength and wisdom of its own people, control its own economic lifelines, and make full use of its resources."[4] He called for selectively importing advanced foreign technologies, paying for them with increased exports of arts and crafts products, industrial products, and mining products, and taking advantage of certain standard international practices like long-term trade credits and compensation trade, whereby China could pay for technology and equipment imports with the resulting products.

Deng's rivals denounced his proposals as currying favor with the capitalist world, promoting old-fashioned arts and crafts in preference to modern industry, and selling off national resources and sovereignty. They argued that Deng's policies would make China "a market where imperialist countries dump their goods, a raw material base, a repair and assembly workshop, and an investment center," placing China in a position of permanent backwardness and dependency on the West.[5]

After returning to power in 1978, Deng renewed his proposals. He argued that bigger foreign exchange earnings would enable China to import more advanced equipment, speed industrialization, and be more independent. In enriching the nation's treasury there was nothing wrong with making use of China's resources, especially labor and raw materials, or with taking advantage of standard business conveniences like trade credits.[6]

Under Mao foreign trade had been monopolized by about a dozen special corporations under the Ministry of Foreign Trade, which processed the paperwork for imports and exports required by the state plan. Deng's government spread the rights to buy and sell commodities abroad among what eventually became thousands of trading companies that belonged to central government ministries, provincial governments, and government-owned enterprises. Step by step China reduced tariffs and lightened administrative controls over imports.

Government trading companies were still not free-market entities, although they were moving in that direction. They followed central or provincial government plans, did overseas business under central government licenses, kept their foreign exchange in the government bank, and exchanged it for domestic currency according to a complex, fluctuating schedule of official rates. But they and their supervising agencies were allowed to keep a portion of the profit they earned. This energized them. China's foreign trade increased at an average annual rate of 15 percent, starting from its takeoff in 1984, and stood at $281 billion in 1995. China ran modest deficits in some years and modest surpluses in others, but the state regulated trade closely enough that imports and exports tracked each other closely from one year to the next.

China's trade is heavily oriented toward the industrialized countries. The main trading partners in 1995 were, in order, Japan, Hong Kong, the United States, Taiwan, South Korea, and Germany.[7] The post-Soviet states remain locally important partners for the border regions because of geographic closeness, but their total share in China's foreign trade was only 2.8 percent in 1994. Trade relations reflect the combination of China's inexpensive labor force and its technological backwardness. China exports chiefly labor-intensive products like toys, footwear, clothing, and inexpensive electronic consumer products. Chinese firms assemble raw materials or components provided by foreign partners, or repay a foreign supplier of technology or equipment with export products produced with that technology or equipment.

On the import side, China purchases high-tech products like airplanes; equipment and machinery to expand the industrial base; fertilizer to expand agricultural productivity; grain to free agricultural land for industrial uses or more-profitable crops; and cotton, yarn, and fabric to supply its textile and garment industries. Following the logic of comparative advantage, China imports semifinished goods from Taiwan and Hong Kong, finishes them in Taiwan- and Hong Kong–owned factories in the mainland, and reexports them; China sells agricultural products to land-poor South Korea, supplies food, beverages, crude oil, and textiles to Japan in return for cars and televisions, and supplies consumer products to the Russian Far East.

As China's integration into the world market advanced, irrationalities flourished at the interface between the half-reformed command economy at home and markets outside. For example, firms exporting products like oil, coal, grain, and cotton, long ago assigned low prices to encourage the growth of new industries, were actually exporting to foreigners subsidies intended for Chinese consumers. On the import side, products like polyester clothing, automobiles, and consumer electronics items, which had been priced high in the 1950s to bring profits to new state enterprises, could fetch windfall profits for importers in the 1980s and 1990s because they were available more cheaply abroad. Yet such imports wasted foreign exchange and damaged domestic producers. Exporters and importers alike traded under a government-controlled exchange rate that inflated the value of the Chinese dollar (renminbi or yuan). As part of state planning the Ministry of Finance was required to subsidize foreign exchange losses that resulted.

The long-run answers to these problems were price reform and foreign exchange reform, matters that were slow, difficult, and controversial because of the many domestic interests affected and the possibility of inflation. Price reform began as soon as the reforms did, and has proceeded since then in fits and starts. Government control of foreign exchange transactions was loosened in the mid-1980s, when certain firms were allowed to trade domestic and foreign currencies at controlled but near-market rates in "swap centers." In 1994 the government introduced a managed floating exchange rate system, in which the official exchange rate merged with the "swap rate" and floated under the influence of supply and demand with loose government supervision.

As reform advanced, the government tried to control surges and patch up irrationalities in foreign trade with ad hoc mechanisms such as import licenses, export subsidies, tariffs, tax rebates, exchange rate manipulations, administrative controls over foreign exchange expenditures, and shifts in the percentages of profit or foreign exchange that trading firms could retain. These measures were not only expensive; they embroiled China in frequent conflicts with trading partners, who accused Beijing of protectionism and dumping (exporting products at below cost). The advanced industrial countries pushed China to accept quotas on the exports of textiles and other products, and to honor foreign standards of hygiene, packaging, labeling, and the environmental friendliness of goods destined for export.

The United States was often the leader in trade-related disputes, although it was not alone in its concerns. America consistently ran a large deficit with China, amounting to $33.8 billion in 1995, by American calculations.[8] Specialists projected that as Japan's trade surplus with the United States declined and China's rose, it would become America's biggest trade imbalance with any country and might top $100 billion by the year 2000. Opening China's markets was a major American concern. Citing provisions of its own law, the United States demanded far-reaching and rapid changes in China's trade regime. In 1992 China agreed to a market access agreement giving the United States unprecedented entry to Chinese markets and exposing the Chinese auto, pharmaceutical, chemical, and other industries to sharp foreign competition. But China was slow to implement its promises. Among other reasons for this, local governments used the powers they had been granted for promoting trade to find ways to restrict trade in order to protect local industries.

The United States and China also engaged in a long struggle over intellectual property rights (patents and copyrights in such intellectual products as chemical and pharmaceutical formulas, computer software, books, music on CDs, and movies on videotape). Under Mao intellectual products had been considered common social property that should be popularized rather than protected. In 1985 the Chinese government implemented its first patent law, but Western businesses considered it inadequate. Corruption and an ineffective legal system prevented the government from fulfilling its commitments. In 1991 the United States gave China an ultimatum to pay copyright fees or suffer trade sanctions. Similar ultimatums were delivered in 1994 and 1996.

In each case China at first threatened countersanctions but then made major concessions. In each case the United States was dissatisfied and demanded more changes and better enforcement. In the course of these negotiations Beijing agreed both to enact new laws and regulations with U.S. advice (such as amendments to the Chinese patent law in 1992) and to allow such international standards as the Berne Convention for the Protection of Literary and Artistic Works to prevail over China's domestic legislation in case of conflict.

From 1986 on, Beijing also found itself embroiled in multilateral negotiations over accession to the World Trade Organization (formerly GATT).[9] China hoped membership would help it gain permanent most-favored-nation trading access to its major market, the United States. Membership would also mean partial relief from bilateral trade negotiations with the United States, since some trade issues would be referred to the world body, where China would often find allies against U.S. demands.[10] And once in the WTO, China would be among the rule makers in an organization that operates by consensus.

To join, China was asked to commit itself to meeting WTO standards of market openness applicable to the world's advanced economies within a specified period. This would have required major changes in trade policy, price administration, foreign exchange controls, customs administration, and banking and currency regulations. Chinese leaders were willing to make some sacrifices but not to abandon protected and inefficient state industries like chemicals, pharmaceuticals, automobiles, and electronics to potentially devastating foreign competition without a long adjustment period. China's negotiators cited poverty and backwardness in asking to prolong many of the reform measures under the concessionary program that the WTO has offered to other countries at similar stages in their economic development, including Japan and South Korea.

The United States and other Western nations retorted that China is too large a world trader to enjoy for an extended period the privileges enjoyed by developing countries. They wanted China to agree to an accession agreement requiring its relatively rapid compliance with the trade norms applicable to the advanced industrial economies. Such a big trader had to be brought into the world trading regime somehow, yet no practicable level of concessions would turn it into a true market economy in the foreseeable future.

China's entry into world markets was unprecedented for its speed and scope, with benefits felt throughout the booming economy. But integration came at a cost to China's autonomy. Foreign officials monitored Chinese tariffs, import quotas, certification requirements, manufacturing hygiene, financial services, and retail networks. American customs, Food and Drug Administration, and Commerce Department officials showed up to inspect Chinese factories. Foreign lawyers pointed out enforcement failures and suggested revisions in Chinese laws and regulations. Each step toward integration with world markets gave greater influence over China's economy to rule makers in Washington and Geneva, Tokyo and Brussels, and to impersonal markets with whom no face-to-face negotiation was possible. At a time when Chinese leaders doubted the benevolence of American attitudes toward their country, each step made the health of China's economy more dependent on the American market and the American dollar, the main currency in which China's foreign exchange reserves are held. China had opened its economy to deeper foreign influence than at any time since the era of Soviet aid in the 1950s.

FOREIGN CAPITAL

The second main element of the open-door reform was a decision to allow foreign capital to enter China. As with trade, the results of importing foreign capital were economically profitable but had political costs.

Some foreign funds came in the form of official development loans and grants. In 1978 China accepted assistance from the UN Development Program (UNDP). In 1980 it joined the International Monetary Fund (IMF) and the World Bank, and in 1986 the Asian Development Bank (ADB). By 1995 China had received $13.9 billion from the World Bank, $325 million from the UNDP, and $322 million from other UN agencies.[11] Around this time Beijing also began to accept aid from foreign governments, especially Japan. In 1993–94 China was the single largest recipient of official development assistance, receiving 6.6 percent of the world total.[12]

Foreign assistance brought foreign influence. In order to become eligible for World Bank assistance, China cooperated with a World Bank study team that gathered sensitive data from government offices and filed a three-volume report containing controversial recommendations to push China in a market reform direction. This was followed by additional studies recommending further market reforms. The key managers of world capitalism, especially the IMF and the World Bank, had inserted themselves into Chinese politics, putting their weight behind the regime's reformists against the conservatives.[13] To join the ADB, China made a concession to Western concerns by agreeing to allow Taiwan to continue as a member under the name of "China, Taipei" (Chapter 12). After the Tiananmen incident of June 1989, the United States used its dominant voting rights in the World Bank and the ADB to block most kinds of new loans to China for several years; Japan postponed some of its official development assistance (ODA) loans. In 1995 Japan suspended its ODA grants (but not loans) to protest China's underground nuclear testing.

Compared with official assistance, private investment was a bigger source of foreign capital. Private investment included portfolio investment (stocks and bonds), commercial lending, and foreign direct investment (FDI); the latter in turn included wholly owned foreign firms, joint ventures, compensation trade, coproduction, and cooperative development, among other forms. The most important form of foreign investment has been joint ventures, which in recent years have accounted for 50 percent of the total FDI in China.[14]

The government initially conceived of foreign investment as a limited tool to accelerate the growth of exports by inserting foreign capital and expertise into the export sector of the state-owned economy. The 1979 joint-venture law encouraged technological upgrading for overseas sales, and policy at the time usually restricted the foreign partner to no more than 49 percent of the enterprise. With only state enterprises available as joint-venture partners on the Chinese side, this left majority control in the hands of the government.

Initial encounters with foreign investors brought unexpected results and required changes in policy. Investors who were willing to meet the Chinese priority for export were usually not the ones who could upgrade Chinese manufacturing technology. They fell chiefly into two categories—natural-resources companies looking for oil, coal, and other raw materials, and Taiwan and Hong Kong firms seeking to move labor-intensive operations onto the mainland so that they could take advantage of cheap labor and, in some cases, of China's textile and clothing quotas for export to the United States and Europe. To critics, such investments either committed natural-resources production on a long-term basis to foreign markets, thus removing it from domestic supply, or put China in the position of a supplier of low-cost labor to outside entrepreneurs, who kept most of the profits.

On the other hand, there were many foreign investors who might provide new manufacturing and managerial technology but had little interest in export, although they might ship some products overseas in order to get a foot in the Chinese door. Because of the low prices of food, housing, and consumer goods, Chinese consumers command more purchasing power than is apparent from the value of their incomes expressed in dollars. Many companies were eager to establish facilities to supply Chinese buyers with televisions, pharmaceuticals, baby food, cosmetics, and cars—or, later, to enter the services market. Cross-purposes about export versus domestic markets bedeviled a number of foreign-invested ventures.

Foreign investors complained about inadequate Chinese ports, roads, railways, electric power, telephones, banking services, laws, and courts; about bureaucracy, corruption, and political instability; about high rents, license fees, and taxes; about distribution problems and obstacles to profit repatriation; and about inadequate living conditions. But in the long run hundreds of American, Japanese, and European companies like Coca-Cola, MacDonald's, Heinz, Toshiba, and Colgate-Palmolive found China a congenial place in which to invest. Western- and Japanese-brand goods manufactured in China reached an estimated 200 million Chinese consumers in 1995, and the distribution networks were expanding constantly.[15] One by one government firebreaks against the extent and type of foreign investment fell. The government raised the ceiling on the size of projects that could be approved at the province and ministry level, encouraged 100 percent foreign-owned enterprises, allowed foreigners to gain virtual ownership of land by means of the purchase of use rights for up to seventy years, made it easier for foreign-invested enterprises to exchange Chinese currency for foreign exchange and to repatriate foreign exchange, provided tax holidays on profits and exemptions from some import duties, and allowed foreign banks, law firms, and other service institutions to set up offices in China.[16]

In 1990 the State Council authorized the establishment of a special zone in Shanghai's Pudong district to serve as a center for foreign financial and services enterprises. In 1994 the government removed restrictions on foreign investment in freeways, power plants, telecommunications, and other infrastructure projects in most provinces. By 1995, except for those related to China's traditional national industries (such as crafts and Chinese medicines), media, and military industries, almost all sectors of the economy were open to foreign investment.

As another way of controlling the impact of FDI, early government policy sought to limit its geographic extent. Both to attract and to quarantine foreign investment, in 1979–80 the government designated four small districts in southern China, including Shenzhen, as special economic zones (SEZs). Their tax concessions and up-to-date infrastructure were intended to lure foreign capital. In the same spirit as the joint-venture policy, the SEZs were meant to be centers for the manufacture of exports. While export-oriented firms did locate there, so did thousands of Chinese trading companies that engaged chiefly in import. Hundreds of hotels and office buildings were also built. In addition, the SEZs attracted investment from inland enterprises seeking to take advantage of the concessions aimed at foreign investors, sometimes by fraudulently channeling funds out of China and back through Hong Kong.

Part of the attraction of SEZs to local governments was the myth that foreign investors would provide not only the tenants but most of the infrastructure for the zones, which had to be built from scratch. But few outside investors wanted to put money into infrastructure in the early years of the open policy, because such projects were expected to take decades to pay back. In the end Shenzhen and the other zones were built chiefly with billions of dollars of central and provincial government money. Singapore, Hong Kong, and Japanese interests later put money into port facilities and industrial parks, mainly in established cities outside the SEZs.

For all these reasons Chinese critics argued that the SEZs were expensive, speculative, and unproductive. Yet the policy spread in response to demand from local governments that wanted a chance to compete for foreign investment. In 1984 SEZ-like investment incentives were extended to fourteen coastal cities and the island of Hainan (later made a province). In 1988 the government opened the entire coastal region from Liaoning in the north to Guangdong in the south, while relaxing conditions for investment. Now both capital and management could come mainly or even wholly from overseas investors rather than be restricted to Chinese-dominated joint ventures. Foreign-invested enterprises were no longer pressured to source their raw materials in China, but were encouraged to import them, so China might supply only cheap labor to such a project. Whereas the old policy emphasized that foreign investors should install advanced modern technology, the new policy was hospitable to labor-intensive industries like clothing, handicrafts, and light-industrial products using old-fashioned technologies. And China eased its demand that foreign investors pay wages far out of line with those paid in China's own enterprises.

In 1992, after Deng Xiaoping reaffirmed his commitment to the open policy with a heralded inspection tour of the southern open zones, the central government further extended foreign investment incentives to the country's major inland river ports and to all provincial capitals, and authorized a horde of new duty-free and high-technology development zones. Local governments throughout the country that lacked central authorization competed to offer comparable tax breaks, factory sites, and conveniences like priority access to electrical power and rail service. In outbidding rivals, some local authorities informally waived pollution control requirements and drove farmers off land that investors wanted. By 1993, governments around the country had reportedly applied to establish 1,200 economic development zones.[17] Although foreign investment and trade remained concentrated in the coastal areas, some Chinese argued that foreign investment was now welcomed so universally that special local concessions were unnecessary. The SEZs might as well be phased out.

Foreign direct investment flowed unabated even after the political disturbances of 1989. Through 1994 China had, according to official statistics, absorbed $95.6 billion in FDI since the initiation of the open policy.[18] But economic liberalization allowed capital to leave China as well as enter it. After subtracting the funds that flowed out of the country in the form of outward-bound investment and certain years' trade deficits, the net inflow of capital was a modest $38.4 billion (in the period 1982–93).[19] The main sources of FDI were Hong Kong (supplying 63 percent in 1993), Taiwan (11 percent in 1993), the United States (7 percent in 1993), and Japan (5 percent in 1993).[20] Hong Kong stood so far in the lead partly because it served as a conduit for investment from Taiwan and elsewhere.

The impact of foreign capital was greater than its face value might suggest. (In the United States, $40 billion is the price of about eight aircraft carriers or twenty B-2 bombers.) Foreign investment had explosive effects because it brought with it technology, management practices, and access to international markets and ways of thinking. According to one official source, by the end of 1994, enterprises with some share of foreign investment employed over 12 million workers and accounted for 13.9 percent of the country's industrial output value and 37 percent of its foreign trade.[21] Foreign-invested world-class hotels and office buildings define the skylines of Beijing and Shanghai. (China claims to have become the fifth-largest tourist destination in the world, welcoming 46.4 million visitors in 1995.) Joint-venture cars fill the streets beneath billboards advertising Japanese-brand television sets and cameras. Local party officials all over the country communicate with one another by Motorola cellular phones. Foreign enterprises exert linkage and demonstration effects throughout the economy on suppliers, consumers, and competitors, as when Chinese hotels improve service to compete and Chinese parts makers raise quality to supply joint-venture car factories.

Along the coast parts of the countryside are spotted with Taiwanese-managed shrimp ponds producing for export. Hundreds of square miles in southern Guangdong have been turned into a virtual Greater Hong Kong, where an estimated three million PRC citizens produce export products for Hong Kong entrepreneurs. People in this region watch Hong Kong television, drink Hong Kong soft drinks, dress in the Hong Kong style, and circulate the Hong Kong dollar. In such areas, consumer China has buried revolutionary China, to the delight of some Chinese and the regret of others.

In interior and mountainous regions where transport is poor and natural resources sparse, it is not the presence but the absence of foreign investment that causes dissatisfaction. Because they cannot compete, these areas are falling further behind even though they are growing faster than before. Tens of millions of their residents have migrated to the coastal regions to work. In a kind of cargo cult, some poor communities have used money painfully levied from the local farmers to clear land and build boulevards, office buildings, hotels, factories, and even railheads, hoping to attract outside tenants, who often do not come.

Like foreign trade, the widespread benefits of foreign investment come at a cost to Chinese autonomy. Moody's and Standard and Poor's pass judgment on the value of China's sovereign credit. Faceless market forces instantaneously set the value of Chinese stocks and bonds with no possibility of appeal. The need to create a good investment climate pushes China to promulgate and revise laws and regulations to meet foreign standards. In 1982 China found it necessary to amend its constitution to include a commitment to protect "the lawful rights and interests" of foreign investors. While the last imperialist lease on Chinese territory was running out in Hong Kong, a new seventy-year lease of land use rights was granted to a Japanese construction firm to build a port city in Hainan.[22] Visiting Shenzhen during the early period of reform, one conservative leader charged that foreign enterprises were demanding so many privileges that China risked returning to the Qing policy of foreign concessions exempt from Chinese law.[23]

The economic opening has had deep effects on Chinese society and culture. Foreign funds have helped the nonstate sector grow faster than the state sector. State enterprises have thrown some of their social-welfare functions overboard in order to compete for foreign markets and investment. Justly or not, some Chinese blame foreign investment at least partly for a widening gap between the inland and the coast and between urban and rural incomes.

By the mid-1990s China had dispatched an estimated 140,000 students and scholars abroad in an effort to acquire advanced world technology, mostly to the United States.[24] Many of these students did not return, but those who did carried advanced knowledge contributing to China's modernization and university reforms. Some Chinese complained that returned intellectuals also brought in Western ideas that undermined official ideology. Western-oriented economists, bankers, lawyers, and traders helped China compete in the world economy, but conservative critics charged that exposure to the West led young people to lose faith in old values and to believe that "even the moon is brighter in the West."

The world economic system thus created constituencies both for and against itself in China's domestic politics, as it has in other trading nations. Many Chinese have profited greatly from integration into the world, and their political power is growing. But controversy has not ended. Some Chinese have been left behind, for others change is too fast, and still others are concerned about China's loss of autonomy in the world system.

CHINA AS AN ECONOMIC POWER

The open-door policy not only made China more vulnerable to the West; it also gave China more economic influence in the world. China had by

1995 become the world's tenth-largest trader, with favorable trade balances with all of its trade partners except Japan, Germany, Italy, and Canada, and had accumulated a foreign exchange reserve estimated at $75.4 billion, fourth largest in the world after those of Japan, Taiwan, and the United States.

China's importance as a trade and investment partner has altered its strategic situation in a fundamental way. It is almost unthinkable that the rest of the world would unite to isolate China as the West did in the era of containment. After the Beijing massacre of 1989, the industrialized world imposed only limited sanctions and quickly lifted most of them (Chapter 10). Economics counts in smaller arenas as well. Trade and investment prospects contributed to South Korea's shift of diplomatic recognition from Taipei to Beijing in 1992. In Hong Kong the business community supported China in most of its battles with the pro-reform British governor, Chris Patten, believing that economic ties with China would do more for Hong Kong than would political reforms. Taiwanese investment in the mainland provides an incentive against independence for the island (Chapter 11).

At the same time, China's importance as a trade partner creates opposition in some countries. For example, in the United States, the European Community, and Japan, labor and industry groups affected by Chinese imports have demanded more antidumping investigations directed at China than at any other country.[25] And such groups often promote opposition to Chinese human rights and defense policies to gain political backing for their trade concerns.

China is a major export competitor for some neighboring economies. In 1994 it exported half the toys on the world market, two-thirds of the shoes, and most of the world's bicycles, lamps, power tools, and sweaters.[26] China also competes with other countries to attract capital, especially development capital at preferential terms. In 1994 China absorbed 15 percent of the world's total FDI, second only to the United States.[27] It had taken 8 percent of cumulative World Bank lending as of June 1995, borrowed 32 percent of Asian Development Bank financing in 1994, and was the largest single aid recipient in the world.[28]

The size of China's population makes the country potentially a major purchaser in world grain markets. Although most Chinese specialists believe their country's grain needs are too large ever to rely substantially on the world market, China uses the world market to supplement domestic production. The high point so far was in 1989, when it absorbed 6 percent of the cereals on the international market, 13 percent of the wheat and wheat flour, and 6 percent of the rice.[29] The future might bring higher numbers. Expanding factories, roads, airports, and housing are chewing up arable land. Water is too scarce to provide the intensive irrigation that green-revolution strains of rice and wheat need in order to supply higher outputs per acre. The population is not only growing in size but changing its diet. As people use their new wealth to buy more eggs, meat, farmed fish, and beer, it takes more grain to meet each person's needs. If production does not keep up with demand, China will have to rely more on overseas purchases. One specialist points out that if China were ever to try to import grain at a per capita level comparable to that of Taiwan or South Korea, it would need more grain than is currently available on world markets.[30]

Energy demand is soaring in China's economy. The country has vast reserves of both coal and oil (some of it offshore), and it is developing them with foreign assistance. The government has also invested heavily in nuclear power. China briefly exported fossil fuels, but now its industrial boom has made it a net importer. If China's demand for imported fossil fuels were to rise rapidly, world prices could be affected. Locally China has emerged as a major supplier of coal to South Korea and a significant supplier of oil to Japan, giving Beijing some economic leverage over these two important neighbors.

China is one of the most polluted countries in the world. Aside from the enormous economic and health costs to the Chinese themselves, some of their environmental problems have international consequences. These include emission of ozone-depleting substances, coastal pollution that pushes Chinese fishermen farther into the Pacific Ocean, ocean dumping of solid waste, and habitat destruction and the reduction of biodiversity.

Burning a ton of coal per person per year, China is a major contributor to the production of carbon dioxide, a greenhouse gas that helps cause global warming. (Rice paddies and herds of grazing cattle emit large amounts of methane, also a greenhouse gas.) Coal burning also contributes to acid rain, carried by prevailing winds to Korea and Japan. But a wholesale switch from domestically produced coal is not an option. China is developing nuclear power, but nuclear plants are expensive, slow to build, require sophisticated safety equipment, and pose the risk of major environmental damage in case of breakdown. Major hydropower projects like the Three Gorges Dam entail habitat damage and population displacements and have proven internationally controversial.

China is increasing oil imports, since domestic production seems to have hit a ceiling. But oil carries its own environmental problems, and these will worsen as Beijing implements its commitment to develop the domestic automobile industry and supply the emerging middle class with private cars. Coal remains the only way to meet a large fraction of China's soaring energy needs.

Beijing has shown a willingness to recognize its shared interest in the global commons and to cooperate with evolving world standards. It has created the National Environmental Protection Administration (NEPA), as well as local environmental protection agencies, and signed a number of international environmental agreements. The government is phasing out the household use of charcoal briquettes and requiring state-owned factories to burn coal more efficiently and to install emissions-scrubbing equipment. But China draws the line at slowing the pace of its own development to ameliorate pollution problems that the Chinese argue were created by the developed world. The Chinese also criticize the use of environmental protection standards by developed countries to erect barriers to Chinese imports (the reverse criticism is that China uses its backward environmental standards to subsidize exports). As in other countries, enforcement of environmental regulations lags behind commitment.

In its poorer days China gave selective but substantial economic aid, including $456 million for a railway between Zambia and Tanzania.[31] Today China's foreign aid hovers in the range of $300 million per year, less than in many years in the past. Terms are generous, and projects focus on achieving economic self-reliance through low-cost, economically practical projects. China's aid program is active in border countries like North Korea, Mongolia, and Myanmar; and in countries in Oceania, Africa, and the Middle East where Beijing competes with Taipei for diplomatic favor.

China is perhaps second only to the United States on the global scene in the degree to which other nations have a stake in its economic health. In one sense the nature of that stake is similar: both countries are important because of the investments, markets, and suppliers that other countries have there. If for large economies like those of the United States and Japan the China factor is only one among many, for certain smaller neighboring economies, including those of Hong Kong, Taiwan, and South Korea, the China boom is a major propellant for economic prosperity.

In another sense the nature of the world's economic stake in China is unique. If American actions set the parameters for commodities prices, rates of inflation, interest rates, and the rise and fall of stock prices around the world, China influences the world most importantly by feeding itself. Its approximate self-sufficiency in grain, cotton, and energy is crucial to world price stability. The steady growth of the Chinese economy helps the world economy stay stable. A sudden downturn could have strong effects elsewhere. It is hard to imagine that major economic troubles could be sealed within China's borders. They might be exported in the form of refugees, pollution, demands on world food supplies, disturbances in currency markets, confiscation of foreign property, or interruption of trade. As one of the few actors on the world scene whose economy is big enough to affect most important markets, China has a special kind of power that it is only beginning to learn how to use.

For the world trading system as a whole, China's integration as a rule-abiding member is important if the system is to survive and grow. The effectiveness of the WTO and other world trade institutions rests on norms that limit protectionism, restrain special treatment of national enterprises, safeguard the interests of foreign enterprises, and establish procedures for the resolution of disputes. Chinese behavior still violates many of these rules. Failure to integrate such a large trading country would challenge the stability of the liberal trade order. With its domestic economies of scale and nearly unlimited supply of cheap labor, China will continue to be a major exporter capable of prevailing in others' domestic markets whether or not it belongs to the WTO. If it fails to offer other trading countries reciprocal opportunities for participation in its market, they may be forced to adopt protectionist measures and even to look for refuge in regional trading blocs. Such reactions to unfair Chinese practices and large trade deficits could gradually undermine the integrity of the entire world trading regime.

MORE OPENING OR LESS?

The impact of the open-door reform on the structure of China's economy is often summarized by the "foreign trade ratio"—the value of merchandise imports and exports as a percentage of GNP. This figure rose in China from 17 percent in 1979 to 38 percent in 1994. By this calculation, China's foreign trade ratio far exceeds that of any other large continental economy, even that of the United States, whose ratio stood at 17 percent in 1994, or that of Japan, whose ratio was 16 percent in the same year. However, economists consider the statistic misleading, partly because it is based on dollar calculations that ignore the different purchasing power enjoyed by each currency within its own country—the Chinese yuan, for example, buys far more at home than it does abroad. Taking this into account, a truer estimate of China's economic openness (as of 1989) might be 10 percent, suggesting that China is considerably less dependent on trade than is Japan or the United States.[32]

At any size, China's foreign trade ratio has enjoyed a rate of increase even higher than that of its surging GNP. The open policy has created an outward-oriented society in large parts of China, where ways of life and thought are becoming closer to those of Taiwan and Hong Kong than to any vision of socialism. Deng wanted to create a "socialist market economy" that combined personal incentives and socialist values, market mechanisms and state control, but his hybrid appears fragile. He has opened his country to the kinds of social and cultural forces that tend to cross borders and topple repressive regimes like his own.

In response to this threat, a partial closing of China's open door is not out of the question. The environment of a succession struggle could amplify anti-foreign voices. Unlike island Japan, continental China could survive without international trade and foreign capital. The results for foreign traders in such a scenario would not be long-lasting, since the size and duration of their exposure are limited. The effects on investors would be more serious, depending on the size and type of their investment.[33] But most observers consider such a reversal unlikely. Closing the door would slow growth, expand unemployment, and demolish the consumer lifestyles of hundreds of millions of Chinese, creating threats to the ruling party's hold on power opposite and roughly equal to the threats created by keeping the door open.

If the open-door strategy continues, it could produce a new economic "dragon" in Asia bigger than all the rest combined. China could replace Taiwan and the other newly industrialized countries (NICs) as the major supplier of many products to the world. Success in this endeavor is dependent not only on reform at home but on world conditions. Even if China's products are competitive in quality and price, its exports may encounter barriers in the United States, Japan, and Europe as well as competition from other manufacturing economies.

The success of the open-door policy would not necessarily turn China into an advanced industrial power. China has not yet developed an indigenous ability to produce high-technology manufacturing equipment. Over 50 percent of Chinese exports are produced by joint ventures using imported manufacturing facilities.[34] The successes of the Malaysian, Singapore, Taiwan, and Thai economies reflect a similar dependence on foreign technology. Unless technology in China takes off as it has in Japan and, to some extent, in South Korea, Chinese export growth will remain dependent on continued foreign investment, and Chinese enterprises will not be able to compete with the United States and Japan in their most profitable markets. If China remains behind technologically, it will not be able to build a first-class military able to project power into Southeast Asia and compete with Japan and the United States in the regional balance of power.

Growing economic integration enhances China's security by creating common interests with economic partners like the United States, Japan, Russia, Taiwan, and Korea, which might otherwise threaten Chinese interests. Those who deal economically with China have become its strongest defenders in the politics of the West. On the other hand, conflicts over economic issues will intensify as China's economic impact on other countries grows.

China's stake in the economic health of its partners reduces its traditional freedom of strategic maneuver. China may need to reconsider its opposition to U.S. dominance in the Middle East, for example, when it takes into account that instability there might affect the economic health of the West via oil prices and damage the markets for Chinese goods. And as we will show in the next chapter, China has had to compromise on human rights issues, which it views as domestic, when foreign partners have linked them to economic ties. Although some constituencies want to slow China's immersion in the world economic system in order to avoid these costs, China has committed itself to an economic strategy that will succeed only through intensified integration into the world economy.

10

HUMAN RIGHTS
IN CHINESE
FOREIGN POLICY

INFLUENCE IN WORLD affairs is not limited to military and economic power. A government can use ideas and values to build support at home and to recruit sympathizers among publics and policymakers abroad.[1] The struggle over beliefs and values may be as complex as the struggle over other forms of power. The human rights issue in Chinese foreign policy exemplifies such a process.[2]

The benchmark of international law on human rights is the Universal Declaration of Human Rights (UDHR), adopted by the UN General Assembly on December 10, 1948. The declaration, representing a compromise among many views, takes the form of a statement of broad principles rather than an enforceable code of conduct.[3] In 1966 the General Assembly adopted the International Covenant on Economic, Social and Cultural Rights and the International Covenant on Civil and Political Rights, which were intended to convert the UDHR into legally binding treaties. Both entered into force in 1976, after ratification by a sufficient number of countries. In addition, nations have negotiated twenty-five major and many lesser human rights conventions, protocols, and other instruments.

Despite its authoritarian political system, nothing in its ideology prevented the Chinese government from championing human rights on the international stage even during the Mao years. The Chinese Communist Party came to power partly as an defender of human rights against the dictatorship of the Kuomintang. Each of the PRC's four constitutions contained extensive rights set forth in a special chapter, conforming to many of the stipulations of the UDHR and the two covenants.[4]

PROMOTING HUMAN RIGHTS IN CHINESE FOREIGN POLICY

For decades, human rights was a useful, if minor, tool of Chinese diplomacy. Placing its emphasis on the rights of self-determination and development, Beijing used human rights advocacy to strengthen friendships with revolutionary movements and Third World nations that shared its interest in opposing domination by the big powers. Throughout the 1950s and 1960s China charged the United States and other Western powers with violating the rights to self-determination, independence, and sovereignty of the peoples of Korea, Laos, Cambodia, South Vietnam, the Philippines, the Arab world, Latin America, Africa, and Cyprus, among other places. France was a frequent target for its policies in North Africa.

China joined African governments in criticizing South African violations. "The rights of the South African people have been encroached upon politically and economically," *People's Daily* stated in 1950. "The [South African] government also enforces a policy of racial discrimination and national oppression, and humiliates the local non-Europeans with violence." A 1964 statement expressed Chinese support for the South African struggle "against colonialism, racial discrimination and for equal rights and national liberation." Another statement the same year censured the South African government for its "most barbarous colonialist and racist rule" and demanded that the authorities "stop immediately their persecution of South African patriots" and release all political prisoners.

After the establishment of the Palestine Liberation Organization in 1964, Israel became a focus of criticism, and China announced support for the Palestinian people's "just struggle." A 1971 mass rally issued a message to "firmly support the Palestinian people in their just struggle to win their national rights and recover their homeland, and firmly support the Arab peoples in their struggle to resist aggression and safeguard state sovereignty and territorial integrity."

Along with its stress on national rights, Beijing did not hesitate to criticize adversaries' civil rights practices. In 1950 a PRC spokesman attacked a crackdown on the Japanese Communist Party by the U.S. occupation in Tokyo as violating "freedom of speech and of thought as well as respect for fundamental human rights." In South Vietnam, China denounced the "U.S.-Diem Clique" for "sanguinary suppression of Buddhists, students, intellectuals, and the mass of the people." On August 8, 1963, Mao Zedong met with an American black radical, Robert Williams, and issued a "statement calling upon the people of the world to unite against racial discrimination by U.S. imperialism and support the American Negroes in their struggle against racial discrimination." The statement supported the American blacks' struggle for "freedom and equal rights." A commentary in the mid-1970s criticized U.S. society for the oppression and exploitation of women, noting that "in the capitalist society of the United States, discrimination against women is a common practice."[5]

Both individual and group rights featured in the Chinese polemics against the Soviet Union. China charged that the Khrushchev regime used "the state machinery for repressing the Soviet working people and the Marxists-Leninists," adding, "In the Soviet Union today, anyone who persists in the proletarian stand, upholds Marxism-Leninism, and has the courage to speak out, to resist or to fight is watched, followed, summoned, and even arrested, imprisoned or diagnosed as 'mentally ill' and sent to 'mental hospitals.' " PRC publications criticized Soviet policies of "discrimination and oppression" against national minorities, "oppression and exploitation" of women, and the use of the KGB "as an important instrument for cracking down on the opposition of the people." *People's Daily* made fun of the Soviet constitution—on which in this regard the Chinese constitution was closely modeled—for granting rights and freedoms and then denying them to those who would use them to infringe on the interests of socialism or the state.

In Southeast Asia, China used human rights arguments to protest the oppression of overseas Chinese. In 1958 China said that the Thai government had "violated fundamental, internationally accepted human rights, persecuted innocent overseas Chinese and infringed upon the legitimate rights of the overseas Chinese." In the 1970s China charged that the Vietnamese government had "resorted to a series of measures of discrimination, ostracism and persecution against the Chinese residents" and had adopted policies that run "counter to general principles of international law."

As part of its backing for what it considered progressive forces around the world, the PRC supported the postwar development of international human rights standards. In June 1950 the All-China Democratic Women's Federation sent a letter to the Women's International Democratic Federation, protesting the persecution of "democratic" women around the world by "imperialist hangers-on and reactionary puppet governments which are opposed to democratic rights, deprive people of their fundamental human rights and are against peace." China attended the International Conference in Defense of Youth Rights in Vienna in March 1953 and spoke in support of youth's struggle for rights in colonial countries. In 1955 China acceded to the Bandung conference final communiqué, which stated, "The Asian-African Conference declared its full support of the fundamental principles of human rights as set forth in the Charter of the United Nations and took note of the Universal Declaration of Human Rights as a common standard of achievement for all peoples and all nations."

The PRC's participation in shaping the international human rights regime intensified after it took the China seat in the United Nations in 1971. A Chinese commentator argued that China should use human rights to promote the interests it shared with other Third World nations, just as the capitalist countries used the idea to promote their interests. One effective method was to get principles serving Third World interests written into UN documents and then press for their implementation. Another was to use the UN as a forum for human rights criticisms against selected countries. The PRC's first statement on the subject stressed the importance of the struggles against imperialism, colonialism, and racism, and for national independence and sovereignty.[6]

After a period of cautious observation, in 1979 China began to attend meetings of the UN Human Rights Commission as an observer, and in 1982 it became a member. The PRC participated in the Subcommission on Prevention of Discrimination and Protection of Minorities and in working groups concerned with the rights of indigenous populations, human rights aspects of communications, the rights of children, the rights of migrant workers, and the issue of torture. With other Third World countries, it promoted the idea of a "right to development," which the UN General Assembly enacted by resolution in 1986. China voted in favor of UN investigations into human rights violations in Afghanistan and Chile. Its UN representatives denounced Israel, South Africa, Vietnam, Afghanistan, and other targets.

Once China entered the international economy under Deng Xiaoping, many forces pushed it toward convergence with the outside world across a broad front of institutions. China began to change its banking, customs, communications, intellectual property rights protection, and other institutions to comply with world standards (Chapter 9). Likewise, the government adopted a criminal code, criminal procedure code, an administrative litigation law, and other laws with provisions relating to human rights. Legal codification brought increasing convergence on paper of China's domestic situation with international human rights standards, even though some of the laws were deficient by international standards or not fully implemented.

China also accelerated its participation in the international human rights regime. Over the course of several years the PRC joined the Convention on Prevention and Punishment of the Crime of Genocide, the Convention relating to the Status of Refugees, the Protocol relating to the Status of Refugees, the International Convention on the Elimination of All Forms of Racial Discrimination, the International Convention on the Suppression and Punishment of the Crime of Apartheid, the Convention on the Elimination of All Forms of Discrimination against Women, and the Convention against Torture and Other Cruel, Inhuman, or Degrading Treatment or Punishment. The 1984 Sino-British joint declaration on Hong Kong committed China to allow the International Covenants on Civil and Political Rights and on Economic, Social, and Cultural Rights to continue in force in Hong Kong for fifty years after 1997, although China itself had not acceded to these covenants. By 1991, when the PRC issued a white paper on its human rights performance, it had acceded to a total of seven of the twenty-five major international human rights conventions, one more than the United States at that time.

HUMAN RIGHTS AND SOVEREIGNTY: THE CHINESE POSITION

As its human rights diplomacy expanded, China drew a theoretical line at the water's edge. The policymakers wanted to see sovereignty gain, not lose, from involvement in the international human rights regime. As a Chinese writer explained, "The development of international law of human rights helps the Third World countries make use of the issue of human rights to oppose hegemonism and colonialism, to preserve sovereignty and independence and to promote the development and prosperity of the national economy."[7]

In international human rights law, the relationship between human rights and sovereignty is complex and contested. On the one hand, the UN Charter states, "Nothing contained in the present Charter shall authorize the United Nations to intervene in matters which are essentially within the domestic jurisdiction of any state." On the other, like much international law, the international human rights regime restricts sovereignty by virtue of its supranational character. The postwar trend has allowed the international community increasing scope to exercise suasion, impose economic sanctions, or even intervene militarily against a state on a growing range of human rights issues. The trend accelerated after the end of the Cold War, with the UN authorizing mandatory sanctions and/or deployment of troops wholly or partly on human rights grounds in or against Iraq, Somalia, Bosnia, and Haiti.

The rise of human rights interventionism sharpened the conflict of interest between countries that saw themselves as potential targets of intervention and those that were its potential executors. This struggle generated debate over the definition of matters "essentially within the domestic jurisdiction" of states.

Chinese scholars wrote little on the issue during the decades when China was largely isolated. Serious study began in the 1980s. The discussions started from the common position that states, not individuals, are the subjects of international law, so individuals' rights cannot be used as a justification to interfere in the sovereignty of a state. But within this framework, Chinese scholars put forth a variety of criteria to allow the international community to protect human rights. None of the several overlapping arguments that emerged has yet been consistently adopted by the government.

First, Chinese scholars say that a human right becomes of international concern when sovereign states enter into treaties or otherwise make themselves subject to international law with regard to the particular right. Second, violations that are particularly heinous, large-scale, or gross and that constitute international crimes can be suppressed by the international community. Examples are genocide, invasion, military occupation, and apartheid. Third, violations that threaten the peace and security of neighboring countries or the world are subject to international intervention, such as racial discrimination, genocide, international terrorism, or violations that create flows of refugees.

Fourth, some scholars have produced a specific list of issues in which the world community can act. These are violations of the rights to self-determination or development, aggression, colonialism and neocolonialism, hegemonism, racial segregation, genocide, slavery, large-scale creation of refugees, and international terrorism. One Chinese source explains that this set of issues consists of the "most urgent" and "major causes for the development of massive and ruthless violation of human rights" and "major human rights issues that attract international attention."[8] Although not clearly stated, criteria for inclusion seem to be that the acts involved operate against collectivities, not individuals, and damage the conditions for national independence and development.

Although proceeding from slightly different premises, these arguments reach roughly the same conclusions. Human rights principles must be used to criticize fascism, hegemonism, and imperialism, but may not be used against socialism and the Third World (both categories including China). But such arguments depend on distinctions that are difficult both to justify and to apply, such as those between group rights and individual rights, rights violated by a state that is party to a convention and rights violated by one that is not, large-scale and gross violations and smaller-scale violations, violations by progressive forces and violations by reactionary forces. China's position is an inconsistent mix, arguing on the one hand for "the struggle of Third World countries and other justice-upholding countries against the large-scale violation of human rights by hegemonism, imperialism, colonialism and autocracy" and on the other that "using alleged charges of human rights violations to vilify and attack China and to interfere in China's judicial and administrative affairs is an act unfriendly to China and the Chinese people and a violation of China's sovereignty."[9]

INTERNATIONAL HUMAN RIGHTS PRESSURE ON CHINA, 1978–1989

Sustained Western attention to Chinese human rights abuses began soon after Deng Xiaoping came to power.[10] In Chinese eyes this was ironic because Deng's regime marked an undoubted human rights improvement over Mao's. It rehabilitated tens of millions of political victims, dissolved the castelike "class status" *(chengfen)* system, promoted economic and social freedoms, and loosened political and religious repression. China made strides in the provision of economic and social rights by increasing incomes and the availability of consumer goods, extending the length of compulsory education from six years to nine, increasing average life expectancy to seventy years, and so on. The government campaigned against torture and ill-treatment of prisoners, cadre abuse of powers, female infanticide, and the kidnaping and sale of women.

Yet the fact remained that under Deng certain types of human rights violations were pervasive and systematic, such as the deprivation of the rights of speech and publication, freedom of association, the right to a fair trial, full religious freedom, and the right to humane treatment in prison. Information about former and current violations of human rights began to appear in Chinese news reports, fiction, and wall posters in the late 1970s. At the same time Beijing gave unprecedented access to Western journalists, who began to report harsh truths about the Chinese system.

The Helsinki accords of 1975 gave new impetus to the international human rights movement and led to the founding of numerous NGOs (nongovernmental organizations) in the human rights field. Amnesty International's 1978 *Political Imprisonment in the People's Republic of China* was the first NGO report on human rights in the PRC. The 1980s saw the formation of Asia Watch (founded in 1985, now called Human Rights Watch/Asia), the Lawyers Committee for Human Rights, the Committee to Protect Journalists, and other organizations that took an interest in China. An active pro-Tibet lobby developed, including the Office of Tibet in New York, the Tibetan Relief Fund and Tibet Information Network in the UK, and the International Campaign for Tibet in Washington, D.C.

Although Chinese human rights was never exclusively an American concern, the dynamics of American politics gave special impetus to the issue (Chapter 4). First raised in Congress, human rights was adopted in 1977 by the new president, Jimmy Carter, as a theme that could restore the national sense of mission after the nightmares of Vietnam and Watergate. The crusade continued under subsequent presidents. Ronald Reagan clothed his anticommunism in human rights garb, calling for "a global campaign for freedom . . . [that would] leave Marxism-Leninism on the ash heap of history as it has left other tyrannies which stifle the freedom and muzzle the self-expression of the people."[11] George Bush stated in his inaugural address, "America is never wholly herself unless she is engaged in high moral principle. We as a people have such a purpose today. It is to make kinder the face of the Nation and gentler the face of the World."[12] Human rights helped generate support for overseas involvements from a public otherwise skeptical about foreign policy.

With the collapse of the Communist parties in the late 1980s in Eastern Europe and the Soviet Union and the end of apartheid in South Africa, and with growing Western involvement in China, Chinese violations moved to the top of the list of American, European and Australian human rights concerns. In the United States the trend was reinforced by trade disputes and criticism of Chinese arms transfers, which contributed to a general antagonism toward China. Although American administrations often preferred to use "quiet diplomacy," societal pressures forced the government to keep human rights on the bilateral public agenda. Human rights organizations publicized a host of violations in other countries, but attention centered on China because of its size, global importance, and Communist ideology. Although the Chinese leaders complained of a double standard, in a sense they were victims of their own success in achieving major-power status while resisting the global trend to abandon Communist ideology.

THE IMPACT OF 1989

In the late 1980s China seemed ready to meet foreign critics partway by expanding its participation in the international human rights regime. Beijing issued favorable press and diplomatic commentaries on the two international covenants, indicating an intent to sign them. On the fortieth anniversary of the UDHR, on December 10, 1988, the document was celebrated at a ceremony in Beijing. By enlarging its involvement in the international human rights regime, China could have highlighted the achievements of reform, contributed to its international respectability, and helped attract foreign investment, without compromising its stance of diplomatic independence and Third World leadership.

The massacre of a thousand or more citizens in Beijing on June 4, 1989, exerted a dramatic effect on China's relations with much of the outside world. Many countries imposed sanctions, including suspension of high-level diplomatic contacts, restriction of exports of military equip-

ment and military-related technologies, and suspension of cultural exchanges, bilateral aid, and loans. Under U.S. leadership the World Bank
and the Asian Development Bank temporarily suspended loans. Negotiations on China's accession to the World Trade Organization came to a
halt that lasted three years. China experienced a two-year decline in its
credit rating, foreign investment, export orders, and tourism.[13] Companies like Levi Strauss, Reebok, Timberland, and Sears, with corporate
good-citizen policies, either imposed human rights standards on Chinese
contractors or reduced or canceled their business in China. Reaction in
Asia and the Third World, however, was limited. Many countries sym-
pathized with Chinese resistance to Western pressure; some would have
been vulnerable to similar charges.

China suffered a series of humiliations in UN bodies concerned with
human rights. In August 1989 the UN Subcommission on Prevention of
Discrimination and Protection of Minorities adopted by secret ballot a
resolution mildly critical of China, marking the first time that a permanent member of the Security Council had been censured for its human
rights performance in a UN forum. In the 1990 session of the Commission on Human Rights, Chinese representatives had to sit through the pre-
sentation of a secretary-general's report on human rights violations based
on material compiled by Amnesty International and other groups, and a
debate on a resolution to condemn China, although the resolution was
ultimately not adopted. In 1991 Beijing came under fire again in the subcommission, which by secret ballot voted to request China to respect the
human rights of the Tibetan people and asked the secretary-general to prepare a report on the situation in Tibet, which he submitted in 1992.

Chinese problems were discussed at one time or another in reports
or meetings of the UN's Special Rapporteur on Religious Intolerance,
Working Group on Arbitrary Detentions, Special Rapporteur on Summary and Arbitrary Executions, Committee against Torture, Special Rapporteur on Torture, and Working Group on Enforced or Involuntary
Disappearances. Each year the UN bodies provided forums for NGOs to
present information disparaging of China. Every year from 1992 through
1996 China staved off action on resolutions presented before the full commission by the United States, Japan, and European and other countries.
China's lobbying included state visits and aid projects for countries holding rotating seats on the UN Human Rights Commission, as well as the
argument that "what is happening to China today will happen to any
other developing country tomorrow."[14]

Although the G-7 nations, led by Japan, moved in 1990 to begin easing economic and political sanctions and to promote enhanced economic cooperation with China, Western governments and politicians felt it politically necessary to maintain verbal pressure. From 1991 onward an endless procession of senior statesmen from nearly all the advanced industrial countries made public representations on human rights. China's achievements seemed to interest a skeptical world less than its failings. In 1993 Beijing's bid to host the Olympics in the year 2000 encountered international opposition on human rights grounds and was defeated. The world press took the 1995 women's conference in Beijing as an occasion not to celebrate improvements in the status of Chinese women but to attack the Chinese government for heavy-handed security measures. The European Union made human rights a centerpiece of its policy of "constructive engagement" with China announced in 1995.

The human rights issue took an indirect toll on Beijing's bargaining position on many issues. The renewal of normal trading rights with the United States ("most-favored-nation privileges") was threatened annually from 1989 on by the public and congressional desire to push China toward human rights improvements. This in turn weakened Beijing's negotiating position in talks on intellectual property rights and market access; as we noted in Chapter 9, in both negotiations, China made major concessions to American demands. Likewise, the fact that China was on the defensive on human rights weakened its ability to block American and French arms transfers to Taiwan in 1992 (Chapter 12) and probably helps explain Britain's replacement of a conciliatory Hong Kong governor with one who confronted Beijing on the issue of Hong Kong democratization (Chapter 11).

China Deals with the Issue

Beijing's response to international human rights pressures demonstrated the attributes of strategic consistency and realism that characterized Chinese policy in other areas. The mix of measures was designed to rally Third World support, especially in multilateral settings, to appeal to advocates of realpolitik in the West, and to construct policy dilemmas for human rights advocates.

China mounted a variety of ideological counterattacks on its critics. Official spokespersons pointed to a series of double standards: that China drew condemnation while other countries whose violations were in some ways worse (for example, Israel, India) were ignored; that Westerners who said nothing about Mao's violations complained about less severe violations under Deng; that prosperous Westerners insisted on immediate implementation of modern standards in a developing China; that the West itself had committed human rights violations more deplorable than those it was criticizing, such as slavery and the Holocaust; and that the West today continues to be rife with human rights problems from which it distracts attention by criticizing others. Such double standards revealed the accusers' bad faith, Chinese spokesmen claimed. As Premier Li Peng told a Beijing audience, "One of the main causes of intranquility in today's world is that some big powers . . . undermine the unity and racial harmony of other countries under the pretext of 'freedom,' 'democracy,' and 'human rights.' "[15]

In addition, Chinese spokespersons argued that cultural standards differ. No culture's concept of human rights has greater claim to be accepted than any other's. Thus the foreigner has no moral right to judge. Interference constitutes cultural imperialism.

Third, Chinese spokesmen raised the issue of sovereignty, arguing that problems foreigners consider human rights violations are matters of domestic Chinese law—for instance, counterrevolutionary crimes or the death penalty. Many of them are not human rights violations at all. Those that are—such things exist in any country—are the purview of the Chinese government to fix, and it is doing so.

Finally, the government argued that China's rights record was excellent, as good as its critics'. Using an expanded definition of human rights that is popular among Third World countries, Beijing argued that the most important rights are those to survival and development. Such rights are better assured in China than in most other places, including the West. Even where the process of achieving socialism has led to mistakes that damaged human rights, only by building socialism can human rights be realized, the argument went. The United States, with many human rights problems of its own, "has no right whatsoever to comment on the human rights situation in other countries," said a Chinese spokesman.[16] "I cannot see [that] those countries who are promoting human rights have a better record than ours," stated Vice Premier Zhu Rongji on a visit to Canada in May 1993.[17] The Chinese press carried extensive coverage of American human rights problems, including the 1992 Los Angeles riots, race relations, police violence, and spousal and child abuse.

Propaganda arguments dovetailed with diplomatic activity carried out in conjunction with like-minded governments. China helped block Western initiatives to strengthen UN human rights mechanisms, such as a 1990 proposal to establish an emergency mechanism to enable the Human Rights Commission to be called into session following a major event like the Tiananmen massacre. In the preparatory work for the 1993 Vienna World Conference on Human Rights, China gained the backing of most Asian countries for the principles of noninterference in the internal affairs of states; nonselectivity (that is, UN bodies should not single out specific countries for criticism); the priority of collective, economic, and social rights encompassed in the notion of a right to development; national sovereignty; and cultural particularism (the nonuniversality of human rights values across regions). These arguments did not carry the day in Vienna, but had some influence over parts of the final declaration.

Despite its rhetorical rejection of human rights interference, the Chinese government's human rights policy offered a series of measured, timed concessions to Western demands. In 1990–91, in an effort to influence the politics of MFN renewal in the United States, Beijing announced the release of three batches of Tiananmen prisoners, totaling 881 persons, lifted martial law in Beijing, permitted the dissident Fang Lizhi to leave his refuge in the U.S. embassy to go abroad, gave assurances to Secretary of State James Baker that Chinese citizens would not be prevented from going abroad for political reasons, and freed the labor activist Han Dongfang when he was in danger of dying in prison. In 1993, in the week prior to the International Olympic Committee's decision on Beijing's application for the 2000 Olympics, China freed its most famous political prisoner, Wei Jingsheng, and other prisoners. In 1994, in the lead-up to the annual American MFN decision, Beijing provided information to American diplomats on political prisoners and held discussions on prison visits with the International Committee of the Red Cross. Indirect concessions included the release without trial of some political prisoners of international note, or the imposition on them of more moderate sentences than would have been likely in the past.

In addition, Beijing agreed to initiate a human rights dialogue with U.S. officials, dispatched two human rights delegations to the West to gather information, and over a period of years issued two white papers on human rights and others on criminal law, the situation in Tibet, children's rights, and the family planning program. Although unyielding in tone, these papers were significant as a sign of willingness to respond to questions raised abroad. At the UN and in other forums, Chinese officials stated their readiness "to engage in discussion and cooperation with other countries on an equal footing on the question of human rights."[18]

But in other selected cases the government spurned international concerns. Many dissidents little known in the outside world received harsh sentences, and so did a few internationally famous political activists. Wei Jingsheng, perhaps the political prisoner given highest priority abroad, was subjected to harsh treatment in jail for years, rearrested shortly after his release, and sentenced to another long prison term. From time to time Beijing interrupted its human rights dialogue with Washington to protest human rights pressure or American policy toward Taiwan. In 1996 Beijing began to experiment with counterlinkage, when Premier Li Peng indicated that a decision to purchase European Airbus rather than American Boeing aircraft was partly a response to American threats to link MFN to progress on human rights. By making selective use of hard-line measures, Beijing tried to remind other governments that human rights pressure was not always productive.

A PERSISTING ISSUE

Beijing's human rights counterpolicies were tactically successful. The West lifted most post-Tiananmen sanctions, and in 1994 the Clinton administration delinked MFN privileges from the human rights issue. Congressional efforts to relink the issues were defeated in 1995 and 1996. Chinese and U.S. officials discussed the possibility of a summit meeting to take place in 1997, symbolically culminating Beijing's return to diplomatic respectability.

But Chinese decision makers have not mastered the politics of human rights in the West. They attribute a strategic quality to Western policy that is more characteristic of their own conduct. By failing to understand the cultural roots of Western human rights policy and the power of the pluralistic public opinion that helps drive it, Chinese leaders may have underestimated the issue's importance and overestimated its negotiability.

Meanwhile, the human rights idea has gained ground at home, leading to some domestic reforms. The trend was propelled partly by China's growing openness to the outside world and partly by the need of its market socialist system for a stronger legal system to resolve economic and social disputes. Chinese lawyers, people's congress staff members, scholars, journalists, and Communist Party liberals argued for the legally binding status of the international law of human rights, the political wisdom of China's joining the world mainstream, and the practical advantages of revising Chinese law to bring it into conformity with international standards. The National People's Congress passed laws to strengthen independence of the judiciary and to place a greater burden of proof on the prosecution in criminal trials. Other issues on the table included ending crimes of counterrevolution and reducing the use of the death penalty.

The Chinese government's assets for the exercise of international cultural and ideological power remain weak. The nature of the Chinese political system forces the government into a defensive international posture on rights, illustrating how a country's domestic regime can constrain its foreign policy. Without a change of regime, human rights is likely to remain a structural weakness for China's diplomacy.

11

TERRITORIAL INTEGRITY: INNER ASIA, TAIWAN, AND HONG KONG

U NTIL THE ARRIVAL of seafaring Europeans in the nineteenth century, Inner Asia rather than the coast dominated China's security concerns. The fertile lowland China of rice- and wheat-growing peasants occupies only about a third of Chinese territory. Although this heartland has diverse topographies, soils, and climates, it is homogeneous compared with China's larger part, the vast western and northern region of high arid plains, steppes, deserts, and mountains. Until this century the west and northwest were dominated by a mosaic of peoples whose cultures were more closely linked to India, Persia, and Turkey than to coastal China. Geographically and culturally, the contrasts between Inner Asian China and heartland China are sharper than those between North and South America or Eastern and Western Europe.

Yet Inner Asia impinges closely on the security of the heartland. Only 500 miles separate Beijing from the Ningxia Hui (Muslim) Autonomous Region to the west and only 125 miles from Inner Mongolia to the north. Five times in its history China was partly or wholly conquered by nations from Inner Asia. In the nineteenth century when Muslim rebels raged through the northwest, a government official warned that they "could breach the Jiayu Pass and threaten Shaanxi, Gansu, and the interior, or they could move by the northern route, and the Mongol tribes would then migrate through the Great Wall: the shoulders and back of Beijing will be broken."[1]

At about the same time a new kind of threat arose in the region. In the nineteenth and early twentieth centuries, Britain moved from its base in India to secure military dominance in Tibet and help it establish administrative autonomy from Beijing. Russia intruded into territories west of Xinjiang, intermittently occupied parts of Xinjiang itself, and promoted Mongolian independence from China. These actions left the heartland exposed from the west, while the same and other foreign powers "carved the Chinese melon" along the coast to create treaty ports and spheres of influence.

As a legacy of its own imperialism, China's population today includes groups that are not ethnically Han, that have traditions of independence from China, whose communities straddle today's international borders, and some of whose members yearn for independence. As a legacy of China's victimization by European, Japanese—and, the Chinese argue, American—imperialism, China has lost control of some territories that it claims. The problem in the first set of regions is to maintain territorial integrity against challenges from within and abroad; in the second set of areas, it is to restore the nation to its full boundaries.

The fundamental dilemma in dealing with issues of territorial integrity is the same one China confronts in dealing with other foreign policy issues: that China is both large and weak. It is large enough to confront numerous problems of the periphery but not strong enough to deal with these issues with a free hand. Problems that China considers essentially domestic interact with its relations with other countries; issues that are international have repercussions in domestic affairs. Problems that the Chinese prefer to view as straightforward issues of sovereignty are defined by foreigners as ones involving human rights and self-determination. China is not strong enough to enforce its own definition of these issues on either domestic minorities or the international community. Strategy must be used where power is not adequate to the task.

RUSSIA

KAZAKHSTAN

UZBEKISTAN

KYRGYZSTAN

TASHKENT
BISHKEK
(FRUNZE)
ALMATY

DUSHANBE

TAJIKISTAN

GHANISTAN

KABUL

ISLAMABAD

AKISTAN

NEW DELHI

KATHMANDU

I N D I A

DHAKA

BANGLADESH

MYANMAR
(BURMA)

MONGOLIA

ULAN BATOR

URUMQI

XINJIANG

C
H
I
N
A

QINGHAI

TIBET

LHASA
THIMPHU BHUTAN

INNER

MONGOLIA

HUHEHOT

GAN
S
U

XINING

LANZHOU

BEIJING

N. KOREA

S. KOREA

SHANGHAI

GUANGZHOU

HONG KONG

TAIWAN

PHILIPPINES

VIETNAM

HANOI

LAOS

GHAZAUD

KAZAKHSTAN

MONGOLIA

TASHKENT

BISHKEK
(FRUNZE)

ALMATY

ZBEKISTAN

KYRGYZSTAN

TAJIKISTAN

DUSHANBE

GHANISTAN

KABUL

ISLAMABAD

PAKISTAN

NEW DELHI

I N D I A

URUMQI

Bosten Lake

XINJIANG

Lop Nur Lake

INNER
MONGOLIA

GANSU

QINGHAI

TIBET

H
I
M
A
L
A
Y
A

NEPAL

KATHMANDU

LHASA

THIMPHU
BHUTAN

CHINA AND
INNER ASIA

1000 km
600 miles

500 km
300 miles

NATIONAL MINORITY TERRITORIES AS
FOREIGN POLICY PROBLEMS[2]

China officially recognizes fifty-five national minorities. Most of these groups are too small, assimilated, or isolated to constitute problems for either domestic security or foreign policy. Three large regions present exceptions: Xinjiang, Inner Mongolia, and Tibet.

The Xinjiang Uighur Autonomous Region in the northwest is China's largest provincial-level unit. About one-fifth the size of the entire United States, it is mostly desert. Xinjiang means "new frontier." The few Chinese who came here before the nineteenth century found Islamic populations whose cultural connections reached away from China toward the Middle East and who saw the Chinese as infidels.[3] In the eighteenth and nineteenth centuries both China and Russia competed for influence in the area. Through the nineteenth and early twentieth centuries, as China tried to tighten its grip on the part of the region it controlled, Xinjiang boiled with rebellions and banditry. In the mid-1940s, when the Chinese presence was weakest, local people declared the short-lived Eastern Turkestan Republic.

Over the centuries China developed a series of methods to tie Xinjiang and other Inner Asian territories to itself. It would later apply them with some modifications to the project of winning back Hong Kong and Taiwan. The methods were trade, colonization, assimilation, administrative integration, and international isolation, backed when necessary by the use of police and military force.

Traders pioneered the Han presence in Xinjiang. Migrants started appearing in large numbers in the 1830s. The region was administratively integrated into China as a province in 1884. The PRC brought the region under state planning and directed its trade entirely to the east. With the Sino-Soviet split, China forbade the trade and migration that had been common across the region's ill-defined and ill-maintained borders. The Han influx was accelerated by the establishment of prison labor camps, whose inmates were forced to settle nearby when released from custody. During the Cultural Revolution in the 1960s, millions of middle school graduates from Chinese cities, especially Shanghai, were "sent down" to Xinjiang to live as farmers. By 1990 the Han constituted 38 percent of Xinjiang's population.

During much of the Maoist period the native Uighurs, Kazaks, Kyrgyz, and smaller local groups were pressured to abandon Islam, learn Chinese, and give up their ways of life. The Chinese garrison suppressed occasional revolts. The largest occurred in 1962. After it was crushed, tens of thousands of Kazaks fled to the Soviet side of the border.

Development had long been postponed because of difficulty, cost, and the region's exposure to the then hostile Soviet Union. Under Deng Xiaoping the coastal development policy discussed in Chapter 9 created a need for Xinjiang's coal and oil reserves, which make it potentially China's largest fossil fuel producer. In the 1990s China started building pipelines to bring far-western oil to interior markets. Xinjiang's living standard increased. Still, Beijing frequently denounces shadowy pro-independence organizations in the region and their alleged foreign backers. Han authorities maintain close supervision of Muslim religious and educational facilities. Demonstrations and riots were reported throughout the 1980s and 1990s. Terror bombings reportedly occurred in the capital, Urumqi, in 1992, and in 1996 the official *Xinjiang Daily* called for stronger repression of what it said was increasing pro-separatist "terrorism."

The breakup of the Soviet Union has removed a once powerful enemy from Xinjiang's borders and improved China's ability to defend the province. But border security is still a long-term concern. Kazakstan, Kyrgyzstan, and Tajikistan have borders touching Xinjiang; these states plus Uzbekistan and Turkmenistan contain populations belonging to the same or similar cultures as some of Xinjiang's people; and all five have growing economic relations with Xinjiang. Events in these five republics could intensify unrest in Xinjiang. Of particular concern to Chinese leaders are Islamic fundamentalist forces active in the Pamir Mountain border region of Tajikistan next to Xinjiang. Central Asia's strategic location, cotton production, and oil, coal, gas, uranium, and gold resources have attracted the interest not only of Russia, China, and the United States but of the main regional powers—Pakistan, India, Iran, Saudi Arabia, and Turkey. While Xinjiang's economic vitality and political stability are among China's main instruments for exerting influence in the Central Asian republics, good relations with the Central Asian governments are among the main tools for keeping Xinjiang under control.[4]

China has similar cross-border concerns in its Inner Mongolian Autonomous Region (460,000 square miles) and the neighboring country of Mongolia (formerly the Mongolian People's Republic, 604,000 square miles). Greater Mongolia was long dominated by the Manchus, whose homeland was next to Mongolia and who founded the Qing dynasty in 1644. In the nineteenth century the Qing permitted the immigration of hundreds of thousands of Chinese to the southern part of Mongolia (now Inner Mongolia). The Mongols responded with uprisings, riots, and looting. These did not threaten Chinese rule until 1912, when Russia gave military and diplomatic support to the Mongolian independence movement. At the nadir of Chinese power in 1924, outer Mongolia declared its independence.

Subsequent Chinese regimes continued to colonize Inner Mongolia. By now Mongols make up only one-sixth of the autonomous region's population. Except in the early 1950s, Beijing pressed for cultural assimilation. The Cultural Revolution rocked Inner Mongolia with purges and battles more violent than those in any other area of China, resulting in the arrest and torture of hundreds of thousands and the deaths of an estimated 16,000 persons, mostly Mongols.[5]

China counters continuing Mongolian independence sentiment with a combination of police repression in Inner Mongolia and economic engagement with outer Mongolia. One of the world's poorest countries and long oriented to the Soviet Union, Mongolia now trades heavily with China and sends much of its foreign trade through the Chinese port of Tianjin. Diplomatic relations are outwardly friendly, but they disguise tension derived from the Mongol fear of Chinese domination, Chinese concern about Mongolian nationalism, and China's mistrust of growing American interest in Mongolia.

The third and most difficult of China's Central Asian problem areas is Tibet. Tibet originally was not a single political unit but a collection of principalities that shared a commitment to Lamaist Buddhism. In the nineteenth century it came together as a theocracy under the Dalai Lama and accepted a tribute relationship to the Chinese empire. In 1904 the British invaded, offsetting Chinese military and political power. From 1913 to 1951 Tibet functioned as a de facto autonomous state, although its independent sovereignty was not internationally recognized. This history gave rise to the contradictory claims that figure in international politics today, both founded on historical fact: that Tibet was legally part of China, and that for a time when it was under British domination it was independent from Chinese authority.[6]

China never abandoned its claim to Tibet. In 1951, after PLA occupation of Tibet, the Dalai Lama's delegates signed an agreement with the People's Republic that Tibet belonged to China although enjoying internal autonomy. But China allocated about half of Tibet's territory to several nearby provinces. Chinese rule, which undermined the position of Tibetan Buddhism, engendered growing dissatisfaction. In 1959 resentment culminated in an armed revolt put down by the PLA. The Dalai Lama took refuge in northern India, where he established the seat of his authority in Dharamsala.

Despite the label of autonomy (Tibet now became the Tibetan Autonomous Region), Chinese civil and military administrators governed the region. During the Mao years the Chinese suppressed Tibetan Buddhism. Under Deng Xiaoping the monastery system was restored, but closely supervised so that it could not openly support allegiance to the Dalai Lama or independence. Chinese traders and workers flooded the territory, especially from the 1980s on, when Deng's reform program created new opportunities for migration and profit. Although they probably make up no more than 10 percent of the population, the Han sojourners are concentrated in Tibet's cities and dominate the modern sectors of the economy.

Independence sentiment in Tibet is the strongest of all China's national-minority areas. Although living standards have improved under Deng's reforms, many Tibetans claim they are being pushed to the economic margins and overwhelmed by Han immigration. They fear the Chinese will solve the Tibetan problem by eliminating Tibetan culture. The Dalai Lama has offered to negotiate with China for cultural, religious, and political autonomy under Chinese sovereignty. China has refused to negotiate until the Dalai Lama unconditionally accepts Chinese rule. Beijing apparently fears that the Dalai Lama is so popular that if he returns to Tibet with any authority the situation in the region would be uncontrollable. In 1995 Beijing refused to accept his designee for the religious post of Panchen Lama, for fear that doing so would legitimate the Dalai Lama's claim to be the final authority in Tibet.[7] China's strategy seems to be to make the Dalai Lama irrelevant through economic modernization and integration, but by all signs resistance increased through the 1980s and 1990s.[8]

No foreign government supports the claim of Tibetan independence, yet the issue has a strong international dimension. In 1989 the Dalai Lama was awarded the Nobel Peace Prize. He has been received by world leaders, including American presidents, and supported by resolutions placed before the UN Human Rights Commission. The Dalai Lama also commands strong support in Mongolia, most of whose residents are adherents of his Yellow Sect Buddhism. Fighting these fires exacts a constant cost from Chinese diplomacy. Yet there is no visible difference of opinion among Chinese leaders over the need to maintain tight control of Tibet for the sake of Chinese security.

CHINA'S HONG KONG PROBLEM

In contrast to China's Inner Asian regions, Hong Kong, Macao, and Taiwan are small territories on the southern coast, populated by Han. Yet the problems they present are no less complicated than those of the interior. They have been separated from China for more than a century, with intense foreign involvement. The task for Chinese diplomacy has been to recover them, while dealing with the entrenched interests of Britain, the United States, and other states.

The crown colony of Hong Kong is about the size of the five boroughs of New York City. Hong Kong island and the small peninsula of Kowloon were ceded to Britain in perpetuity in the nineteenth century. But nearly 90 percent of the colony consists of an area called the New Territories that Britain leased in 1898 for a period of ninety-nine years, expiring in 1997. Macao is a nearby Portuguese colony of 6.5 square miles. Neither territory would be militarily or politically viable as an independent state without Chinese acquiescence, nor has Chinese sovereignty been seriously questioned. Perhaps for these reasons, for years Beijing gave little urgency to their recovery. But in 1982 Prime Minister Margaret Thatcher of Britain visited China and suggested to Deng Xiaoping that international business confidence in Hong Kong's future would improve if China agreed to extend British rule beyond the lease's expiration date. She misjudged the mood of China's leaders.

Deng insisted on the return of sovereignty to China. To negotiate the terms, London and Beijing held talks without representation of the residents of Hong Kong. In the joint declaration of 1984, the British accepted Deng Xiaoping's formula of "one country, two systems." They agreed that Hong Kong would become a special administrative region (SAR) of China under a basic law written by China's national legislature. The joint declaration initiated a transition period that would end with the transfer of sovereignty on July 1, 1997. A separate Chinese agreement with Portugal established that Macao would revert to Chinese control in 1999.

Beijing had an economic interest in a smooth transition. Because of its role as a regional financial center and entrepôt, Hong Kong's GDP is 20 percent of the mainland's. Hong Kong capitalists are the largest foreign investors in China (Chapter 9), employing an estimated three million mainland Chinese in factories whose products are trucked to Hong Kong's state-of-the-art container terminals for transshipment to the United States and other markets. Multinational corporations use the territory as their base for mainland business activities. Taiwan and Southeast Asian businesses use Hong Kong subsidiaries and bank accounts to trade with and invest in China. The spread of mainland corruption to Hong Kong, or disruption of Hong Kong's sophisticated financial, communications, transportation, and legal infrastructures, could drive the lucrative foreign presence to another regional center like Singapore, Tokyo, or even Taipei. To prevent this, China provided in the joint declaration that Hong Kong would "enjoy a high degree of autonomy" for at least fifty years after 1997. It would be governed by Hong Kong people and preserve its social and economic systems unchanged.

For political reasons as well, China needed a smooth transition. In calling for the continuation of Hong Kong's political system beyond 1997, the joint declaration suggested that the Chinese would inherit the executive-led structure that the British had found so workable for 150 years. Since Beijing would choose the chief executive, it could expect to dominate the Hong Kong government as easily as London had done. Beijing also expected the Hong Kong people to be as pragmatic and apolitical as they had always been.

The situation changed soon after the signing of the joint declaration. A democratic movement developed in Hong Kong in response to the 1989 Tiananmen incident. Led by the English-trained barrister Martin Lee, it won a strong victory in elections for Hong Kong's Legislative Council (LegCo) in 1991. Britain responded by trying to move Hong Kong as far as it could toward democracy within the constraints of the joint declaration and basic law. To serve as the territory's last governor, the British government replaced a cautious Foreign Office diplomat with a populist Tory politician, Chris Patten. Without consulting Beijing, Patten proposed to empower all Hong Kong citizens above the age of eighteen with a direct vote for LegCo representatives and to create a LegCo majority of directly rather than indirectly elected and appointed members. The proposals were consistent with the letter of the joint declaration but violated the Chinese understanding of its intent.[9]

Beijing faced a dilemma. To acquiesce to British challenges would call into question China's determination to resist further challenges to its interests in Hong Kong or elsewhere. To tolerate dissent or disorder would give encouragement to the democracy movement at home and to separatists in Tibet, Xinjiang, and Taiwan. On the other hand, to wrangle with the British and suppress Hong Kong democrats would worsen China's human rights image in the West, sap the appeal of unification on Taiwan, and increase vigilance against China throughout Asia.

China chose toughness. To Beijing, Patten's reforms seemed a poison pill, designed to transfer a turbulent Hong Kong vulnerable to Western influence. Even before the last elections under British rule, in 1995, Beijing announced that this LegCo would be dissolved as soon as China took control, to be replaced by a provisional legislature that would oversee the election of a new LegCo expected to be more responsive to PRC wishes. Despite this announcement, Hong Kong voters gave a majority to Martin Lee's Democratic Party and its allies. The stage was set for a confrontation between the Chinese rulers and the popular Hong Kong democracy activists after 1997.

Besides being threatened by the substance of Patten's reforms, China was stung by London's failure to consult Beijing before proposing them. Britain read the joint declaration and its annexes as providing that London would continue to rule with full authority until the date of the handover. China viewed the agreements as committing Britain to consult on decisions affecting the transition, a practice followed by Patten's predecessor. To force the British to return to this precedent, China insisted on its right to be consulted over plans for a new airport and container terminal, land use, legal reform, and other issues whose consequences would extend beyond 1997.

Hong Kong will continue to be a foreign policy problem after it reverts to PRC control. As cosigner of the joint declaration, Britain claims an interest in Hong Kong's future. It has given some Hong Kong residents semirestricted British passports, and all others the right of visa-free entry to Britain. So political, economic, or administrative mismanagement of Hong Kong could lead to an exodus of Hong Kong residents to Britain and produce a political crisis.

The Americans, too, have asserted an interest in Hong Kong's post-1997 political welfare. The territory is a significant trading partner and the base for many American corporations dealing with China. It is the home of the largest American chamber of commerce outside the United

States, and one of the few places in Asia with which the United States enjoys a trade surplus. In the 1992 McConnell Bill (the U.S.–Hong Kong Policy Act), Congress stated that the United States has an interest in Hong Kong's economic autonomy, political stability, and human rights. American officials have warned that if China does not respect Hong Kong's autonomy after 1997, the United States might treat Hong Kong as part of China for trade purposes. This is important because the United States now plans to extend beyond 1997 Hong Kong's own textile quotas, aviation agreements, and other privileges separate from those of China. If these were canceled, it would cost Hong Kong billions of dollars a year.[10]

The bruising conflicts that attended the Hong Kong transition demonstrated China's vulnerability in a world where economic interests and the power of ideas have become as important as military power. China could have taken Hong Kong long ago just by turning off the water, which comes from across the border. It chose to negotiate a peaceful transfer because its interests there were so large and so intertwined with foreign interests. But when faced by challenges from Britain, the United States, and the Hong Kong people, China's leaders gave higher priority to political control than to Hong Kong's economic welfare and Beijing's smooth relations with other powers.

THE TAIWAN PROBLEM

Of all the issues of territorial integrity, Taiwan carries the highest risk of Chinese failure. Taiwan is the only piece of its contested territory that China does not dominate militarily and that would be viable without its acquiescence as an independent political entity. Indeed, the Republic of China (ROC) has functioned as an independent international actor based on Taiwan since 1949. It has a complete foreign policy of its own, the chief goal of which is to frustrate Beijing's efforts to control it. We consider Taiwan's foreign policy in Chapter 12. Here we discuss the problem from the mainland's point of view.

The Taiwan-China relationship differs from that of some other divided nations, such as Korea and Germany. These were long-unified countries whose temporary division was imposed by the superpowers and formally accepted by both sides at the end of World War II. In these two countries each government eventually recognized the existence of the other as legitimate, although temporary. No foreign power or domestic political force challenged the ultimate goal of unification.

Taiwan's case is different. China laid claim to the island in 1683 and made it a province in 1885. But in 1895 China ceded Taiwan to Japan as a colony. During World War II, in both the Cairo declaration of 1943 and the Potsdam proclamation of 1945, the Allied leaders pledged the return of Taiwan to China. At the end of the war the ROC took over Taiwan and reaffirmed that it was a Chinese province. Driven out of mainland China by Chinese Communists in 1949, the government of the ROC retreated to its last province. The ROC government on Taiwan refused to recognize the legitimacy of the authorities in Beijing, calling them "Communist bandits," and expressed its determination to "retake the mainland." Beijing denied the legitimacy of the government in Taipei, calling it the "Chiang Kai-shek clique." The PRC prepared to invade Taiwan in 1950 to finish off the rival regime, but the United States intervened after the outbreak of the Korean War to prevent military conflict sparked by either side.

For decades the ROC and PRC governments made it a common project to insist on Taiwan's status as part of China. Both governments refused to accept recognition from any government that recognized the other. Until 1971 the ROC occupied the China seat in the United Nations and was recognized as the government of China by most countries. In 1971 the UN General Assembly voted to give the China seat to the PRC, and most governments subsequently switched their diplomatic recognition to Beijing.

The United States, however, resisted pressure from both the mainland and Taiwan to express agreement with their common position on Taiwan's status. After the Chinese Communists had taken control of the mainland and the Korean War was under way, the United States backed away from its positions at Cairo and Potsdam. It arranged for Japan, in the San Francisco peace treaty of 1951, to renounce its claims to Taiwan without saying to whom it ceded them. Over the objections of both the PRC and Taiwan, it took the position that "sovereignty over Taiwan and the Pescadores [small islands near Taiwan] is an unsettled question subject to future international resolution."[11]

When the question came up again during the process of U.S.-China rapprochement, the United States still refused fully to accept the Chinese position. In both the 1972 Shanghai communiqué and the 1978 normalization communiqué, Washington acknowledged the Chinese claim to Taiwan without either endorsing or challenging it (Chapter 4). Moreover, both communiqués asserted an American interest in the peaceful resolution of the Taiwan issue, in effect claiming a voice in what the Chinese considered a domestic political issue.

Without the American defense commitment, Taiwan's bargaining position would be more like Hong Kong's, and Taiwan might have been integrated into the PRC long ago. This is why Beijing considers that the heart of the "Taiwan problem" is not Taiwan's separation from the mainland but the American role in perpetuating it. The world community has determined as a matter of practice that Taiwan is part of China, and it would take a diplomatic earthquake for the legal position to change. Yet an earthquake can never be ruled out so long as the United States continues to provide a security guarantee that prevents China from enforcing unification on Taiwan. Many Chinese believe that the United States wants to separate Taiwan from China permanently. While this is not the expressed intent of U.S. policy, so far it has been the policy's effect. However problematic, the American commitment to the security of Taiwan has roots in both grand strategy and domestic politics. It has been maintained by Republican and Democratic administrations and supported by Congress for half a century, and is not likely to change.

China's concern about Taiwan separatism is not baseless. Since colonial times there has been an active independence movement there. Most of the current inhabitants are descendants of eighteenth- and nineteenth-century immigrants from southeastern China. Their sense of separateness was further shaped by fifty years of Japanese colonial rule. The island became more modernized than the mainland and built up an educated middle class whose members spoke Japanese and thought of themselves as Japanese citizens. When Taiwan returned to Chinese control in 1945, the demoralized KMT army that came over from the mainland repaid the initial welcome of Taiwan's residents with repression and corruption. The mainlander ROC regime imposed martial law until the late 1980s. Eventually prosperity, generational change, and intermarriage eased conflicts between mainlanders and native Taiwanese. The KMT undertook "Taiwanization" by recruiting and promoting Taiwanese party members and government officials from the 1970s on, and in 1986 President Chiang Ching-kuo initiated a democratic reform that led, ten years later, to the first direct election of a president in Chinese history.

These developments did nothing to increase Taiwan residents' enthusiasm for unification with mainland China. On the contrary, the more economic and cultural contacts occurred across the Taiwan Strait from the late 1980s on, the more Taiwan residents, both native Taiwanese and those of mainlander origin, valued Taiwan's autonomy. They felt like strangers when they visited the mainland and were repelled by the backwardness and corruption they found there. The majority of Taiwan residents remain opposed to any form of reunification in which the mainland authorities could exercise power over them.

Opposition to reunification is not equivalent to support for a declaration of independence. Many believe that a declared "Republic of Taiwan" would not survive against the likely PRC military retaliation. American support has been promised only for Taiwan's defense against unprovoked mainland attack, not for independence. Most voters back candidates who in one form or another promise to put Taiwan's interests first, by which they mean maintaining and enlarging Taiwan's de facto autonomy without provoking a PRC attack.

The Evolution of PRC Policy

China's interest in Taiwan is often viewed as emotional and nationalistic, linked to China's resentment of its century of humiliation by imperialism. Mao Zedong once said that resolution of the Taiwan issue might take a hundred years, implying that China would never give up the goal.[12] Deng Xiaoping refused to waver on the principle of Chinese sovereignty even to get diplomatic recognition from the United States. The weaker governments that are likely to follow Deng's are even less likely to compromise on this politically sensitive issue.

But the issue is more than political and sentimental. There is no serious dissent in China to the view that China has a firm legal claim to Taiwan. The Taiwan issue thus involves the same principle that governs the status of Xinjiang, Inner Mongolia, Tibet, Hong Kong, and the South China Sea islands. If China were to allow self-determination for one of its major territories on the grounds that its people see themselves as culturally distinct, it would set a precedent for other territories where populations feel estranged and might claim the right to break away.

Legal considerations are fortified by hard motives of national security. Control of Taiwan is crucial for defense of the mainland against external enemies. General Douglas MacArthur called Taiwan an "unsinkable aircraft carrier and submarine tender."[13] One hundred miles from the Chinese coast, the island is equipped with major air bases and ports. It sits astride China's southeastern coastal shipping channels and overlooks the navigation routes from Europe and the Middle East to China, Japan, Korea, and Siberia. Since 1949 the island has been used as a base from which to land amphibious KMT attack teams on the Chinese coast, to spy on China, to broadcast anti-Communist propaganda into China, and to support the American role in the Korean and Vietnam Wars.

Lying across from a region of China that is difficult to defend and increasingly prosperous, Taiwan is always in a position to threaten the mainland, especially by offering military, intelligence, or propaganda facilities to a great power. Just as the United States is determined to prevent a rival's military access to Cuba, Chinese leaders are determined to prevent Taiwan from once again becoming a strategic asset of a rival great power.

Taiwan presents not only a potential military threat to the mainland but a present political threat. The government on Taiwan has avoided direct political provocations, such as a Taiwan-based seaborne radio station that pro-democracy Chinese wanted to establish to broadcast programs into the mainland. It has given support to mainland dissidents in a limited and quiet way. A larger subversive potential comes from Taiwan's simply being what it is, a modern Chinese society that is economically prosperous and politically democratic. So long as the Taiwan problem is not solved, Taiwan remains an unsinkable carrier not only of military force but of subversive values and ideas that are widely attended to on the mainland.

During the 1950s PRC Taiwan policy focused on influencing Washington's commitment to Taiwan. Beijing's efforts in 1954 and 1958 to deter American cooperation with Taiwan by creating military tension in the Taiwan Strait failed (Chapter 4). Only in the process of developing security cooperation with the United States in the 1970s did China succeed in creating some strategic distance between the United States and Taiwan. Although the United States proclaimed its continuing commitment to Taiwan, other countries began diplomatically to desert the ROC as soon as Henry Kissinger's secret 1971 visit to the PRC became public. In 1970 China had been rejected in its annual bid for the UN China seat; in 1971 it was voted in by an overwhelming vote. More and more countries, including Japan and many West European countries, switched their diplomatic recognition to the PRC. The American transfer of recognition to the PRC in 1979 culminated the process of isolating Taiwan internationally.

By 1979 Beijing's policy had achieved much. The United States agreed to abrogate its defense treaty with Taiwan and to withdraw its remaining military personnel. The residual American defense commitment, as expressed in the Taiwan Relations Act, came from Congress, not the administration. De-recognition struck a blow to the prestige of the KMT government, which was also being tested by the rise of a large, anti-authoritarian Taiwanese middle class. The end of the year saw the worst episode of violent political repression since the 1940s, when police beat and arrested demonstrators in Kaohsiung. Eight were given long jail terms. Their cases became a rallying cry for further growth of the opposition movement and intensified international criticism of Taiwan's human rights violations.

Normalization of relations with the United States thus allowed China to focus greater attention on directly influencing Taiwan, at the same time that Deng Xiaoping's incipient domestic reforms and recently launched open-door economic policy made room for new thinking. On January 1, 1979, the date of the establishment of U.S. diplomatic relations with the PRC, Beijing issued a "Letter to Taiwan Compatriots." It called for an end to the state of enmity between the two sides and quick, peaceful reunification; announced the end of the light, symbolic bombardment of the offshore islands of Jinmen and Mazu, which had continued since 1958; and called for "three contacts and four exchanges" (commercial, postal, and aviation contacts and cultural, art, sports, and science and technology exchanges).

The new policy targeted the mainlander KMT leaders still governing Taiwan, especially President Chiang Ching-kuo. Their claim to be the legitimate government of China had lost all credibility, and they faced demands for an end to authoritarian rule. If the ruling party accepted mainland control, the mainland would license them as local rulers, offering an escape from the twin dilemmas of international isolation and political challenges at home. The "three contacts and four exchanges" also offered incentives to mainlanders yearning to return home and to businessmen who wanted to trade or invest in China.

China promulgated a series of regulations and preferential policies to encourage Taiwanese travel and investment. Taiwan's prosperity makes it an important potential asset for China's policy of open-door development. With less than 2 percent of China's population, Taiwan in the mid-1990s had a GDP that was 40 percent of the mainland's, exports that were 77 percent of the mainland's, and a foreign currency reserve that was 120 percent of the mainland's. The manufacturing-based, export-oriented model of China's coastal economic miracle is modeled in many respects on the Taiwan experience. There is a precise fit between the mainland's development needs and the island's technological capabilities, management expertise, manufacturing and packaging skills, and international marketing channels.

The PRC gambled that economic links would tie Taiwan's prosperity to the mainland economy, thus increasing mainland leverage over Taiwan's foreign policy. Travel and other person-to-person contacts would reduce the Taiwanese sense of estrangement and build political support for closer links. Beginning in 1981, PRC troops in the province of Fujian, across from Taiwan, were redeployed inland, in an effort to reduce the sense of threat and to calm international concern about Taiwan's security.

To sweeten the offer, in 1981 the PRC head of state, Ye Jianying, announced "nine points," which offered Taiwan a "high degree of autonomy" (a phrase later to be incorporated into the Sino-British agreement on Hong Kong). The 1982 PRC constitution included a new provision for the establishment of special administrative regions, of which Taiwan (like Hong Kong) could become one. In 1983 Deng Xiaoping stated that Taiwan's high degree of autonomy would include the right to maintain its own defense forces, and that the mainland would not send military or civilian officials there. Finally, in 1984, when Deng articulated the theory of "one country, two systems" as the principle for reincorporating Hong Kong into China, he added that the principle would also apply to Taiwan.

"Smiling diplomacy," as some called it, was supplemented with a tough side. The threat of force had always been part of China's Taiwan policy. In the 1950s Beijing refused American demands to foreswear the use of force, insisting that the right to use military power within one's own territory was an inalienable attribute of sovereignty. In the 1980s Chinese leaders stated that the mainland would use force against Taiwan if it declared independence, offered itself as a base for a foreign power, or developed nuclear weapons. When Taiwan's opposition party adopted a platform calling for independence in 1991, President Yang Shangkun stated that "those who play with fire will perish by fire." And when Party Secretary Jiang Zemin renewed China's call for peaceful unification in early 1995, he also renewed the threat of force.

Chinese leaders have calculated that giving up the right to use force against Taiwan would be tantamount to inviting Taiwan to declare independence. Yet the threat of force was also turned against Beijing by others. Taiwan independence forces cited the threat as evidence of Beijing's hostility to Taiwanese interests, and the United States used it to justify continuing arms sales to Taiwan despite the 1982 communiqué commitment to reduce arms supplies as tensions over Taiwan diminished.[14]

Beginning in 1987, Deng's Taiwan policy appeared to bear fruit. In response to voter demands the KMT loosened restrictions on individual and trade contacts across the Strait. Cross-strait economic ties mushroomed. China became a major market for Taiwan's inexpensive consumer goods, including textiles and foodstuffs, and Taiwan businesses moved manufacturing operations to the mainland to avoid rising labor costs at home. By March 1996 the mainland was Taiwan's second-largest market, attracting 21 percent of Taiwan's exports, and the major target of Taiwan's overseas investments. Taipei policymakers were concerned that Taiwan was becoming economically dependent on the mainland, yet found no effective way to counteract its economic magnetism.

The Kuomintang regime, however, decided to spurn help from across the Taiwan Strait to stay in power. The KMT chose instead to strengthen its position through democratic reform at home.[15] Over the course of a decade starting in 1986, the last mainlander ruler of Taiwan, Chiang Ching-kuo, and his successor, the Taiwanese-born Lee Teng-hui, lifted martial law, released political prisoners, ended controls on speech and the press, allowed the formation of opposition parties, and conducted full-scale elections for the National Assembly, the Legislative Yuan, and the presidency. By restructuring its legitimacy on a democratic footing, the government gained the domestic base to withstand the mainland diplomatic offensive and international isolation. This development alarmed Chinese leaders and introduced a new element of instability in Taiwan-mainland relations. On newly democratizing Taiwan, it was no longer illegal to advocate Taiwan independence, and some politicians campaigned for votes by catering to anti-PRC sentiments among the electorate.

The emergence of new political obstacles to reunification within Taiwan was supplemented by a reverse course in American Taiwan policy. Growing U.S.-China discord in the 1990s increased sympathy in the

United States for Taiwan's defense and diplomatic needs. In 1992 President George Bush all but openly breached the 1982 communiqué by agreeing to sell 150 F-16 fighter planes to Taiwan. In 1994 the Clinton administration upgraded the protocol status of Taiwan officials in the United States. Finally, under congressional pressure in 1995 the White House authorized an unofficial visit by President Lee Teng-hui to his alma mater, Cornell University, to receive an honorary degree.

Faced with challenges to its policy both on Taiwan and in the United States, and concerned that if unchecked Taiwan would seek formal independence, China began a series of military exercises in the Taiwan Strait in July 1995. By demonstrating its capacity to use force, Beijing sought to compel Taiwan to restrain its challenge to PRC policy.

A FRAGILE BALANCE

U.S. policy after 1949 succeeded in avoiding the worst outcomes in the Taiwan Strait, and since 1972 the United States has been able to avoid choosing sides openly. Yet the American policy of ambiguity may be rendered bankrupt if Taiwan and China gravitate into crisis. Most policymakers in Beijing and Washington would like to maintain the framework of U.S.-China communiqués as a way of neutralizing the Taiwan issue as a problem in U.S.-China relations. But now that Taiwan is a democratic system, its leaders are neither willing nor able to let others determine the island's fate. With their eye on elections, Taiwan politicians seek new ways to enhance Taiwan's international standing.

If the United States has to chose sides, it will be a painful choice. In the eyes of many Americans Taiwan has an appealing claim to some form of sovereign status. Yet Washington must avoid war with China and try to integrate it into the world. The preferred policy is still avoidance and delay, but it may no longer be within Washington's reach.[16]

For China the dilemma is to deter Taiwan from challenging mainland sovereignty without creating a crisis in U.S.-China relations or undermining support among other countries for accepting the PRC into the international system. Every PRC show of force against Taiwan reinforces the China threat scenario in the West, Japan, and elsewhere in Asia. Force also makes it harder to promote economic and cultural ties with Taiwan. So long as its economic dynamism and political confidence are increasing, Taiwan will remain a challenge to Chinese security.

12

THE FOREIGN POLICY OF TAIWAN

Nowhere are the linkages between foreign policy and domestic policy more intimate than on Taiwan. And these two levels of policy are connected by a middle level, Taiwan's policy toward the Chinese mainland. In all three policy arenas the island itself is the contested prize: at home, among reunification-oriented and independence-oriented politicians; across the Taiwan Strait, between the two parties in the Chinese civil war; and internationally, between mainland China and Taiwan's main protector, the United States. At each level the central struggle is over increasing or decreasing Taiwan's separateness from China. Actions taken at one level affect power relations on both of the others.

Although there are many domestic issues in Taiwan politics (social welfare, government control of the media, environmental pollution, nuclear power), the central issue is how to assure security in the face of the threat from the mainland. Unification is favored only by a small group of Kuomintang (KMT) conservatives, mostly of mainlander origin. Even they want to join the mainland only in the long run and on favorable terms. Unambiguous Taiwan independence advocates who favor the establishment of an independent Taiwanese state in the near term also command limited support.

The recognition of mainland power and the need to appeal to the voting public have brought most politicians toward the center. The "mainstream" faction of the KMT is led by officials of Taiwanese origin, with their electoral base in the party's urban and rural political machines. They are nominally committed to one China, but in practice they seek to assure Taiwan's autonomy for the indefinite future by maintaining formal continuity as the Republic of China (ROC) while improving Taiwan's international standing. The large moderate faction of the opposition Democratic Progressive Party (DPP) wishes to build on the basis of Taiwan's de facto autonomy to move toward independence, but at a pace slow enough to prevent radical deterioration of relations with the PRC. The New Party, with an electoral base of mainlanders, criticizes recklessness in relations with the mainland but does not argue for immediate unification.

The common core of most positions is to avoid unification with the mainland in the foreseeable future. Taiwan residents see mainland China as too backward, turbulent, and authoritarian to be a safe partner, and prefer to have their own government. All factions seek to enhance Taiwan's ability to maintain its own political system, set the terms for relations with China, and prosper in the international economy.

The complexity of Taiwan's politics is shaped by its contradictory position in the world. It alternates among the top three positions in foreign exchange reserves, ranks thirteenth in foreign trade, has the sixteenth-largest army, stands eighteenth in GNP and twenty-fourth in GDP per capita, and belongs among the top one-third of countries in population size.[1] Yet it is excluded from the United Nations, recognized by only thirty-one countries, geographically small, and tucked close to China, its main antagonist, and far from the United States, its main supporter. Within China, Taiwan is again both large and small. Despite its large GNP and foreign trade, it is the second-smallest Chinese province in size and sixth smallest in population.[2] Taiwan is large as a country but small as part of China; wealthy economically but exposed diplomatically and militarily; a prize and a threat for mainland China; for the rest of the world, a legal anomaly that can neither be abandoned nor protected.

Taiwan's politics and diplomacy are dominated by the search for security from a fraternal enemy. Long-term possibilities for the future—reunification, independence, confederation, commonwealth—are matters of theory rather than policy so long as conditions are not ripe for any of them. For now, Taiwan's mainland and foreign policies are devoted not to resolving its future but to keeping it open.

TAIWAN'S MAINLAND POLICY

Until 1979, when Beijing launched its unification offensive, Taipei's and Beijing's policies mirrored each other. Both sides held that Taiwan's separation from the mainland was a feature of an unfinished civil war, that Taiwan belonged to China, and that the end of the civil war would bring reunification. While Beijing proposed a KMT surrender, Taipei awaited a CCP collapse. Chiang Kai-shek built up Taiwan as a military base from which to retake the mainland by force when the Beijing regime showed signs of weakness. His son and successor, Chiang Ching-kuo, shifted to a political strategy that called for "uniting China under the Three People's Principles"—that is, returning to the mainland as rulers when the KMT's free-market, democratic policies were accepted there, whenever that might be.

For years mainland-Taiwan relations revolved around the issue of contacts. The mainland offered party-to-party meetings, private friendly talks, secret negotiations, any form of encounter consistent with Taiwan's status as a rebel province. For Taipei to negotiate on such terms would have been to acknowledge that the PRC, not the ROC, was the real China, weakening both the KMT's support in the United States and its base among the Taiwanese, who were always alert to the possibility that the mainland rulers would sell them out to Beijing. Taipei created a firebreak to talks by defining the CCP as "Communist bandits." The rare KMT members who broke with this policy to pursue private encounters with mainland officials became enemies and exiles.

Taiwan was able to resist PRC blandishments because the United States was committed to Taiwan's defense. From 1949 to 1979 Taiwan's security was guaranteed not by how well it managed relations with the mainland but by how well it managed relations with the United States. Twice Washington threatened the mainland with nuclear attack when it seemed that Beijing was intent on using force to unify Taiwan. In such circumstances Taiwan's best efforts went into cultivating relations with Washington rather than with Beijing. The Taiwan lobby helped delay U.S.-

China rapprochement by threatening domestic political repercussions for any administration that opened relations with China (Chapter 4). But by 1979 the workings of strategic necessity weakened the American tie and exposed Taiwan to the blandishments of PRC smiling diplomacy.

Taipei now needed a creative mainland policy. An inflexible response could cost Taiwan its remaining American support. Within Taiwan the mainland's offers met a positive response from just those local people who had always been most fearful of KMT-CCP contacts. They were still not interested in unification, but wanted to take advantage of Beijing's flexibility to increase their freedom to travel and do business on the mainland and abroad. They also saw an opportunity to score points in the increasingly open internal politics of Taiwan by criticizing the KMT for a clumsy response to the mainland.

Taipei attempted jujitsu diplomacy. While offering a series of conciliatory moves that created a thaw with the mainland, the KMT kept attempting to enhance Taiwan's domestic and international viability as a separate political system. At home the government began the political reform that would relegitimate it as a locally based rather than a mainland-based regime. Toward the mainland it opened a wide range of contacts but limited them to those that could be labeled unofficial.

In 1987 the government started to allow mainlander residents of Taiwan to visit relatives on the mainland. Visits had reached a total of 5.9 million by 1993. Taipei also gave permission for the exchange of mail via the Red Cross and allowed the import to Taiwan of most publications from the mainland. The government then opened the island to limited visits from mainland residents. These started with humanitarian visits to close relatives who were seriously ill and for funerals; then they broadened to include selected mainland scholars, selected PRC students studying abroad, prominent mainland dissidents living in exile, a few mainland reporters, and Red Cross officials.

In April 1989 Taipei announced that it would participate in meetings of international organizations of which it was a member even when these meetings took place in the PRC, although it would continue to refuse invitations for meetings convened by the PRC itself. In May 1989 Taiwan's minister of finance attended a meeting in Beijing of the Asian Development Bank, stood at attention during the PRC anthem, and shook hands with the PRC president, all without acknowledging any change in the position that there were no official party-to-party or government-to-government contacts.

In 1990 Taipei established the Straits Exchange Foundation (SEF), a nominally private but government-funded organization charged with handling technical and functional relations with the mainland. Although preferring official-level contacts, Beijing eventually established the quasi-official Association for Relations across the Taiwan Strait (ARATS), headed by the retired Shanghai mayor Wang Daohan. He met with Taipei's delegate Koo Chen-fu in Singapore in 1993 and signed several minor agreements. China proposed an official meeting between the leaders of the two sides on "Chinese" soil (mainland or Taiwan). Taiwan countered with an offer to meet in an "international" venue. The underlying issue over the framework for meeting was always status. Beijing insisted that any meeting take place in a way that reaffirmed Taiwan's place as a subordinate part of China, while Taipei sought a symbolic acknowledgment of its status as an equal governmental entity.

In 1991 President Lee Teng-hui revoked the "state of Communist rebellion" that Chiang Kai-shek had declared decades earlier. This move appeared conciliatory, yet it also vacated Taiwan's claim to the mainland. Lee acknowledged the PRC as a "political entity which controls the mainland area" and described the ROC as "a sovereign state on Taiwan." On their face simple statements of fact, these formulas differed critically from Taipei's traditional claim to be the sole legitimate government of all China. Without using the term "independence," they pointed to the existence of two separate sovereignties.

In March 1991 Taipei issued Guidelines for National Unification. The guidelines envisioned unification taking place in three phases stretching into the remote future. In the first phase, Taiwan would continue people-to-people contacts. In return, the mainland was to cease threatening the use of military force, denying Taiwan's existence as a political entity, and restricting its activities in the international arena, while carrying out economic reform and democratization to make itself a more acceptable partner for unification. Had the mainland met these conditions, it would have set Taiwan free to pursue as much autonomy as it wanted, up to and including independence. The guidelines put off to the second and third phases the establishment of government-to-government contacts and final consultations toward unification. In effect, the guidelines asked the mainland to disarm itself of all forms of leverage as the precondition to the start of negotiations over Taiwan's relations with China.

Of all Taiwan's initiatives toward the mainland, none carried greater risk than the decision to open economic relations. If Taiwan had denied itself access to the thriving mainland market just as its traditional markets were becoming more protectionist, its ability to maintain its high rate of growth would have been compromised. A refusal to open trade relations with China would also have made Taiwan seem the obstinate party in the conflict. So in 1988 Taiwan legalized certain forms of trade and later allowed some kinds of investment. Both legal and illegal cross-strait trade and investment boomed, reflecting the complementarity between Taiwan's high-tech, export-oriented economy and the mainland's cheap labor and hunger for funds, technology, and access to international trade channels.

Trade reached an annual level of $34 billion in 1993, and cumulative Taiwan investment on the mainland was estimated at $25 billion by 1996. The growth of economic ties between the smaller Taiwan economy and the massive mainland economy gave the PRC new leverage over Taiwan's domestic economy and politics. The 1995–96 Taiwan Strait crisis, which we describe further below, reminded Taiwan of its large neighbor's power and willingness to affect its economy.

"Flexible Diplomacy"

Corresponding to its mainland initiatives, Taiwan developed a foreign policy that sought to reinforce its ambiguous position as a political entity neither juridically independent from China nor subject to it. Labeled "pragmatic," "substantive," or "flexible" diplomacy, the new approach sought a position somewhere between the traditional stance that the ROC must be recognized as the government of all China and the German and Korean models, which would have allowed foreign governments to recognize two Chinese states pending unification.

Taipei now argued that the ROC was a distinct system or "political entity" within China, with historically continuous sovereignty since its founding on the mainland in 1912 and still maintaining effective control over the territory of Taiwan. China was therefore for the time being "one country with two governments." Taipei made known that it would accept recognition as the ROC from countries that recognized the PRC without, as in the past, requiring them to break relations with Beijing. This put the onus for breaking relations on Beijing. To raise Taiwan's international profile, President Lee Teng-hui made state visits to several countries; he also made quasi-state visits, labeled private, to friendly countries that did not recognize Taiwan.

Taiwan's diplomatic relations had sunk to twenty-two mostly small countries by 1978. The number rose and fell as some countries switched their ties to the PRC and a few recognized the ROC. Some did so to benefit from Taiwan's well-funded International Economic Cooperation and Development Fund, prompting Beijing to accuse Taipei of "dollar diplomacy." Saudi Arabia broke relations with Taipei in 1990 and South Korea in 1992. As of late 1996 Taipei had diplomatic relations with thirty countries. Its most important foreign diplomatic partner was South Africa, which announced that it would switch recognition to Beijing by the end of 1997. Taiwan's other formal ties were with small countries and ministates in Africa, Latin America, the Caribbean, and the South Pacific.[3]

Taiwan increased its subdiplomatic representation around the world. From rapprochement in 1972 to the establishment of formal diplomatic relations in 1979, the United States and China were represented in each other's capitals by liaison offices staffed by diplomats but lacking embassy status. In 1979 the United States reversed the picture. After officializing ties with Beijing, it established the unofficial American Institute in Taiwan to handle relations with Taipei, and Taiwan established the Coordination Council for North American Affairs (later renamed the Taipei Economic and Cultural Representative Office). Elsewhere in the world Taipei's delegates were welcomed in the capitals of most trade- and aid-hungry post-Communist states and even in the capital of Communist Vietnam, although these countries shunned formal diplomatic ties. As of 1995 Taiwan had representative offices in 61 countries and formal commercial relations with 150 nations.

Taiwan cultivated membership in as many nongovernmental and intergovernmental organizations as possible. Taipei joined all conceivable international and regional sports organizations, performing especially well in the international Little League movement. It gave high priority to its membership in the Olympic movement as a powerful symbol of nationhood. It belongs to intergovernmental organizations, including the Asian Development Bank, the Asia Pacific Economic Cooperation forum (APEC), and the Permanent Court of Arbitration. It sought to join the International Monetary Fund, the Organization for Economic Cooperation and Development (OECD), and the World Trade Organization. Since 1993 Taiwan has mounted an annual effort to ask the UN to study the terms under which it might regain a seat in the world organization.

While opposing Taiwan's membership in the UN, Beijing on a case-by-case basis dropped its opposition to Taiwanese participation in certain international and intergovernmental organizations in pursuit of its goal of enticing Taiwan into increased contacts. It considered Taiwan participation in these organizations as an acceptable price for cross-strait cooperation. To find a rubric acceptable to both Taipei and Beijing under which Taiwan could participate in such organizations, the two sides played the "name game," with China refusing names that imply Taiwan is a state in the international system and Taiwan rejecting those that imply it is a local government in China. The most widely used name is the "Olympic formula," which refers to Taiwan as "Chinese Taipei" (sometimes with a hyphen).[4]

Taiwan's ingenuity and full purse gained it a statelike presence in many world arenas. Yet Chinese diplomats managed to keep the ambit of Taiwan's diplomatic ties narrow. The key to each government's strategy in dealing with the other was the United States.

TAIWAN'S U.S. POLICY

The U.S. relationship occupies a unique place in Taiwan's foreign policy because it alone guarantees Taiwan's security. Yet that guarantee as expressed in the 1979 Taiwan Relations Act (TRA) is less reliable than it was in the U.S.-ROC Mutual Defense Treaty that the TRA replaced. Whereas the Mutual Defense Treaty was rooted in Washington's global anti-Communist strategy, the TRA runs counter to the American strategy of engagement with China. It contradicts some of the commitments undertaken by American presidents in the three U.S.-China communiqués; was decided by Congress rather than the administration; has the character of domestic legislation rather than an international treaty; and leaves ambiguous the nature of an American response to a threat to Taiwan.[5] To be sure that the United States will offer real support when it is needed, Taipei needs to cultivate its American ties tirelessly.

U.S.-Taiwan relations reached a low in the mid-1980s because of political, human rights, and trade issues, but the subsequent democratization of Taiwan's political system turned many congressional and media critics into admirers. Taiwan worked to remove irritants in its economic relations with the United States. To reduce its trade surplus with the

United States, which rose to a high of $17 billion in 1987, Taiwan sent "Buy America missions"; tightened its enforcement of copyright protection for American books, software, and other intellectual property; allowed the New Taiwan dollar to appreciate, thus raising the cost of Taiwan's exports to the United States and lowering the cost of imports; reformed its banking and insurance systems to permit more American involvement; and lowered many tariffs and other barriers to imports. Many of the measures coincidentally buttressed Taiwan's application for membership in the World Trade Organization.

By 1994 America's trade deficit with Taiwan had been more than halved, to $9.6 billion. Meanwhile, the PRC replaced Taiwan as the country with which the United States had its second-largest trade deficit, and was on its way to replacing Japan as first on the list. This happy (for Taiwan) event was partly the result of growing Taiwan-PRC economic ties: much of Taiwan's production for the American market, and thus its trade surplus, had been relocated on the mainland to take advantage of cheaper labor.

As U.S.-China relations worsened in the 1990s, American politicians became more sympathetic to Taiwan. Taiwan's economic miracle and the contrast of its blossoming democracy with repression on the mainland reenergized Taiwan's supporters in the United States. The well-organized and vocal Taiwanese-American community, which at one time worked at cross-purposes with the KMT government, has become its political ally. Taiwan's representative office, with headquarters in Washington and thirteen consulate-like branches around the country, conducts an effective public relations effort by sponsoring cultural events, conferences, exhibits, and visits to Taiwan by influential public figures. Taiwan's investment is spread throughout the country. It deposits most of its foreign exchange reserves in the United States and in the 1990s conducted a six-year, $220 billion infrastructure program that awarded many contracts to American firms. Taiwan cultivates academic ties in America through its grant-giving Chiang Ching-kuo Foundation, its conference-sponsoring Institute of International Relations and Institute for National Policy Research, and a variety of exchange relations between U.S. and Taiwan institutions.

American China policy in the 1990s shifted in a way more favorable to Taiwan (Chapter 4). In addition, foreign policy specialists advocated stretching or abandoning the communiqué framework in order to pursue closer economic ties with Taiwan, strengthen Taiwan's security, or pressure Beijing to adopt policies more satisfactory to the United States. But none of these successes offset Taiwan's growing economic dependency on the mainland or its international isolation.

Only in 1995, when the White House reversed previous policy by granting President Lee Teng-hui a visa to make a personal visit to Cornell University did Taiwan's fortunes seem on the brink of fundamental change. This apparently innocuous event caused a crisis in U.S.-China-Taiwan relations. Although an unofficial visit, it had high political significance. Taiwan was about to cap its ten-year democratic reform with the first open, competitive direct election of a head of state in Chinese history. Running for reelection, Lee had made clear to Taiwan voters his intent to resist mainland pressure for unification on Beijing's terms and to expand Taiwan's presence in world affairs.

The trends in Washington and Taipei did not elude policymakers in Beijing. Beijing read the Cornell trip as evidence both of Lee's determination to enlarge flexible diplomacy and of Washington's willingness to support him in doing so. China faced the prospect that a quarter century's effort to box Taipei into a shrinking diplomatic space was about to crumble. If the trend continued, influential groups in Taipei and Washington might conclude that the time was ripe to push for formal independence.

To remind the Taiwanese and Americans of the risks of that course, Beijing denounced Lee for moving toward independence and mounted a series of threatening military exercises in the Taiwan Strait beginning in July 1995 and extending through Taiwan's March 1996 presidential election. The exercises occurred close to Taiwan and its offshore islands, used live weaponry and missiles, and interfered with shipping and air traffic in the strait and near Taiwanese ports. During the height of the crisis, the Taipei stock market fell, investors sold Taiwan currency to buy gold and U.S. dollars, and capital flowed to foreign bank accounts until the Taipei government intervened to stabilize the economy.

Beijing's strategy seemed directed less at influencing the election itself, which Lee won, than at influencing Lee's post-election mainland policy and Washington's post-election Taiwan policy. Beijing seemed to hope that Lee and the United States would return to the framework of earlier policies, which limited Taiwan's diplomatic leeway. The United States sent two aircraft carrier battle groups to the region, signaling that Washington had the capability to intervene if Beijing launched a direct invasion of Taiwan. But the exercises demonstrated to Taiwan that the United States cannot easily prevent China from closing the Taiwan Strait and damaging Taiwan's economy, and to the United States that China is determined to prevent erosion of the limits it has placed on U.S.-Taiwan ties.

THE CROSS-STRAIT MILITARY BALANCE

A direct military clash with Taiwan would be at best costly to China and its economy, and at worst unwinnable. Even if China could occupy Taiwan, it would gain uneasy dominion over a hostile population and a devastated economy; if it failed, the attempt to invade would have done great damage to the goal of reunification. Win or lose, belligerency would enlarge fears of a Chinese threat throughout Asia and in the United States. Yet the military option is real because of Taiwan's strategic and political importance to China. On matters of crucial national interest, PRC policymakers traditionally have spoken with one voice and have not uttered empty threats. Warnings of force in Chinese diplomacy have usually signaled commitments to real strategic interests.

China's military options in the Taiwan Strait include invasion and blockade. In an invasion attempt, mainland fighter planes would have to defeat Taiwan's fighter planes to open the Taiwan Strait for an invasion force. After the opponent's air force was destroyed, Chinese sea forces would seek to overwhelm Taiwan's navy, although Taiwan's submarines and frigates could wreak great damage. The third step would be to land the infantry, which would hope to overwhelm Taiwan's 290,000-man ground force. The defending side would have a good chance of prolonging the conflict by picking apart the attacking forces. The complex operation would have to be completed quickly to minimize the cost to China, the damage to Taiwan, and the risk of international intervention.

In the blockade scenario, mainland air and naval forces would enforce a ban on shipping to and from Taiwan's ports. The navy would stand picket off Taiwan's main ports on the north, south, and west of the island and might also mine the harbors. Taiwan's navy is too small to break a full blockade, but its submarines could sink some Chinese warships. The air force would be Taiwan's major weapon of defense, so long as it could keep control of the air in the battle with mainland fighter planes. A blockade would run considerable risk of foreign, especially American intervention, because it would interfere with foreign shipping interests and impinge on the freedom of navigation in international waters.

Either invasion or blockade could be a surprise, or it might be the last step in a series of warnings, threatening gestures, and escalations, designed to test Taiwan's military readiness and political determination. The chief deterrent to both options for the time being is Taiwan's air force. It is smaller than the mainland's but currently has better fighter planes, navigational equipment, and pilot training. The mainland's acquisition of Su-27s from Russia (Chapter 8) will merely slow the rate at which Taiwan's air superiority grows.

China has other military options in which its air inferiority would be less important. It could repeat the 1995–96 drama of testing ground-to-ground missiles and conducting exercises in the seas near Taiwan; make feint attacks by air and naval craft in the direction of Taiwan territory; create incidents around the detention or harassment of Taiwan fishing boats, shipping, or aircraft; attack any of the eighty-five smaller islands other than Taiwan that belong to the ROC, including Jinmen (Quemoy) and Mazu (Matsu); dispatch waves of mainland refugees to Taiwan; increase smuggling to Taiwan, perhaps including drugs and firearms; and fire missiles or drop bombs on selected targets on Taiwan.

Actions like these—or the mere verbal announcement of a blockade without military action—would frighten off shipping, push up insurance costs, and alarm Taiwan stock market and real estate investors. Such actions would be difficult for the Taiwan army to defend against and would make U.S. intervention difficult both militarily and politically. The goal of such escalations might not be military conquest but to create economic disorder and psychological panic and to demonstrate to Taiwan that the United States will not come to its aid in an effective manner. Beijing could give itself a period of several years to intensify psychological pressure on Taiwan step by step, while keeping the United States off balance.

In strategy, success or failure is measured first in the effectiveness of deterrence, and only if that fails in the outcome of fighting. Taiwan's deterrence rests on superiority in technology and training. Taiwan maintains a 468,000-man armed force with a 1.6 million-man reserve. Its defense budget exceeds that of India ($11.3 billion versus $7.3 billion), and it ranks among the top countries in the percentage of GDP devoted to defense (4.6 percent). It has superiority over the mainland in all the relevant technical fields except submarine warfare. With chiefly American technology Taiwan has developed its own surface-to-air missile, air-to-air missile, and a surface-to-surface missile capable of destroying warships at long range. Taiwan also coproduces with an American shipyard advanced frigates with sophisticated antisubmarine warfare capabilities. Its effort to build its own indigenous defense fighter (IDF), the Ching-kuo, modeled on the U.S. F-16, has encountered difficulties, but the plane is being gradually improved. Taipei canceled a nascent nuclear weapons program in 1988 after the United States discovered it.

But Taipei remains dependent on foreign suppliers for key weapons systems. In the late 1980s the United States sold Taiwan advanced tanks, transport planes, frigates, and various kinds of short-range missiles, and licensed the export to Taiwan of the advanced technology it needed to manufacture the Ching-kuo fighter plane. In the 1990s, after the end of the Cold War, Washington sold Taiwan 150 F-16 fighter planes, 200 Patriot antimissile missiles, eight E-2T early-warning planes, 41 Harpoon antiship missiles, Stinger surface-to-air missiles, advanced targeting and navigation systems for fighter jets, and M60A3 tanks. Taiwan's access to U.S. weaponry was partly the result of the Defense Department's evaluation of Taiwan's self-defense needs under the Taiwan Relations Act. It also reflected successful lobbying of the White House and congressional representatives of districts where the arms were manufactured. Taiwan also purchased from France, despite PRC objections, 6 Lafayette class frigates and 60 Mirage-2000 jet fighters.

China's military is relatively backward, and its forces are deployed, armed, and trained chiefly for territorial defense (Chapter 8). Yet the mainland holds certain immutable advantages. Relative to Taiwan, the mainland's geographic and demographic size would enable it to sustain a long conflict and withstand severe losses, while island Taiwan is vulnerable not only to military but to economic and psychological attrition. A war's impact on the mainland would be limited to a few coastal provinces, while Taiwan's entire society and economy would rapidly suffer catastrophic losses. Despite Washington's security commitment, it is not clear that the United States would go to war to protect Taiwan, especially if the conflict was provoked by diplomatic assertiveness on the part of Taipei that the United States counseled against.

TAIWAN'S FUTURE

Taiwan-mainland relations are dominated by a dilemma of mutual vulnerability. Each side is potentially able to do vital damage to the security of the other, and in trying to improve its own security each increases the sense of threat on the other side. The more the mainland tries to constrain Taiwan's options, the less safe Taiwan feels; the more Taiwan tries to increase its freedom of action, the less safe the mainland feels. For now, Taiwan has escaped from the trap of passivity to assert a measure of control over its own fate. But given the island's centrality to Chinese interests, tampering with the status quo is risky. In attempting to protect its interests against the mainland, Taiwan may stir China to defend its interests in ways that pose a still greater threat.

Mutual trust might dissolve this dilemma, but the dilemma itself makes trust hard to achieve. Future generations of Chinese leaders may feel less nationalist fervor about recovering Taiwan than the cohorts of Mao and Deng did, but they will still want to control Taiwan's international relations in order to prevent the island from being used by others as a base for hostile action. Mainland economic prosperity and political reform may reduce the Taiwanese sense of estrangement, but the residents of Taiwan will still want to maintain their own political system, way of life, and foreign policy without domination from across the strait. A solution that serves the needs of both sides is imaginable in theory, but hard to reach in practice. Meanwhile there is little prospect that the United States will extricate itself from its decades-long involvement in what has become the most tenacious international issue of the post–World War II era, or from that involvement's pervasive, baneful influence on U.S.-China relations.

13

CHINESE SECURITY AND WORLD ORDER

C HINA IS STRONGER today and its borders are more secure than at any other time in the last 150 years. To the north Chinese land forces are better equipped and better trained than their Russian counterparts. In Central Asia the PLA dominates Xinjiang, despite unrest there, and China's military and economic influence deters the new post-Soviet republics from challenging Chinese interests. Sino-Indian relations are better today than at any time since the 1950s. Beijing continues to bolster Pakistan's security with arms transfers. China has a near-monopoly of influence in North Korea. Its political and economic relations with South Korea continue to develop, on the basis of complementary economies and shared mistrust of Japan. Having ousted French, American, and Soviet forces, China has no strategic competitor in mainland Southeast Asia. Vietnam and Thailand, as well as the smaller states of Burma, Laos, and Cambodia, have accommodated to Chinese interests.

But in its relations with the great powers the PRC remains vulnerable to challenge. Relations with Japan have the potential to deteriorate. Japanese trade, direct investment, and low-interest loans contribute to

Chinese development, and Japanese diplomats value stable relations with China. But China sees cause for concern in Japan's military potential, its improving strategic relationship with the United States, its deepening economic ties with Taiwan, and its growing criticism of Chinese human rights abuses. Japan's public opinion increasingly focuses on a potential threat in the rise of China, and China policy, including the Taiwan issue, is more and more politicized in Japan's multiparty political system.

U.S.-China relations are difficult. Trade relations improved after the Clinton administration delinked China's MFN status from its human rights record and after a bipartisan consensus emerged in the 1996 presidential campaign on maintaining China's MFN status. The U.S. market continues to play a vital role in Chinese modernization, and U.S.-China educational, cultural, and scientific exchanges are expanding. But the Taiwan issue has become more difficult to manage. Washington's reappraisal of U.S.-China agreements on Taiwan, its sympathy for Taiwan's economic and political successes, and the growing assertiveness of Taiwan's democratically elected leadership have the potential to undermine cooperation between China and the United States. Frequent clashes between the two countries over economic and arms proliferation issues, even when successfully resolved, fuel American antagonism and talk of a new containment policy.

Chinese leaders remain wary of Russia's military capabilities. Despite growing Sino-Russian economic and political cooperation and Russian domestic instability and economic difficulties, the Russian military still possesses a massive nuclear arsenal that could threaten Chinese security. When Russia eventually stabilizes its political system, it will be able to mobilize vast economic and human resources and reassert itself as a power in Asia. The long Sino-Russian border could once again become a source of insecurity.

There is also uncertainty in China's strategic environment in maritime Southeast Asia. Its states have been the least susceptible to Chinese influence of China's smaller neighbors. They have close economic relations with Japan and the United States, but they have minimal economic ties with China and experience little immediate pressure from the PLA. They are able to challenge Chinese territorial claims in the South China Sea, confident that China lacks the capability to retaliate. For now this situation poses no major threat to the PRC. The region is distant from China's borders, and the South China Sea serves as a natural buffer. Japan and the United States have not used their economic influence to turn the ASEAN countries against China, nor has the United States used its naval supremacy in the South China Sea to deny China commercial or naval access to the sea-lanes. But if Beijing's relations with Washington or Tokyo worsen, maritime Southeast Asia could be used in a regional effort to isolate and contain China.

CHINA AND THE FUTURE: THREAT OR THREATENED?

Does China's growing strength portend a threat? Some observers point to China's territorial and demographic size, its modernizing economy, and its increasing defense budget as evidence that China is becoming a major world military power, capable of dominating Asia and challenging American interests. They cite China's sovereignty disputes with many of its neighbors, including with Southeast Asian states over the Paracel and Spratly Islands and with Japan over the Diaoyutai/Senkaku Islands, and its assertiveness toward Taiwan as evidence of an intent to realize territorial ambitions. Some scholars suggest that China's imperial past, its "Middle Kingdom" culture, or its Communist ideology will support a drive for regional or even global supremacy. They further argue that once China develops sufficient military power it will not shrink from using force to achieve its ambitions.[1]

These commentators call on the United States to take the lead to maintain international stability against the Chinese challenge. They argue that it should contain Chinese power by strengthening U.S. military capabilities, deploying antimissile systems on the Chinese perimeter, and consolidating regional alliances. Otherwise Asia will come under Chinese economic, political, and military dominance, and U.S. security will depend on maintaining good relations with China's authoritarian leadership.

There is no question that China is a powerful country. Its size, location, and population guarantee this. In 1950 the PLA held the U.S. Army to a standstill on the Korean peninsula. Since then China has become more powerful, achieving a degree of territorial security unknown in recent Chinese history. It has been the dominant power in Indochina since 1975, when American forces withdrew from Vietnam, and in mainland Northeast Asia since the decline of Soviet power in the late 1980s. There is also no question that China is growing stronger. By reducing the size of the

PLA and providing improved training and weaponry for its specialized infantry units, China has developed a more efficient army capable of carrying out sophisticated logistical and combined military operations. The PLA's modernization is consolidating China's conventional military supremacy on the Asian mainland.

But China's strength on mainland Asia does not constitute a threat to regional stability. On the contrary, the current balance of power is widely accepted as an appropriate foundation for building a stable post–Cold War regional order. In order for China to become a threat to the regional balance of power, it would have to develop the military strength to contend with the other great powers and the power projection capabilities to influence developments across the open seas.[2] In the ability to project power China remains by far the weakest of the four great powers in Asia. Although Beijing is upgrading its air force by purchasing Russian equipment, this force is composed mainly of 1950s and 1960s generation aircraft, and remains dependent on foreign powers for advanced military technology. The Chinese air force is still inferior to Taiwan's and ranks even further behind those of Japan and the United States. Without aircraft carriers, Chinese battleships and patrol boats operating beyond coastal waters are easy targets for the land-based aircraft of local powers, including Malaysia, Indonesia, and Singapore, and the carrier-based aircraft of the United States. Since China will likely not possess its first limited-capability aircraft carrier until 2010, it is hard to imagine that the United States could lose its naval supremacy in the western Pacific within even a quarter century, even if it stood still while China advanced, unless it chose to withdraw from the region. Russia built aircraft carriers as recently as 1992 and will be able to do so again when it stabilizes its economy and political system. Japan too is in a better position to develop power projection capabilities than China, if it opts to do so.

Given that the PRC's competitors possess a technological head start and that developing an indigenous high-technology manufacturing base is extremely difficult, China's technological level and military capabilities may fall even further behind those of its great-power rivals. Nor, despite the size of its economy and its rapid rate of growth, is China able to use economic power to advance an aggressive foreign policy. Access to the China market makes a contribution to the economies of the United States, Europe, and Northeast Asia, but these markets are more important to China than China's market is to them. China has frequently been compelled to compromise its policies to maintain access to these markets.

In the ASEAN countries China's economic influence pales besides that of the United States and Japan.

China is not a satisfied power. It has a number of outstanding territorial claims that it wants recognized by its neighbors, and it seeks veto power over Taiwan's foreign alignments. It exerts less influence than it wants in the regional balance of power and in the international nonproliferation trade, and human rights regimes. The PRC's security remains hostage to the behavior of potential adversaries and unreliable neighbors, such as the two Koreas and Vietnam. Yet these considerations give China stronger interests in favor of than against regional stability, and for rather than against cooperative relations with its potential great-power rivals. They create stronger incentives for China to accept a voice in shaping the global order than to opt out of it. Only by doing so will China be able to continue to focus its domestic resources on economic modernization while attracting the foreign trade, investment, aid, and technical assistance needed to sustain the long process of military modernization and bring its historical search for security to a satisfactory conclusion.

Since its 1979 attack on Vietnam, China has been a reactive power, striving not to alter but to maintain regional patterns of power. Its diplomacy has been in support of the status quo, aiming not to undermine but to join international regimes. China's policies toward Russia, the new Central Asian republics, India, the two Koreas, Japan, and the countries of Indochina have sought to consolidate bilateral relationships and to stabilize subregional power balances. Its military threats against Taiwan were aimed at deterring Taiwan from changing the status quo rather than at compelling it to accelerate the pace of reunification. In the South China Sea, China has acted to maintain historical claims when others challenged them, rather than to extend new claims. Friction in U.S.-China relations has come chiefly from American dissatisfaction with Chinese trade, human rights, and arms transfer policies rather than from Chinese attempts to change American behavior. While voicing criticisms of international rules of the game in all these areas, China has moved toward compliance with each set of regimes. The disputes over these regimes now involve mostly Chinese demands to enter them, as in the case of the World Trade Organization (WTO), or to shape them, as in the case of the antiproliferation and human rights regimes, rather than efforts to deny their applicability to China.

The potential remains for China to change course and adopt destabilizing policies. China's current leaders lack the revolutionary experience and political credentials of their predecessors. They are disposed to allow personal political considerations to influence policy choices. They require PLA support to stay in power. Political instability may encourage policymakers to prefer hard-line positions on nationalistic issues, including territorial disputes, Taiwan, reintegration of Hong Kong, and policy toward the United States. Chinese intransigence could contribute to heightened conflict with the West over otherwise manageable issues.

Political and economic decentralization in China will also influence its role in world affairs. China is not on the verge of disintegration. Local politicians and soldiers are loyal to the center, and the military remains an effective instrument of domestic stability and social control. But some of China's conflicts with Western nations have been exacerbated by the central government's inability to enforce international commitments on local authorities. Weak Chinese leadership and institutions will continue to plague international cooperation on a wide range of issues.

Seizing the Opportunity

The challenge posed to the West by the rise of Chinese power is thus not to frustrate China's ambitions but to respond to its interest in a stable international environment by integrating China into a post–Cold War order that serves Chinese interests and those of other countries. The problem, for both the Chinese and their neighbors, is to find the balance point of common interests where security can be achieved for all. China can no longer protect itself behind a Great Wall that deters foreign invasion and fends off foreign influence. Nor can it achieve its goals by challenging more-powerful enemies with claims to be stronger than it actually is. China as well as its neighbors can be secure only when China is part of a world system that it has a hand in shaping.

China's integration into the global order requires that the West develop three distinct agendas for its China policy. First, in defense policy, America needs to maintain current deployments in order to prevent destabilizing changes in the regional balance of power. The United States possesses strategic superiority throughout Asia. Its navy faces no challenger, and it enjoys cooperative security relations with Japan, the second-most-powerful country in the region, and with other states there. The American presence reassures Japan that America is a reliable partner and reassures the smaller powers that they do not have to placate either Japan or China to maintain their security. For now, Beijing views the U.S. military presence in Asia as a force for stability, especially because it inhibits Japan from developing an independent military policy. The United States should maintain its forces at current levels, avoiding reductions that suggest that it is withdrawing from Asia.

But Washington should also avoid unnecessary measures that would diminish Chinese security. While maintaining their security relationship, the United States and Japan should take care to assure China that they are willing to give it a voice in establishing the post–Cold War regional order. If Beijing were to conclude that Tokyo and Washington are cooperating to "contain" the "China threat," it might adopt adversarial policies imposing unnecessary economic and military costs on Washington and Tokyo, such as unrestrained weapons proliferation, obstructionism on the Korean peninsula, and enhanced strategic cooperation with Russia. The current level of U.S.-Japan cooperation is suited to present circumstances. Barring a significant worsening of regional tensions, Washington should not deploy a theater missile defense system in Asia. Such weapons systems perfectly embody the security dilemma. While they might be useful in intercepting Chinese or North Korean missiles launched preemptively against their neighbors in Asia, their presence would also deprive China of its second-strike deterrent capability. China might well respond by withdrawing from international arms control agreements and deploying additional ICBMs.

Second, the integration of China into a stable international order requires effective management of conflicts of interests. Despite the broad congruence of Chinese and Western interests in building such an order, many issues permit no immediate solution that gives each side all it wants. Progress entails some loss and some gain for each side. Current examples of such disputes involve trade, weapons proliferation, human rights, and Taiwan. In these cases the West should combine a clear sense of policy direction with a tactical mix of firmness and compromise. While negotiations go forward on matters in dispute, cooperation on matters of common interest should also be pursued, to lay the basis for an easier resolution of future conflicts.

On trade the United States and its economic partners should continue to push China to expand foreign access to its market and to protect Western copyrights and patents. Step-by-step goals must be realistic, since the Chinese government lacks the ability fully to control local authorities and since some issues, such as trade imbalances, reflect economic dynamics beyond short-term government control. Western policies should also take into account Chinese interests, lest China simply decide to opt out of the WTO system and adopt destabilizing protectionist or even mercantilist policies. In combination with Chinese self-interest, trade friction creates an important incentive for Beijing to reform its economic system. Meanwhile, the Western nations should facilitate increased consultation between their own specialists and Chinese regulators, bankers, lawyers, insurance officials, customs officials, and others, contributing to the long-term reform of China's economic, legal, and administrative systems involved in trade.

On proliferation the West must continue to challenge Chinese arms exports that damage Western interests. American policy has persuaded Chinese leaders that missile and nuclear weapons sales to U.S. adversaries, including such states as Syria and Iran, would undermine relations. Washington must maintain the credibility of this policy, continue to warn the PRC of the costs of disregarding U.S. interests, and impose sanctions when Chinese leaders ignore important U.S. interests. Chinese assistance to the Pakistani nuclear weapon and missile programs is going to be an especially hard problem to resolve because it serves a fundamental Chinese security interest. Final resolution of this issue will probably not come until arms control or other arrangements in South Asia offer an improvement in Pakistan's security. Meanwhile, exchanges between Chinese and Western military and arms control establishments can help create a common language in which technical arms control issues can be discussed with less misunderstanding. The United States should also acknowledge that some Chinese arms exports reflect vital PRC strategic interests and do not affect vital U.S. interests. Washington should deal differently with exports that reflect central PRC government policies and those that reflect decisions made by autonomous local actors. Western assistance can be helpful in strengthening China's arms export control institutions so that the government is better able to make good on its antiproliferation commitments.

Human rights diplomacy must also be a central component of Western policy toward China. Failure to speak out for human rights in China would not only ignore the fate of courageous Chinese proponents of democratic values but also undermine the support of the American public for U.S.-China cooperation on a wide range of issues. Moreover, the promotion of human rights serves the West's interests in a more stable world order. Just as the West seeks to create international trade and nonproliferation regimes that are robust and effective, so too a solid international human rights regime can contribute to stability. Such a regime may help ameliorate the internal and international behavior of states. It cannot be effective without encompassing the world's largest country[3]. In addition, rule of law is essential to protect Western business and other interests in China.

Chinese human rights abuses should be part of the agenda of all high-level meetings with Chinese leaders. The United States should cooperate with other Western countries to mobilize international pressure in multilateral settings, including the United Nations Commission on Human Rights in Geneva.[4] The United States and other Western countries should not underestimate the important successes they have achieved in promoting reform in China. Contemporary Chinese society is more open and freer from government involvement than at any time since 1949, and it continues to improve. A major impetus behind this development has been international involvement in the Chinese economy and the exposure of Chinese society to Western values and culture. Educational exchanges have enabled China's intellectual community to develop an understanding of Western political and legal institutions. Many members of China's next generation of political leaders received training in the West, where they learned how an open political system can contribute to political stability. To promote continued political liberalization in China and stable U.S.-China relations, Western governments should expand educational and cultural exchanges with China.

The most explosive issue in Chinese foreign policy concerns Taiwan. Washington must maintain a Taiwan policy that enables the United States to protect both common U.S.-Taiwan interests and America's interest in stable relations with the PRC. In the 1970s and 1980s the United States developed cooperative relations with China while providing Taiwan with the security it required to ward off mainland pressures and thrive economically and politically. Washington must continue to keep Taiwan secure. It can do so by reminding Beijing of the costs of any use of force against Taiwan, by supplying Taiwan with sufficient military equipment to stabilize the mainland-Taiwan balance of power, and by maintaining economic and cultural ties with Taiwan.

At the same time the United States must accommodate China's interest in preventing international recognition of Taiwan as a sovereign state. This requires that the United States persist in its one-China policy. Taiwan flourished under this policy during the 1980s and early 1990s, despite the absence of Taiwan leadership visits to the United States and participation in the United Nations, and can do so in the future. If Washington impresses on Taipei the limits to U.S. support and the cost to Taiwan of disregarding mainland interests, Taiwan can continue to prosper in a stable regional environment. In short America should continue not to take sides in the mainland-Taiwan conflict but to insist on a peaceful solution arrived at by the two parties.

The third element of U.S. policy should be to integrate China into multilateral institutions. Beijing wants to play by the rules of the international community but also to help develop the rules. It is in the interest of the United States and its allies that China join the international community on these terms and that Chinese membership be based on accommodation of Chinese interests as well as Chinese accommodation of the interests of other nations. Chinese participation with Russia, Central Asian countries, and India in significant confidence-building measures indicates that Beijing can be a constructive partner in developing a stable international order. China is not yet a member of the major functional international institutions that regulate international trade and weapons proliferation. It is not a member of the WTO or the Missile Technology Control Regime. It has also not been invited to attend Group of Seven meetings, bringing together the world's major economies, although Russia participates. It has not been asked to help formulate new post–Cold War arms control institutions, including the Zangger Committee and the Nuclear Suppliers Group, which are concerned with exports of nuclear-related technologies, the Australia Group, which deals with the proliferation of dual-use chemicals and biological agents, and the Wassenar Arrangement, regarding the transparency of weapons exports. Since these institutions are new, PRC participation would not be complicated by a need to bring China into compliance with preexisting rules and would give Beijing the voice it seeks in drawing up the rules of the emerging post–Cold War international order.

Negotiations over Chinese membership in preexisting and well-established multilateral institutions will require complex bargaining. Yet is imperative that China be brought in. When China is excluded, it is under no obligation to adhere to their rules, yet it loses minimal benefits, other than prestige. This is true of its membership in the WTO—Beijing is in no hurry to join the WTO since it already enjoys full access to the markets of the advanced industrial powers.[5] It is also true of the various arms control groups; for the most part exclusion costs Beijing only prestige. On the other hand, membership can impose on China regulations it has agreed to follow. Multilateral pressure on China to comply with international norms can be more effective than unilateral U.S. pressure, when Chinese leaders understand that other countries will support U.S. sanctions. It is also politically easier for them to compromise with the international community than with the United States.

CHINA'S PLACE IN THE WORLD

Does Chinese power threaten the rest of the world? The issue is misstated when it is posed as a question about China alone. The China threat is a matter not of absolute Chinese capabilities but of Chinese capabilities relative to those of others, not of Chinese interests in isolation but of how these can be served in tandem with the interests of others. The question is not whether China has the capability to damage other countries' interests if it feels it needs to, but whether its interests can be accommodated so that it does not need to do so to ensure its security.

The outcome will depend on the power structure that the United States, Japan, Russia, and China shape in Asia. If these four countries accommodate each other's interests and help strengthen regional and global institutions that set rules for some aspects of interstate relations, China will find that its security lies in cooperation with the other powers. If the powers are unable to establish a consensual regional order, the result will be at best an armed and fragile peace.

Widening cycles of suspicion could lead to polarization. China might find itself contained by the United States and its allies, including Japan— or by Japan alone if the United States withdraws from the region—and Russia might choose to stand on either side of the divide. In this eventuality China would both be threatened and pose a threat to others. Barring an American economic collapse or withdrawal from Asia, China would continue to be weaker than its enemies. But it would be capable of wreaking great damage.

Management of the transition to a new power structure in Asia will not be easy. Just as China's international role is growing, its capacity for unified political leadership is weakening. The post–Deng Xiaoping regime is likely to be more divided than Mao's or Deng's, less able to coordinate its bureaucracies, and less able to follow a consistent foreign policy strategy. So far, Chinese foreign policy remains less politicized than that of the

West. Still, its further politicization will make the transition in Asia more difficult.

That is why it is important for the West itself to pursue a more strategic policy toward China. To understand what motivates Chinese foreign policy is not to counsel yielding to all Chinese demands. Precisely because China's security concerns are real, they cannot be resolved by sympathetic understanding, symbolic reassurance, or even substantive concessions. China's vulnerability is a fact; it will remain a fact for a long time under any plausible scenario for the future of the international system. Understanding its causes and consequences should help Western policymakers accommodate China when they should, persuade China when they can, and resist China when they must.

NOTES

FOREWORD

1. Robert Gilpin, *War and Change in International Politics* (Cambridge: Cambridge University Press, 1981), chap. 5.
2. Samuel S. Kim, "China and the World in Theory and Practice," in Kim, ed., *China and the World: Chinese Foreign Relations in the Post–Cold War Era,* 3rd ed. (Boulder: Westview Press, 1994), chap. 1; Friedrich W. Wu, "Explanatory Approaches to Chinese Foreign Policy: A Critique of the Western Literature," *Studies in Comparative Communism* 13, no. 1 (Spring 1980): 41–62; Bin Yu, "The Study of Chinese Foreign Policy: Problems and Prospect," *World Politics* 46 (January 1994): 235–61.
3. Robert O. Keohane, ed., *Neorealism and Its Critics* (New York: Columbia University Press, 1986).
4. Diplomatic historians who argue that China's "Middle Kingdom syndrome" affects current policy stress that Chinese culture inhibits realist behavior; see John King Fairbank, ed., *The Chinese World Order: Traditional China's Foreign Relations* (Cambridge: Harvard University Press, 1968). For the argument that Chinese realism reflects Chinese culture rather than anarchy, see Alastair Iain Johnston, *Cultural Realism: Strategic Cultural and Grand Strategy in Chinese History* (Princeton: Princeton University Press, 1995).
5. Robert Jervis, *Perception and Misperception in International Relations* (Princeton: Princeton University Press, 1976), chap. 3.
6. Robert D. Putnam, "Diplomacy and Domestic Politics: The Logic of Two-Level Games," *International Organization* 42 (Summer 1988): 427–60; Peter B. Evans,

Harold K. Jacobson, and Robert D. Putnam, eds., *Double-Edged Diplomacy: International Bargaining and Domestic Politics* (Berkeley: University of California Press, 1993); James N. Rosenau, *Linkage Politics: Essays on the Convergence of National and International Systems* (New York: Free Press, 1969).

1 CHINA'S PLACE IN THE WORLD

1. The coastal provinces have a combined population of 468 million, while the combined population of Japan, Indonesia, South Korea, Malaysia, Thailand, Taiwan, Singapore, and Hong Kong comes to 458 million.
2. World Bank, *The World Bank Atlas 1996* (Washington, D.C.: World Bank, 1995), pp. 18–20.
3. China has verbally assured the Indonesians that their claims in the South China Sea do not overlap, although the exact boundaries of both sides' claims remain unclear. According to Eric Hyer (personal communication, June 13, 1996), there is some evidence that the boundary with North Korea was settled by secret treaty, but also evidence that some in the Chinese government are questioning that settlement. Useful accounts of Chinese border agreements and disputes are Byron N. Tzou, *China and International Law: The Boundary Disputes* (New York: Praeger, 1990), and Eric Hyer, "The South China Sea Disputes: Implications of China's Earlier Territorial Settlements," *Pacific Affairs* 68 (Spring 1995): 34–54.
4. A good discussion of China's security situation is Gerald Segal, *Defending China* (London: Oxford University Press, 1985).
5. "Third front" is also sometimes translated as "third line." Local "small third fronts" were established in many provinces by moving industries from coastal and plains cities to remoter areas. Barry Naughton, "The Third Front: Defence Industrialization in the Chinese Interior," *China Quarterly*, no. 115 (September 1988): 351–86.
6. There are also large concentrations on the Chengdu Plain and along the Yangtze River.
7. The number of autonomous administrative units is given as of 1990. *The National Economic Atlas of China* (Hong Kong: Oxford University Press, 1994), "Notes to the Maps," bk. 1, pp. 3–4.
8. Ping-ti Ho, *Studies in the Population of China, 1368–1953* (Cambridge: Harvard University Press, 1959), p. 281.
9. Michael B. Yahuda, *China's Role in World Affairs* (London: Croom Helm, 1978), p. 13.
10. Michael R. Chambers, "Explaining China's Alliances: Balancing against Regional and Superpower Threats" (Ph.D. diss., Columbia University, in progress). Minor exceptions include Nepal, Bhutan, Sikkim, and Laos.
11. Yahuda, *Role*, p. 11.
12. United Nations Development Programme, *Human Development Report 1995* (New York: Oxford University Press, 1995), p. 156.

2 LEGACIES

1. Wolfram Eberhard, *China's Minorities: Yesterday and Today* (Belmont, Calif.: Wadsworth, 1982), pp. 8–10; Ying-shih Yü, "Minzu yishi yu guojia guannian" (Ethnic consciousness and the state concept), *Mingbao yuekan* 18, no. 12 (December 1983): 3.

2. John King Fairbank, ed., *The Chinese World Order: Traditional China's Foreign Relations* (Cambridge: Harvard University Press, 1968); Mark Mancall, *China at the Center: 300 Years of Foreign Policy* (New York: Free Press, 1984).
3. Joseph Fletcher, "Ch'ing Inner Asia *c.* 1800," "Sino-Russian Relations, 1800–62," and "The Heyday of the Ch'ing Order in Mongolia, Sinkiang and Tibet," in *The Cambridge History of China,* vol. 10, ed. John K. Fairbank (Cambridge: Cambridge University Press, 1978), pp. 35–106, 318–50, 351–408; Owen Lattimore et al., *Pivot of Asia: Sinkiang and the Inner Asian Frontiers of China and Russia* (Boston: Little, Brown, 1950); Morris Rossabi, *China and Inner Asia from 1368 to the Present Day* (London: Thames and Hudson, 1975).
4. Morris Rossabi, "Traditional Chinese Foreign Policy and Intersocietal Cooperation," in Harry Harding, ed., *Patterns of Cooperation in the Foreign Relations of Modern China* (forthcoming); also see Joseph F. Fletcher, "China and Central Asia, 1368–1884," in Fairbank, ed., *World Order,* pp. 206–24.
5. Arthur Waldron, *The Great Wall of China: From History to Myth* (Cambridge: Cambridge University Press, 1990).
6. The quotations come from Sun Tzu, *The Art of War,* trans. Thomas Cleary (Boston: Shambhala, 1988), pp. 64, 59, and 75. The quotation in the next paragraph is from p. 112.
7. "The Present Situation and Our Tasks," in *Selected Works of Mao Tse-tung* (Peking: Foreign Languages Press, 1961), vol. 4, p. 161.
8. Growth rates except for Hong Kong: Angus Maddison, *Monitoring the World Economy, 1820–1992* (Paris: Development Centre of the Organisation for Economic Co-operation and Development, 1995), p. 83; Hong Kong growth rate: *Hong Kong Economic and Trade Statistics (1947–1987)* (Hong Kong: Haren Trade Consulting, 1988), p. 3; per capita GNPs except for Taiwan: World Bank, *World Tables, 1989–90 Edition* (Baltimore: Johns Hopkins University Press, 1990), pp. 180, 328, 340, giving China's GNP per capita in 1978 as $220, South Korea's as $1,190, and Hong Kong's as $3,750; Taiwan per capita GNP of $1,559 given in *National Income in the Taiwan Area: The Republic of China: National Accounts for 1951–1985 and Preliminary Estimates for 1986* (Taipei: Directorate-General of Budget, Accounting and Statistics, Executive Yuan, Republic of China, 1986), p. 15.
9. Andrew J. Nathan, "Beijing Blues," *New Republic,* January 23, 1995, pp. 34–40.
10. R. Randle Edwards, "Imperial China's Border Control Law," *Journal of Chinese Law* 1 (Spring 1987): 33–62.
11. Fletcher, "Ch'ing Inner Asia," pp. 105, 377–85, 395–407.
12. Current estimates of overseas Chinese in the world are 25–30 million and 36 million, respectively, from Wang Gungwu, "Greater China and the Overseas Chinese," *China Quarterly,* no. 136 (December 1993): 927; and *The Republic of China Yearbook 1995* (Taipei: Government Information Office, 1995), p. 189. The classic work on the early phase of the PRC's overseas Chinese policy is Stephen Fitzgerald, *China and the Overseas Chinese: A Study of Peking's Changing Policy, 1949–1970* (Cambridge: Cambridge University Press, 1972). For a discussion of the overseas Chinese as a liability in PRC diplomacy, see Robert S. Ross, "Ethnic Chinese in Southeast Asia: Political Liability/Economic Asset," in Joyce K. Kallgren, Noordin Sopiee, and Soedjati Djiwandono, eds., *ASEAN and China: An Evolving Relationship* (Berkeley: Institute for East Asian Studies, University of California, Berkeley, 1988), pp. 147–76.
13. Eberhard, *China's Minorities;* Edward Friedman, "Reconstructing China's National Identity: A Southern Alternative to Mao-Era Anti-Imperialist Nationalism,"

Journal of Asian Studies 53 (February 1994): 67–91; Emily Honig, *Creating Chinese Ethnicity: Subei People in Shanghai, 1850–1980* (New Haven: Yale University Press, 1992).

14. June Teufel Dreyer, *China's Forty Millions: Minority Nationalities and National Integration in the People's Republic of China* (Cambridge: Harvard University Press, 1976), pp. 141–46; David Yen-ho Wu, "The Construction of Chinese and Non-Chinese Identities," *Daedalus* 120, no. 2 (Spring 1991): 159–79; Dru C. Gladney, *Muslim Chinese: Ethnic Nationalism in the People's Republic* (Cambridge: Council on East Asian Studies, Harvard University, 1991).

15. Su Xiaokang and Wang Luxiang, *Deathsong of the River: A Reader's Guide to the Chinese TV Series "Heshang,"* introduced, translated, and annotated by Richard W. Bodman and Pin P. Wan (Ithaca: East Asia Program, Cornell University, 1991).

16. Now these are common in world trade, and what is exceptional is not granting but withholding MFN status, as America has threatened to do several times from China because of human rights concerns; see Chapter 10.

3 The Rise and Decline of the Russian Threat

1. *Selected Works of Mao Tse-tung* (Peking: Foreign Languages Press, 1961), vol. 4, p. 415.

2. Steven I. Levine, *Anvil of Victory: The Communist Revolution in Manchuria, 1945–1948* (New York: Columbia University Press, 1987), chaps. 1–2.

3. *The Secret Speeches of Chairman Mao: From the Hundred Flowers to the Great Leap Forward,* ed. Roderick MacFarquhar, Timothy Cheek, and Eugene Wu (Cambridge: Harvard University Council on East Asian Studies, 1989), p. 142. Other sources give higher figures; e.g., R. J. Rummel, *China's Bloody Century: Genocide and Mass Murder since 1900* (New Brunswick: Transaction, 1991), pp. 219–36.

4. "Minutes, Conversation between Mao Zedong and Ambassador Yudin, 22 July 1958," in *Cold War International History Project Bulletin,* nos. 6–7 (Winter 1995–96): 156.

5. Nicholas R. Lardy, "Economic Recovery and the 1st Five-Year Plan," in *The Cambridge History of China,* vol. 14, ed. Roderick MacFarquhar and John K. Fairbank (Cambridge: Cambridge University Press, 1987), p. 179; Zhang Shuguang, "The Collapse of Sino-Soviet Economic Cooperation, 1950–1960: A Cultural Explanation" (paper prepared for the Cold War International History Project Hong Kong Conference on the Cold War in Asia, January 9–12, 1996); Sergei Goncharov, John W. Lewis, and Xue Litai, *Uncertain Partners: Stalin, Mao, and the Korean War* (Stanford: Stanford University Press, 1993).

6. The negotiations over nuclear cooperation are discussed in John Wilson Lewis and Xue Litai, *China Builds the Bomb* (Stanford: Stanford University Press, 1988), pp. 60–65.

7. "Minutes, Conversation between Mao Zedong and Ambassador Yudin, 22 July 1958," pp. 155–59.

8. William Taubman, "Khrushchev vs. Mao: A Preliminary Sketch of the Role of Personality in the Sino-Soviet Dispute" (paper prepared for the Cold War International History Project Hong Kong Conference on the Cold War in Asia, January 9–12, 1996), pp. 8–9.

9. Lewis and Xue, *China Builds the Bomb,* pp. 64–65; Mark Kramer, "The Soviet Foreign Ministry's Appraisal of Sino-Soviet Relations on the Eve of the Split"

(paper prepared for the Cold War International History Project Hong Kong Conference on the Cold War in Asia, January 9–12, 1996).

10. Khrushchev, quoted in Steven M. Goldstein, "The Sino-Soviet Alliance, 1937–1962: Ideology and Unity," in Harry Harding, ed., *Patterns of Cooperation in the Foreign Relations of Modern China* (forthcoming).

11. John Gittings, *Survey of the Sino-Soviet Dispute: A Commentary & Extracts from the Recent Polemics, 1963–1967* (New York: Oxford University Press, 1968).

12. Thomas Robinson, "China Confronts the Soviet Union: Warfare and Diplomacy on China's Inner Asian Frontiers," in *The Cambridge History of China*, vol. 15, ed. Roderick MacFarquhar and John K. Fairbank (Cambridge: Cambridge University Press, 1991), chap. 3.

13. Richard H. Solomon and Masataka Kosaka, eds., *The Soviet Far East Military Buildup: Nuclear Dilemmas and Asian Security* (Dover, Mass.: Auburn House, 1986); Harry Gelman, *The Soviet Far East Buildup and Soviet Risk-Taking against China* (Santa Monica: RAND, 1982).

14. Xiong Xianghui, "Dakai ZhongMei guanxi de qianzou" (Prelude to the opening of U.S.-China relations), *Zhonggong dangshi ziliao*, no. 42 (Beijing: Zhonggong dangshi chubanshe, 1992), pp. 56–96.

15. Michael B. Yahuda, "The Significance of Tripolarity in China's Policy toward the United States since 1972," in Robert S. Ross, ed., *China, the United States, and the Soviet Union: Tripolarity and Policy Making in the Cold War* (Armonk, N.Y.: M. E. Sharpe, 1993), pp. 11–37.

16. Owen Lattimore et al., *Pivot of Asia: Sinkiang and the Inner Asian Frontiers of China and Russia* (Boston: Little Brown, 1950); Herbert J. Ellison, "Political Transformation of the Communist States: Impact on the International Order of Asia," in Robert S. Ross, ed., *East Asia in Transition: Toward a New Regional Order* (Armonk, N.Y.: M. E. Sharpe, 1995), pp. 295–324; Steven I. Levine, "Second Chance in China: Sino-Soviet Relations in the 1990s," *Annals of the American Academy of Political and Social Science* 519 (January 1992): 26–38.

17. James Rupert, "Dateline Tashkent: Post-Soviet Central Asia," *Foreign Policy*, no. 87 (Summer 1992): 189.

18. *ITAR-TASS*, June 26, 1995, in Foreign Broadcast Information Service (FBIS)/CIS, June 26, 1995, p. 4.

19. Bates Gill and Taeho Kim, *China's Arms Acquisitions from Abroad: A Quest for "Superb and Secret Weapons,"* SIPRI Report, no. 11 (Oxford: Oxford University Press, 1995).

20. *Interfax*, August 24, 1995, in FBIS/CIS, August 25, 1995, p. 15. On the size of the Chinese population in eastern Russia and for an extensive analysis of border relations, see James Clay Moltz, "Regional Tension in the Russo-Chinese Rapprochement," *Asian Survey* 35 (June 1995): 511–27.

21. *Zhongguo tongxun she*, December 16, 1993, in FBIS/China, December 17, 1993, pp. 6–7.

4 THE AMERICAN PUZZLE

1. Michael H. Hunt, *The Making of a Special Relationship: The United States and China to 1913* (New York: Columbia University Press, 1983).

2. Dorothy Borg and Waldo Heinrichs, eds., *Uncertain Years: Chinese-American Relations, 1947–1950* (New York: Columbia University Press, 1980); Nancy Bernkopf Tucker, *Patterns in the Dust: Chinese-American Relations and the Recognition Controversy, 1949–1950* (New York: Columbia University Press, 1983).

3. Sergei N. Goncharov, John Lewis, and Xue Litai, *Uncertain Partners: Stalin, Mao, and the Korean War* (Stanford: Stanford University Press, 1993). For the courtyard quotation, see *Mao Zedong waijiao wenxuan* (Selected documents on Mao Zedong's diplomacy) (Beijing: Zhongyang wenxian chubanshe and Shijie zhishi chubanshe, 1994), p. 79.
4. Chen Jian, *China's Road to the Korean War: The Making of the Sino-American Confrontation* (New York: Columbia University Press, 1994); William Stueck, *The Korean War: An International History* (Princeton: Princeton University Press, 1995).
5. Gordon H. Chang, *Friends and Enemies: The United States, China, and the Soviet Union, 1948–1972* (Stanford: Stanford University Press, 1990).
6. Nancy Bernkopf Tucker, *Taiwan, Hong Kong, and the United States, 1945–1992: Uncertain Friendships* (New York: Twayne, 1994).
7. Thomas E. Stolper, *China, Taiwan, and the Offshore Islands* (Armonk, N.Y.: M. E. Sharpe, 1985); Thomas J. Christensen, *Useful Adversaries: Grand Strategy, Domestic Mobilization, and Sino-American Conflict, 1947–58* (Princeton: Princeton University Press, 1996).
8. "Talk with the American Correspondent Anna Louise Strong," *Selected Works of Mao Tse-tung*, vol. 4 (Peking: Foreign Languages Press, 1961), p. 100.
9. Chang, *Friends and Enemies*, pp. 241–43.
10. Robert S. Ross, *Negotiating Cooperation: U.S.-China Relations, 1969–1989* (New York: Columbia University Press, 1995); Harry Harding, *A Fragile Relationship: The United States and China since 1972* (Washington, D.C.: Brookings Institution, 1992); Rosemary Foot, *The Practice of Power: U.S. Relations with China since 1949* (Oxford: Oxford University Press, 1995).
11. Robert M. Gates, *From the Shadows: The Ultimate Insiders' Story of Five Presidents and How They Won the Cold War* (New York: Simon & Schuster, 1996), pp. 122–23; Eden Y. Woon, "Chinese Arms Sales and U.S.-China Military Relations," *Asian Survey* 29 (June 1989): 600–618.
12. Robert S. Ross, "National Security, Human Rights, and Domestic Politics: The Bush Administration and China," in Kenneth A. Oye, Robert J. Leiber, and Donald Rothchild, eds., *Eagle in a New World: American Grand Strategy in the Post–Cold War Era* (New York: HarperCollins, 1992), pp. 281–313.
13. Nicholas R. Lardy, *China in the World Economy* (Washington, D.C.: Institute for International Economics, 1994).
14. James Shinn, ed., *Weaving the Net: Conditional Engagement with China* (New York: Council on Foreign Relations, 1996), p. 86.

5 Difficult Friends: Japan and the Two Koreas

1. Chae-Jin Lee, *Japan Faces China: Political and Economic Relations in the Postwar Era* (Baltimore: Johns Hopkins University Press, 1976).
2. Chae-Jin Lee, *China and Japan: New Economic Diplomacy* (Stanford: Hoover Institution Press, 1984).
3. *Zhongguo duiwai jingji maoyi nianjian: 1984* (Yearbook of Chinese foreign economics and trade) (Beijing: China's Foreign Economics and Trade Press, 1984), IV-184; *China's Foreign Economic Statistics* (Beijing: China Statistical Information and Consultancy Center, 1992), pp. 333–35.
4. Richard J. Samuels, *Rich Nation/Strong Army: National Security and the Technological Transformation of Japan* (Ithaca: Cornell University Press, 1994); Michael J. Green, *Arming Japan: Defense Production, Alliance Politics, and the Postwar Search for Autonomy* (New York: Columbia University Press, 1995).

5. Allen S. Whiting, *China Eyes Japan* (Berkeley: University of California Press, 1989).
6. *Renmin ribao* (overseas edition), June 29, 1987, p. 1; *Beijing Review,* July 20, 1987, pp. 21–22.
7. Whiting, *China Eyes Japan,* pp. 154, 155.
8. Allen S. Whiting, "China and Japan: Politics versus Economics," *Annals of the American Academy of Political and Social Science* 519 (January 1992): 39–51.
9. Robert S. Ross, *Managing a Changing Relationship: China's Japan Policy in the 1990s* (Carlisle, Penn.: Strategic Studies Institute, U.S. Army War College, 1996); Michael J. Green and Benjamin L. Self, "Japan's Changing China Policy," *Survival,* summer 1996, pp. 35–58.
10. Kyodo, June 23, 1995, in FBIS/China, June 26, 1995, p. 1; Kyodo, June 24, 1995, in FBIS/China, June 27, 1995, p. 13.
11. *Xinhua,* September 21, 1995, in FBIS/China, September 21, 1995, p. 1; *Ta Kung Pao,* September 23, 1995, in FBIS/China, October 16, 1995, p. 4.
12. *Sankei shimbun,* March 14, 1996, in FBIS/EAS, March 15, 1996, p. 7; *Nihon keizai shimbun,* March 17, 1996, in FBIS/EAS, March 18, 1996, p. 20; Kyodo, March 19, 1996, in FBIS/China, March 19, 1996, pp. 1–2.
13. Da Jun, "Where Will Japan Go?" *Xinhua,* December 7, 1995, in FBIS/China, December 7, 1995, pp. 4–5; Chen Lineng, "The Japanese Self-defense Forces Are Marching toward the 21st Century," *Guoji zhanwang,* no. 2, 1996, in FBIS/China, May 1, 1996, p. 12.
14. Chen Zhijiang, "Japan-U.S. Joint Declaration on Security—A Dangerous Signal," *Guangming ribao,* April 18, 1996, in FBIS/China, April 23, 1996, p. 2; Zhang Guocheng, "Japan's Constitution Is Facing a Test," *Renmin ribao,* April 23, 1996, in FBIS/China, April 29, 1996, pp. 3–4.
15. Liu Huaqing, "Evaluation and Analysis of China's Nuclear Arms Control Policy," *Xiandai junshi,* November 11, 1995, in FBIS/China, December 22, 1995, pp. 6–11.
16. *Zhongguo xinwen she,* January 18, 1996, in FBIS/China, January 19, 1996, p. 32; *Yomiuri shimbun,* April 1, 1996, in FBIS/EAS, April 3, 1996, p. 14.
17. Zhang Jing, "Reform of the UN Security Council," *Beijing Review,* October 23–29, 1995, in FBIS/China, October 23, 1995, p. 6.
18. Kyodo, March 2, 1996, in FBIS/EAS, March 4, 1996, p. 43.
19. Thomas P. Bernstein and Andrew J. Nathan, "The Soviet Union, China and Korea," in Gerald L. Curtis and Sung-joo Han, eds., *The U.S.-South Korean Alliance: Evolving Patterns in Security Relations* (Lexington, Mass.: Lexington Books, 1983), pp. 89–127; Hao Yufan, "China and the Korean Peninsula: A Chinese View," *Asian Survey* 27 (August 1987): 862–84.
20. Robert A. Scalapino, "Korea in the Cold War and Its Aftermath," in Robert S. Ross, ed., *East Asia in Transition: Toward a New World Order* (Armonk, N.Y.: M. E. Sharpe, 1995) pp. 183–215.
21. *Xinhua,* February 27, 1996, in FBIS/China, February 27, 1996, pp. 4–5.
22. *Wen Wei Po* (Hong Kong), February 14, 1996, in FBIS/China, February 16, 1996, pp. 4–5.
23. *Ta Kung Pao* (Hong Kong), June 3, 1994, in FBIS/China, June 6, 1994, pp. 9–10; June 2, 1994, statement by the PRC Foreign Ministry spokesman, Agence France Presse, June 2, 1994, in FBIS/China, June 3, 1994, p. 1.
24. For example, Assistant Secretary of State Winston Lord's October 11, 1995, testimony before the Senate Foreign Relations Committee, Asian and Pacific Affairs Subcommittee.

6 NEIGHBORS TO THE SOUTH

1. The original members of ASEAN are Thailand, Malaysia, Singapore, Indonesia, and the Philippines. Brunei joined ASEAN in 1984; Vietnam, in 1995. For most of the period discussed in this chapter, Vietnam was not a member of ASEAN.
2. William J. Duiker, *The Communist Road to Power in Vietnam* (Boulder: Westview Press, 1981).
3. Zhai Qiang, "China and the Geneva Conference of 1954," *China Quarterly*, no. 129 (March 1992): 103–22.
4. Chen Jian, "China's Involvement in the Vietnam War, 1964–1969," *China Quarterly*, no. 142 (June 1995): 356–87.
5. D. P. Mozingo and T. W. Robinson, *Lin Biao on People's War* (Santa Monica: RAND, 1965).
6. Robert S. Ross, *The Indochina Tangle: China's Vietnam Policy, 1975–1979* (New York: Columbia University Press, 1988).
7. Richard H. Solomon and Masataka Kosaka, *The Soviet Far East Military Buildup: Nuclear Dilemmas and Asian Security* (Dover, Mass.: Auburn House, 1986); Donald S. Zagoria, ed., *Soviet Policy in East Asia* (New Haven: Yale University Press, 1982).
8. Robert S. Ross, "China and the Cambodian Peace Process: The Value of Coercive Diplomacy," *Asian Survey* 31 (December 1991): 170–85.
9. David Mozingo, *Chinese Policy toward Indonesia, 1949–1967* (Ithaca: Cornell University Press, 1976); Marshall Green, John H. Holdrige, and William N. Stokes, *War and Peace in China: First-hand Experiences in the Foreign Service of the United States* (Bethesda, Md.: Dacor Press, 1994).
10. Melvin Gurtov, *China and Southeast Asia—The Politics of Survival: A Study of Foreign Policy Interaction* (Baltimore: Johns Hopkins University Press, 1971).
11. Jay Taylor, *China and Southeast Asia: Peking's Relations with Revolutionary Movements*, 2nd ed. (Boulder: Westview Press, 1976); Peter Van Ness, *Revolution and Chinese Foreign Policy: Peking's Support for Wars of National Liberation* (Berkeley: University of California Press, 1970).
12. Stephen Fitzgerald, *China and the Overseas Chinese: A Study of Peking's Changing Policy, 1949–1970* (New York: Cambridge University Press, 1972).
13. Alexander J. Yeats, *China's Foreign Trade and Comparative Advantage: Prospects, Problems, and Policy Implications*, World Bank Discussion Papers, no. 141 (Washington, D.C.: World Bank, 1991); Fred Herschede, "Trade between China and ASEAN: The Impact of the Pacific Rim Era," *Pacific Affairs* 64 (Summer 1991): 179–93.
14. Stephen Leong, "Malaysia and the People's Republic of China in the 1980s: Political Vigilance and Economic Pragmatism," *Asian Survey* 27 (October 1987): 1119.
15. Mark J. Valencia, *China and the South China Sea Disputes: Conflicting Claims and Potential Solutions in the South China Sea*, Adelphi Paper, no. 298 (London: Oxford University Press, 1995).
16. Allen S. Whiting, *The Chinese Calculus of Deterrence: India and Indochina* (Ann Arbor: University of Michigan Press, 1975).
17. J. D. Armstrong, *Revolutionary Diplomacy: Chinese Foreign Policy and the United Front Doctrine* (Berkeley: University of California Press, 1977), pp. 159–64; also Yaacov Y. I. Vertzberger, *China's Southwestern Strategy: Encirclement and Counterencirclement* (New York: Praeger, 1985), pp. 21–45.

18. Carnegie Task Force on Non-Proliferation and South Asian Security, *Nuclear Weapons and South Asian Security* (Washington, D.C.: Carnegie Endowment for International Peace, 1988).
19. T. Karki Hussain, "China's Calculus in South Asia," in Naranarayan Das, ed., *Contemporary Chinese Politics and Foreign Policy* (London: Sangam Books, 1989), pp. 169–71; Steven I. Levine, "China and South Asia," *Strategic Analysis* (New Delhi) 21 (January 1989): 1107–26.
20. Surjit Mansingh and Steven I. Levine, "China and India: Moving beyond Confrontation," *Problems of Communism* 38, nos. 2–3 (March–June 1989): 37–38.

7 POLICY-MAKING

1. Paul H. Kreisberg, "China's Negotiating Behavior," in Thomas W. Robinson and David Shambaugh, eds., *Chinese Foreign Policy: Theory and Practice* (Oxford: Clarendon Press, 1994), pp. 453–77; Richard H. Solomon, *Chinese Political Negotiating Behavior, 1967–1984: An Interpretive Assessment* (Santa Monica: RAND, December 1985).
2. For an overview of the structure, see Kenneth Lieberthal, *Governing China: From Revolution through Reform* (New York: Norton, 1995).
3. Roderick MacFarquhar, *The Origins of the Cultural Revolution*, vol. 2, *The Great Leap Forward, 1958–1960* (New York: Columbia University Press, 1983).
4. "On Questions of Party History," *Beijing Review,* July 6, 1981, p. 29.
5. Li Zhisui, with the editorial assistance of Anne F. Thurston, *The Private Life of Chairman Mao* (New York: Random House, 1994).
6. Andrew J. Nathan, "A Factionalism Model for CCP Politics," *China Quarterly,* no. 53 (January–March 1973): 34–66; Andrew J. Nathan, *Peking Politics, 1918–1923: Factionalism and the Failure of Constitutionalism* (Berkeley: University of California Press, 1976); Andrew J. Nathan and Kellee S. Tsai, "Factionalism: A New Institutionalist Restatement," *China Journal* 34 (July 1995): 157–92.
7. Robert S. Ross, "From Lin Biao to Deng Xiaoping: Elite Instability and China's U.S. Policy," *China Quarterly,* no. 118 (June 1989): 265–99.
8. Michael D. Swaine, *The Role of the Chinese Military in National Security Policymaking* (Santa Monica: RAND, 1996).
9. A. Doak Barnett, *The Making of Foreign Policy in China* (Boulder: Westview Press, 1985); David Shambaugh, "China's National Security Research Bureaucracy," *China Quarterly,* no. 119 (June 1987): 276–304.
10. Philip Snow, "China and Africa: Consensus and Camouflage," and Lillian Craig Harris, "Myth and Reality in China's Relations with the Middle East," in Robinson and Shambaugh, eds., *Chinese Foreign Policy,* pp. 283–321, 322–47.

8 MILITARY POWER AND FOREIGN POLICY

1. The classic statement on the three kinds of power is Amitai Etzioni, *The Comparative Analysis of Complex Organizations* (New York: Free Press, 1961).
2. John W. Lewis and Xue Litai, *China Builds the Bomb* (Stanford: Stanford University Press, 1988); John W. Lewis and Hua Di, "China's Ballistic Missile Programs: Technologies, Strategies, Goals," *International Security* 17, no. 2 (Fall 1992): 5–40.
3. Gordon H. Chang, *Friends and Enemies: The United States, China, and the Soviet Union, 1948–1972* (Stanford: Stanford University Press, 1990); Henry Kissinger, *White House Years* (Boston: Little, Brown, 1979).

4. For an interval between Mao's death and the rise of Deng, the chairmanship of the CMC was occupied by Mao's successor, Hua Guofeng, and then by Deng's ally Ye Jianying.

5. Fang Zhu, "Party-Army Relations in Maoist China, 1949–1976" (Ph.D. diss., Columbia University, 1994), forthcoming as *Factional Politics and Party-Army Relations in Maoist China* (Oxford: Oxford University Press).

6. Harlan W. Jencks, *From Muskets to Missiles: Politics and Professionalism in the Chinese Army* (Boulder: Westview Press, 1982).

7. Paul H. B. Godwin, "Force and Diplomacy: Chinese Security Policy in the Post–Cold War Era," in Samuel S. Kim, ed., *China and the World: Chinese Foreign Relations in the Post–Cold War Era*, 3rd ed. (Boulder: Westview Press, 1994), pp. 171–86. On the immediate post-Mao reforms, see Ellis Joffe, *The Chinese Army after Mao* (Cambridge: Harvard University Press, 1987).

8. Jonathan D. Pollack, "Structure and Process in the Chinese Military System," in Kenneth C. Lieberthal and David M. Lampton, eds., *Bureaucracy, Politics, and Decision Making in Post-Mao China* (Berkeley: University of California Press, 1992); June Teufel Dreyer, "The Demobilization of PLA Servicemen and Their Reintegration into Civilian Life," in June Teufel Dreyer, ed., *Chinese Defense and Foreign Policy* (New York: Paragon House, 1989); Arthur S. Ding, "The PRC's Military Modernization and a Security Mechanism for the Asia-Pacific," *Issues and Studies* 31, no. 8 (August 1995): 1–18.

9. Kenneth W. Allen, Glenn Krumel, and Jonathan D. Pollack, *China's Air Force Enters the 21st Century* (Santa Monica: RAND, 1995).

10. Harlan W. Jencks, "Chinese Evaluations of 'Desert Storm': Implications for PRC Security," *Journal of East Asian Affairs* 6, no. 2 (summer–fall 1992): 447–77.

11. Richard Bitzinger and Chong-Pin Lin, "Off the Books: Analyzing and Understanding Chinese Defense Spending" (paper, Fifth Annual AEI Conference on the People's Liberation Army, Staunton Hill, Va., June 17–19, 1994).

12. For an attempt to consider all the complexities involved in estimating China's defense budget, see Paul H. B. Godwin, " 'PLA Incorporated': Estimating China's Military Expenditures" (conference paper).

13. Bates Gill and Taeho Kim, *China's Arms Acquisitions from Abroad: A Quest for "Superb and Secret Weapons,"* SIPRI Research Report, no. 11 (Oxford: Oxford University Press, 1995).

14. Paul H. B. Godwin, "Technology, Strategy, and Operations: The PLA's Continuing Dilemma" (paper prepared for the SIPRI workshop "Military Technology and Offensive Capability in Southern Asia," Solna, Sweden, September 22–24, 1995); Allen, Krumel, and Pollack, *China's Air Force*, pp. 147–55.

15. Godwin, "Technology, Strategy, and Operations"; John Caldwell, *China's Conventional Naval Capabilities, 1994–2004* (Washington, D.C.: Center for Strategic and International Studies, 1994); Christopher D. Yung, *Peoples' War at Sea: Chinese Naval Power in the Twenty-first Century* (Alexandria, Va.: Center for Naval Analysis, 1996).

16. John Caldwell, "China's Nuclear Modernization Program," *Strategic Review* 23, n. 4 (fall 1995): 27–37. For an alternative view, see Alastair Iain Johnston, "China's New 'Old Thinking': The Concept of Limited Deterrence," *International Security* 20, no. 3 (Winter 1995–96): 5–42.

17. John Wilson Lewis and Xue Litai, *China's Strategic Seapower: The Politics of Force Modernization in the Nuclear Age* (Stanford: Stanford University Press, 1994).

18. John W. Lewis, Hua Di, and Xue Litai, "Beijing's Defense Establishment: Solving the Arms-Export Enigma," *International Security* 15, no. 4 (Spring 1991):

87–109; Karl W. Eikenberry, *Explaining and Influencing Chinese Arms Transfers*, McNair Paper, no. 36 (Washington, D.C.: Institute for National Strategic Studies, National Defense University, 1995); Richard A. Bitzinger, "Arms to Go: Chinese Arms Sales to the Third World," *International Security* 17, no. 2 (Fall 1992): 84–111; Zachary S. Davis, "China's Nonproliferation and Export Control Policies: Boom or Bust for the NPT Regime?" *Asian Survey* 35 (June 1995): 587–603.

19. Alastair Iain Johnston, "Learning versus Adaptation: Explaining Change in Chinese Arms Control Policy in the 1980s and 1990s," *China Journal*, no. 35 (January 1996): 27–61.

20. "White Paper on Arms Control and Disarmament in China," by the Information Office of the State Council, November 16, 1995, in FBIS/China, November 16, 1995, pp. 20–31.

9 Dilemmas of Opening: Foreign Economic Relations

1. Susan L. Shirk, *The Political Logic of Economic Reform in China* (Berkeley: University of California Press, 1993); Andrew J. Nathan and Tianjian Shi, "Left and Right with Chinese Characteristics: Issues and Alignments in Deng Xiaoping's China," *World Politics* 48 (July 1996): 522–50.

2. Nicholas R. Lardy, *Foreign Trade and Economic Reform in China, 1978–1990* (Cambridge: Cambridge University Press, 1992); Bruce Reynolds, "China in the International Economy," in Harry Harding, ed., *China's Foreign Relations in the 1980s* (New Haven: Yale University Press, 1984), p. 83.

3. Even though China claims political sovereignty over Hong Kong and Taiwan, it treats them as separate entities for the purposes of trade and investment policy and statistics, as we do in this chapter.

4. "Chairman of Delegation of People's Republic of China Deng Xiaoping's Speech at Special Session of U.N. General Assembly," *Peking Review,* supplement to no. 15, April 12, 1974, p. iv.

5. *Red Flag* magazine, quoted in Alexander Eckstein, *China's Economic Revolution* (Cambridge: Cambridge University Press, 1977), p. 242.

6. For example, Deng Xiaoping, "Guanyu jingji gongzuo de jidian yijian" (Several opinions on economic work), in *Deng Xiaoping wenxuan* (Selected works of Deng Xiaoping), vol. 2 (Beijing: Renmin chubanshe, 1994), pp. 194–202.

7. However, American statistics place the United States in first place, buying about one-third of Chinese exports and supplying about one-tenth of China's imports. The disparity between American and Chinese figures comes partly from different ways of counting products originating in China and further processed in Hong Kong.

8. The Chinese government disputes the U.S. calculation of the deficit, saying it unfairly includes goods shipped from China to the United States through Hong Kong, which should be listed in Hong Kong's export statistics, and excludes goods shipped from the United States to China through Hong Kong.

9. Technically, China was applying to rejoin GATT, since it was a founding member in 1948 whose membership was interrupted in 1950.

10. Both of these things would happen, however, only if Congress agreed to give WTO commitments to China domestic legal effect. Among other things, this would involve repealing or exempting China from the Jackson-Vanick amendment, under which China's MFN rights are subject to annual reconsideration by president and Congress. Jackson-Vanick was written to apply trade pressure on the Soviet Union in connection with the problem of Jewish emigration. Later it

was applied to China in connection with human rights and other problems (Chapter 10).

11. William R. Feeney, "China and the Multilateral Economic Institutions," in Samuel S. Kim, ed., *China and the World: Chinese Foreign Relations in the Post–Cold War Era*, 3rd ed. (Boulder: Westview Press, 1994), pp. 226–51. We have updated Feeney's figures from *Almanac of China's Foreign Economic Relations and Trade 1994* (Beijing: Editorial Board of the Almanac of China's Foreign Economic Relations and Trade, 1994), p. 880; World Bank, *The World Bank Annual Report 1995* (Washington, D.C.: World Bank, 1995), p. 144.

12. James H. Michel, *Development Co-operation* (Paris: Organisation for Economic Co-operation and Development, 1996), p. A61.

13. Samuel S. Kim, "China and the World in Theory and Practice," in Kim, ed., *China and the World*, p. 31; Harold K. Jacobson and Michel Oksenberg, *China's Participation in the IMF, the World Bank, and GATT: Toward a Global Economic Order* (Ann Arbor: University of Michigan Press, 1990).

14. *Zhongguo tongji nianjian 1994* (China Statistical Yearbook 1994) (Beijing: Zhongguo tongji chubanshe, 1994), p. 528; Margaret M. Pearson, *Joint Ventures in the People's Republic of China: The Control of Foreign Capital under Socialism* (Princeton: Princeton University Press, 1991).

15. The number comes from Craig S. Smith, "Doublemint in China: Distribution Isn't Double the Fun," *Wall Street Journal*, December 5, 1995, p. B1. Western presumably includes Japanese.

16. James V. Feinerman, "Chinese Law relating to Foreign Investment and Trade: The Decade of Reform in Retrospect," *China's Economic Dilemmas in the 1990s: The Problems of Reforms, Modernization and Interdependence*, Joint Economic Committee, Congress of the United States (Washington, D.C.: Government Printing Office, April 1991), vol. 2, pp. 828–40.

17. *China Daily* August 18, 1993, p. 1; also *New York Times*, August 15, 1993, p. 7, quoting *People's Daily*. Both sources say most of the applications were rejected, but informal visits around the country suggest to us that many local governments went ahead anyway.

18. *Zhongguo tongji nianjian 1995* (China statistical yearbook 1995) (Beijing: Zhongguo tongji chubanshe, 1995), p. 554. According to the same source, cumulative contracted FDI was $304.5 billion. Chinese economists say the official figures of both paid-in and contracted investment are exaggerated by two, three, or more times. Local governments have an interest in overestimating foreign investment to improve their performance reports; the central government has an interest in overestimating the figures to encourage more investment. An undetermined, perhaps large, amount of investment classified as foreign consists of Chinese funds channeled through Hong Kong to take advantage of tax and tariff incentives. Lincoln Kaye, "This Money Has Wings," *Far Eastern Economic Review*, July 15, 1993, pp. 72–73, reports the research of Frank R. Gunter, who estimates that $15–25 billion of "hot money" was exported from China in 1990, $13–28 billion in 1991, and a still larger amount in 1992.

19. Nicholas R. Lardy, "The Role of Foreign Trade and Investment in China's Economic Transformation," *China Quarterly*, no. 144 (December 1995): 1073.

20. *Almanac of China's Foreign Economic Relations and Trade 1994*, pp. 742–44.

21. Xinhua report in FBIS/China, July 24, 1995, p. 58. Nicholas Lardy estimates that foreign-invested enterprises were responsible for 28.7 percent of all Chinese exports in 1994; Lardy, "Role of Foreign Trade", p. 1074.

22. *New York Times*, March 23, 1993, p. D1. Of course, this lease was not for sovereignty, but for land use rights to build infrastructure.

23. Hu Qiaomu in 1985, quoted in *Zhongguo fazhi bao* 28 June 1985, p. 2, in FBIS/China, July 8, 1995, pp. K18–K19.

24. The figure, as of the mid-1990s, is from Hua Wenge, "Economic Causes and Consequences of Nonreturn of Students Studying Abroad," *Jiaoyu pinglun,* no. 64, August 20, 1994, pp. 20–22, in FBIS/China, November 17, 1995, p. 29. Hua says 40,000 have returned, confirming the estimated 70 percent nonreturn rate, which is found in many sources. Also see Chen Changgui and David Zweig, "The Impact of the Open Policy on Higher Education in China," paper presented to the Association for Asian Studies annual meeting, Los Angeles, March 25–28, 1993.

25. Wang Tu-tsun, "The Transformation of Mainland China's Economic System in a Bid to Reenter GATT," *Issues and Studies* 31, no. 3 (March 1995): 11–12.

26. *Wall Street Journal,* November 13, 1995, p. 1.

27. United Nations Conference on Trade and Development, Division on Transnational Corporations and Investment, *World Investment Report 1995: Transnational Corporations and Competitiveness* (New York: United Nations, 1995), pp. 391–94.

28. *World Bank Annual Report 1995,* pp. 144–45; Michel, *Development Cooperation,* pp. A61, A76.

29. *UNCTAD Commodity Yearbook 1995* (New York and Geneva: United Nations Conference on Trade and Development, 1995), pp. 115, 119, 123.

30. Vaclav Smil, *Environmental Problems in China: Estimates of Economic Costs,* East-West Center Special Reports, no. 5 (Honolulu: East-West Center, April 1996), pp. 56–57; also Lester R. Brown, *Who Will Feed China? Wake-up Call for a Small Planet* (New York: Norton, 1995); Vaclav Smil, "Who Will Feed China?" *China Quarterly,* no. 143 (September 1995): 801–13.

31. George T. Yu, "The Tanzania-Zambia Railway: A Case Study in Chinese Economic Aid to Africa," in Warren Weinstein and Thomas H. Henriksen, eds., *Soviet and Chinese Aid to African Nations* (New York: Praeger, 1980), p. 130.

32. Nicholas Lardy, *Foreign Trade,* appendix B.

33. Andrew J. Nathan, *China's Crisis* (New York: Columbia University Press, 1990), chap. 3.

34. Barry Naughton, "The United States and China: Management of Economic Conflict" (paper prepared for the Conference on Domestic Factors in U.S.-China Relations, Fairbank Center for East Asian Research, Harvard University, and Research Center for Contemporary China, Peking University, June 24–25, 1996).

10 HUMAN RIGHTS IN CHINESE FOREIGN POLICY

1. Joseph S. Nye, Jr., "Soft Power," *Foreign Policy* 80 (Fall 1990): 153–71.

2. A longer version of this chapter, with fuller details and citations, is Andrew J. Nathan, "Human Rights in Chinese Foreign Policy," *China Quarterly,* no. 139 (September 1994): 622–43.

3. Louis Henkin, *The Rights of Man Today* (Boulder: Westview Press, 1978), chap. 3.

4. R. Randle Edwards, Louis Henkin, and Andrew J. Nathan, *Human Rights in Contemporary China* (New York: Columbia University Press, 1986).

5. For more examples, see R. David Arkush and Leo O. Lee, eds., *Land without Ghosts: Chinese Impressions of America from the Mid-Nineteenth Century to the Present* (Berkeley: University of California Press, 1989), pp. 241–57.

6. See further Hungdah Chiu, "Chinese Attitudes toward International Law of Human Rights in the Post-Mao Era," in Victor C. Falkenheim, ed., *Chinese Pol-*

itics from Mao to Deng (New York: Paragon House, 1989), pp. 237–70; Samuel S. Kim, *China, the United Nations, and World Order* (Princeton: Princeton University Press, 1979).

7. Gu Yan, "On Human Rights in International Relationships," *International Strategic Studies* (Beijing Institute for International Strategic Studies) 1991, no. 3 (September 1991): 10.

8. Guo Qing, "China's Basic Position on and Practice of Human Rights," *Qiushi*, December 1, 1991, pp. 14–19, in FBIS/China, February 5, 1992, p. 15.

9. Shen Baoxiang, Wang Chengquan, and Li Zerui, "Guanyu guoji lingyu de renquan wenti" (On the question of human rights within the international sphere), *Hongqi*, April 16, 1982, pp. 46–47, translated in *Beijing Review,* July 26, 1982, pp. 15, 17.

10. James D. Seymour, "Human Rights in Chinese Foreign Relations," in Samuel S. Kim, ed., *China and the World: Chinese Foreign Relations in the Post–Cold War Era,* 3rd ed. (Boulder: Westview Press, 1994), chap. 10; Roberta Cohen, "People's Republic of China: The Human Rights Exception," *Human Rights Quarterly* 9 (November 1987): 447–549.

11. "Promoting Democracy and Peace," speech by President Ronald Reagan before the British Parliament, June 8, 1982, in U.S. Department of State, *Current Policy,* no. 399 (June 1982): 4.

12. *American Foreign Policy: Current Documents, 1989* (Washington, D.C.: Department of State, 1990), p. 5.

13. James D. Seymour, "Human Rights and the World Response to the 1989 Crackdown in China," *China Information* 4, no. 4 (Spring 1990): 1–14.

14. The Chinese delegate Wu Jianmin at the UN Human Rights Commission in April 1996, quoted in *New York Times,* April 24, 1996, p. A12.

15. Li Peng, "Upholding the Purposes and Principles of the UN Charter, and Promoting the Lofty Cause of Peace and Development," Beijing Xinhua Domestic Service in Chinese, October 24, 1995, in FBIS/China, October 25, 1995, p. 9.

16. Zhang Yishan, Chinese representative to the UN Commission on Human Rights, quoted in *Beijing Review,* March 2–8, 1992, p. 27.

17. *South China Morning Post,* May 25, 1993, p. 10, in FBIS/China, May 25, 1993, p. 7.

18. Li Peng's UN statement, in PRC Mission to the UN Press Release, New York, January 31, 1992, p. 4.

11 TERRITORIAL INTEGRITY: INNER ASIA, TAIWAN, AND HONG KONG

1. Wenxiang, quoted in Kwang-Ching Liu and Richard J. Smith, "The Military Challenge: The North-West and the Coast," in *The Cambridge History of China,* vol. 11, ed. John K. Fairbank and Kwang-Ching Liu (Cambridge: Cambridge University Press, 1980), p. 238.

2. This section draws on Joseph Fletcher, "Ch'ing Inner Asia *c.* 1800" and "The Heyday of the Ch'ing Order in Mongolia, Sinkiang and Tibet," in *The Cambridge History of China,* vol. 10, ed. John K. Fairbank (Cambridge: Cambridge University Press, 1978), pp. 35–106, 351–408; Morris Rossabi, *China and Inner Asia: From 1368 to the Present Day* (London: Thames and Hudson, 1975); June Teufel Dreyer, *China's Forty Millions: Minority Nationalities and National Integration in the People's Republic of China* (Cambridge: Harvard University Press, 1976).

3. Fletcher, "Heyday," 407.

4. J. Richard Walsh, "China and the New Geopolitics of Central Asia," *Asian Survey* 33 (March 1993): 272–84.

5. W. Woody [pseud.], *The Cultural Revolution in Inner Mongolia: Extracts from an Unpublished History,* ed. and trans. Michael Schoenhals, (Stockholm: Center for Pacific Asia Studies at Stockholm University, December 1993).
6. Melvyn C. Goldstein, with Gelek Rimpoche, *A History of Modern Tibet, 1913–1951: The Demise of the Lamaist State* (Berkeley: University of California Press, 1989); Melvyn C. Goldstein, *Tibet, China, and the United States: Reflections on the Tibet Question* (Washington, D.C.: Atlantic Council, 1995).
7. Lamas are considered reincarnations and are supposed to be recognized by religious rituals. Since the Qing the Chinese authorities have tried to influence the selection of lamas. The Panchen Lama is the second-most-important leader in Tibetan Buddhism. When the Dalai Lama designated a young boy as the eleventh Panchen Lama, Beijing insisted that the selection committee choose someone else and placed the Dalai Lama's choice under house arrest.
8. Tibet Information Network and Human Rights Watch/Asia, *Cutting Off the Serpent's Head: Tightening Control in Tibet, 1994–1995* (New York: Human Rights Watch, 1996).
9. Michael B. Yahuda, *Hong Kong: China's Challenge* (New York: Routledge, 1996), pp. 62, 68.
10. *South China Morning Post,* November 8, 1995, p. 1, in FBIS/China, November 9, 1995, p. 39, reporting a speech by U.S. Consul-General Richard Muller.
11. State Department spokesman, April 28, 1971, quoted in Jerome Alan Cohen et al., *Taiwan and American Policy* (New York: Praeger, 1971), p. 184.
12. Henry Kissinger, *White House Years* (Boston: Little, Brown, 1979), p. 1062. Before 1949 the Chinese Communist Party took the position that minority peoples and Taiwan could choose independence if they wanted to, but it abandoned this position upon taking power.
13. Among other places, in "Memorandum on Formosa," June 14, 1950, *Foreign Relations of the United States, 1950,* vol. 7, *Korea* (Washington, D.C.: Government Printing Office, 1976), p. 162. His argument was that if access to Formosa was not denied to the Soviets, they could use it to threaten U.S. positions in Japan, Okinawa, and the Philippines. But the logic applies even more forcefully to the use of Taiwan by American or other forces to threaten China.
14. At the same time the United States gave "six assurances" to Taiwan: it would not set a date for ending arms sales, hold prior consultation with Beijing on U.S. arms sales to Taiwan, play a mediating role between Beijing and Taipei, revise the Taiwan Relations Act, alter the U.S. position regarding sovereignty over Taiwan, or exert pressure on Taiwan to enter into negotiations with Beijing.
15. Andrew J. Nathan and Yangsun Chou, "Democratizing Transition in Taiwan," *Asian Survey* 27 (March 1987): 277–99; Andrew J. Nathan, "The Effect of Taiwan's Political Reform on Taiwan-Mainland Relations," in Tun-jen Cheng and Stephen Haggard, eds., *Political Change in Taiwan* (Boulder: Lynne Reinner, 1992), pp. 207–19; Andrew J. Nathan and Helena Ho, "Chiang Ching-kuo's Decision for Political Reform," in Shao-chuan Leng, ed., *Chiang Ching-kuo's Leadership in the Development of the Republic of China on Taiwan* (Lanham, Md.: University Press of America, 1993), pp. 31–61.
16. *Managing the Taiwan Issue: Key Is Better U.S. Relations with China: Report of an Independent Task Force* (New York: Council on Foreign Relations, 1995).

12 THE FOREIGN POLICY OF TAIWAN

1. Economic figures are for 1994, from World Economic Forum, *The World Competitiveness Report* (Geneva: World Economic Forum, 1995), pp. 360, 364.

2. The size and population comparisons exclude cities that have provincial-level rank.

3. They were the Bahamas, Belize, Burkina Faso, the Central African Republic, Costa Rica, Dominica, the Dominican Republic, El Salvador, the Gambia, Grenada, Guatemala, Guinea-Bissau, Haiti, the Holy See, Honduras, Liberia, Malawi, Nauru, Nicaragua, Panama, Paraguay, St. Kitts and Nevis, Saint Lucia, St. Vincent and the Grenadines, Senegal, the Solomon Islands, Swaziland, Tonga, and Tuvalu. Three of these states are so small they are not even members of the UN: the Holy See and the Pacific island nations of Nauru and Tuvalu.

4. Byron S. J. Weng, "Divided China and the Question of Membership in International Economic Organizations," in Yun-han Chu, ed., *The Role of Taiwan in International Economic Organizations* (Taipei: Institute for National Policy Research, 1990), pp. 27–61.

5. The best analysis of the meaning of the TRA's security commitment is Richard Bush, "Helping the Republic of China to Defend Itself," in Ramon H. Myers, ed., *A Unique Relationship: The United States and the Republic of China under the Taiwan Relations Act* (Stanford: Hoover Institution Press, 1989), pp. 79–118. Also see Parris H. Chang and Martin L. Lasater, eds., *If China Crosses the Taiwan Strait: The International Response* (Lanham, Md.: University Press of America, 1993).

13 CHINESE SECURITY AND WORLD ORDER

1. Nicholas D. Kristof, "The Rise of China," *Foreign Affairs* 72, no. 5 (November–December 1993): 59–73; Ross H. Munro, "Awakening Dragon: The Real Danger in Asia Is from China," *Policy Review,* no. 62 (Fall 1992): 10–16; David Shambaugh, "Growing Strong: China's Challenge to Asian Security," *Survival* 36, no. 2 (Summer 1994): 43–59.

2. On this controversial point, the authors do not agree with one another. It seems to Ross that the call for a "robust and effective" human rights regime is reminiscent of the 1928 Kellogg-Briand Pact outlawing war—if we promote better values, the world would be a more peaceful place. Even if such a regime were possible, it is not clear that it would contribute to stability; it might even have the opposite effect. The scholarly literature suggests that democratic states do not fight each other, but it offers no evidence that countries that respect human rights conduct more peaceful foreign policies.

3. Robert S. Ross, "Beijing as a Conservative Power," *Foreign Affairs* 76, no. 2 (March/April 1997): 35–44.

4. Andrew J. Nathan, "China: Getting Human Rights Right," *Washington Quarterly* 20, no. 1 (January 1997): 135–51; and Andrew J. Nathan, "China and the International Human Rights Regime," in Michel C. Oksenberg and Elizabeth Economy, eds., *Constructive Engagement with China* (New York: Council on Foreign Relations Press, forthcoming).

5. Robert S. Ross, "Enter the Dragon," *Foreign Policy,* no. 104 (September 1996): 18–25.

INDEX